From Past-Present to Future-Perfect: A Tribute to Charles A. Bunge and the Challenges of Contemporary Reference Service

From the Past-Present to Future-Perfect: A Tribute to Charles A. Bunge and the Challenges of Contemporary Reference Service has been simultaneously co-published as *The Reference Librarian*, Number 66 1999.

From Past-Present to Future-Perfect: A Tribute to Charles A. Bunge and the Challenges of Contemporary Reference Service

Chris D. Ferguson
Editor

From Past-Present to Future-Perfect: A Tribute to Charles A. Bunge and the Challenges of Contemporary Reference Service has been simultaneously co-published as *The Reference Librarian*, Number 66 1999.

Routledge
Taylor & Francis Group
NEW YORK AND LONDON

First published 1999 by The Haworth Press, Inc.
10 Alice Street, Binghamton, NY 13904-1580 USA

This edition published 2013 by Routledge
711 Third Avenue, New York, NY 10017
2 Park Square, Milton Park, Abingdon, Oxon OX14 4RN

First issued in paperback 2016

Routledge is an imprint of the Taylor & Francis Group, an informa business

From Past-Present to Future-Perfect: A Tribute to Charles A. Bunge and the Challenges of Contemporary Reference Service has been co-published simultaneously as *The Reference Librarian*, Number 66 1999.

Cover design by Thomas J. Mayshock Jr.

Library of Congress Cataloging-in-Publication Data

From past-present to future-perfect: a tribute to Charles A. Bunge and the challenges of contemporary reference service/Chris D. Ferguson, editor.

p. cm.

Published also as no. 66, 1999 of The reference librarian.

Includes bibliographical references and index.

ISBN 0-7890-0767-3 (alk. paper)

1. Reference services (Libraries–United States. 2. Bunge, Charles A. 3. Public libraries–Reference services–United States. 4. Research libraries–Reference services–United States. I. Ferguson, Chris D., 1951- . II. Bunge, Charles A. III. Reference librarian.

Z711.F76 1999

025.5′2–dc21 99-27773

CIP

ISBN 13: 978-1-138-97478-4 (pbk)

ISBN 13: 978-0-7890-0767-4 (hbk)

From Past-Present to Future-Perfect: A Tribute to Charles A. Bunge and the Challenges of Contemporary Reference Service

CONTENTS

ABOUT THE EDITOR

Chris D. Ferguson is Executive Director of the Public Services Core in the University of Southern California's Information Services Division. Previous positions include director of USC's Thomas and Dorothy Leavey Library; head of Research Services and head of the undergraduate library at the University of California, San Diego; and reference-bibliographer at the University of California, Irvine and the University of Mississippi. He has written and edited several works on reference service in academic libraries and on the bibliography of medieval and ancient history. Ferguson may be contacted at cdf@usc.edu or Information Services Division, University of Southern California, Los Angeles, CA 90089-0182.

Introduction

Charles Bunge made a difference. From broad-ranging and numerous publications to leadership in professional organizations to the mentoring of countless graduate students, Bunge's presence has been felt in both public and academic library reference service for more than three decades. His confidence in the goodness of people, optimism for the future, and ability to bring keen insight and analytical skills to bear on complicated and often emotional issues has greatly influenced a generation of librarians.

This volume is a tribute to an especially rich dimension of Charles Bunge's career, his contributions to the literature of reference service. It begins with a comprehensive bibliography of his published works, then moves into a medley of topical sections. It is difficult to force his works into patterns or categories, but four categories do emerge where he has had especially key impact: measuring the effectiveness of reference service, the reference environment, reference sources, and reflections on the past and future of reference work.

Each section includes a select bibliography of Bunge's relevant works accompanied by a brief narrative overview of them, one or two reprints of important but less-accessible articles (this was Charles's suggestion; even in retirement he remains committed to intellectual access and the convenience of his readers), and an article or articles by admirers who have been impressed and influenced by his work.

Each generation of librarians has acknowledged leaders, and each generation's leaders have grateful admirers who seek to acknowledge them. He is ours, and we are his.

Chris D. Ferguson

[Haworth co-indexing entry note]: "Introduction." Ferguson, Chris D. Co-published simultaneously in *The Reference Librarian* (The Haworth Information Press, an imprint of The Haworth Press, Inc.) No. 66, 1999, p. 1; and: *From Past-Present to Future-Perfect: A Tribute to Charles A. Bunge and the Challenges of Contemporary Reference Service* (ed: Chris D. Ferguson) The Haworth Information Press, an imprint of The Haworth Press, Inc., 1999, p. 1. Single or multiple copies of this article are available for a fee from The Haworth Document Delivery Service [1-800-342-9678, 9:00 a.m. - 5:00 p.m. (EST). E-mail address: getinfo@haworthpressinc.com].

Chronological Bibliography of Works Published by Charles A. Bunge

Chris D. Ferguson

1965-1972

"Statewide Public Library Surveys and Plans, 1944-64." *ALA Bulletin* 59 (May 1965): 364-74.

"Statewide Library Surveys and Plans, Development of the Concept and Some Recent Patterns." *Library Quarterly* 36 (January 1966): 25-37.

"Library Education and Reference Performance." *Library Journal* 92 (15 April 1967): 1578-81.

Professional Education and Reference Efficiency. Illinois State Library Research Series, no. 11. Springfield, IL: Illinois State Library, 1967.

Library Cooperation for the Madison Area. Madison: University of Wisconsin Library School, 1969.

"Charting the Reference Query." *RQ* 8 (Summer 1969): 245-50.

"Flow-Chart Analysis." In: *Introduction to Reference Work*, vol. 2, edited by W.A. Katz. New York: McGraw-Hill, 1969. Reprint, 1974.

Chris D. Ferguson is Executive Director, Public Services Core, Information Services Division, University of Southern California.

[Haworth co-indexing entry note]: "Chronological Bibliography of Works Published by Charles A. Bunge." Ferguson, Chris D. Co-published simultaneously in *The Reference Librarian* (The Haworth Information Press, an imprint of The Haworth Press, Inc.) No. 66, 1999, pp. 3-7; and: *From Past-Present to Future-Perfect: A Tribute to Charles A. Bunge and the Challenges of Contemporary Reference Service* (ed: Chris D. Ferguson) The Haworth Information Press, an imprint of The Haworth Press, Inc., 1999, pp. 3-7. Single or multiple copies of this article are available for a fee from The Haworth Document Delivery Service [1-800-342-9678, 9:00 a.m. - 5:00 p.m. (EST). E-mail address: getinfo@haworthpressinc.com].

"Research in Reference." *RQ*, 1969-72. Column.

"Reference Service in the Information Network." In: *Interlibrary Communication and Information Networks*, edited by J. Becker. Chicago: American Library Association, 1971.

"What Difference Will Public Library Systems Make–Really?" *Wisconsin Library Bulletin* 68 (July-August 1972): 203-06.

1972-81

"Current Reference Books." *Wilson Library Bulletin*, 1972-81. Column.

"Seekers vs. Barriers." *Wisconsin Library Bulletin* 70 (March-April 1974): 76-78.

"The Library School: Education for Librarianship at the University of Wisconsin-Madison." In: *A Resourceful University*. Madison: University of Wisconsin Press, 1975.

"Library Education at Madison: The University of Wisconsin Library School: Through Its Last 25 Years." *Wisconsin Library Bulletin* 71 (November-December 1975): 335-38.

"Wisconsin." In: *The ALA Yearbook*. Chicago: American Library Association, 1977, 1978, 1979, 1980.

"Approaches to the Evaluation of Library Reference Services." In: *Evaluation and Scientific Management of Libraries*, edited by F.W. Lancaster & C.W. Cleverdon. Leyden: Noordhoff, 1977.

"Library Education for Library Instruction." In: *Putting Library Instruction in Its Place*. Ann Arbor: Pierian Press, 1978.

"Reference Services." *ALA World Encyclopedia of Library and Information Services*. Chicago: American Library Association, 1980.

"Beliefs, Attitudes, and Values of the Reference Librarian." *Musings* 5 (1980): 7-15.

"The Reviewing of Adult Reference Materials for General Libraries." *The Reference Librarian* 1-2 (Fall-Winter 1981): 21-29.

1982-1986

"Strategies for Updating Knowledge of Reference Resources and Techniques." *RQ* 21 (Spring 1982): 228-32.

"If I Had to Choose." *RSR: Reference Services Review* 10 (Fall 1982): 11-13.

"The Publishing of Heavily Illustrated Reference Books." *RSR: Reference Services Review* 11 (Spring 1983): 89-98.

"The Measurement and Evaluation of Reference and Adult Services." *RQ* 22 (Spring 1983): 251-54.

"The Personal Touch: A Brief Overview of Reference Services in American Libraries." In: *Reference Service: A Perspective*, edited by S.H. Lee. Ann Arbor: Pierian Press, 1983.

"Planning, Goals, and Objectives for the Reference Department." *RQ* 23 (Spring 1984): 306-14.

"Interpersonal Dimensions of the Reference Interview." *Drexel Library Quarterly* 20 (Spring 1984): 4-23.

"Potential and Reality at the Reference Desk." *Journal of Academic Librarianship*, 10 (July 1984): 128-32.

(with M. Murfin) "Evaluating Reference Service from the Patron Point of View." *The Reference Librarian* 11 (Fall-Winter 1984): 175-82.

"Information Service in the Real World." *Journal of Academic Librarianship* 11 (May 1985): 77-78.

"Factors Related to Reference Question Answering Success." *RQ*, 24 (Summer 1985): 482-86.

"Reference Desk Staffing Patterns: Report of a Survey." *RQ*, 26 (Winter 1986): 171-79.

1987-1990

(with E. Cortez) "The Communication Audit as a Library Management Tool." *Journal of Library Administration* 8 (Summer 1987): 41-64.

"Reference Questions: Data from the Field." *RQ* 27 (Fall 1987): 15-18.

"Stress on the Job: Reports from Library Staff Members." *Library Journal* 112 (15 September 1987): 47-51.

(with M. Murfin) "Paraprofessionals at the Reference Desk: Some

Findings from Academic Libraries." *Journal of Academic Librarianship* 14 (March 1988): 10-14.

(with M. Murfin) "Responsible Standards for Reference Service in Ohio Public Libraries." *Ohio Libraries* 1 (March-April 1988): 11-13.

"Stress in the Library Workplace." *Library Trends* 38 (Summer 1989): 92-102. [Same as following item.]

"Stress in the Library Workplace." In: *Critical Issues in Library Personnel Management: Papers Presented at the Allerton Park Institute, 1987,* edited by R. Rubin. Champaign: University of Illinois Graduate School of Library and Information Science, 1989.

(with J. Krikelas) "Herbert Goldhor: A Tribute and a Bibliography." *Library Trends* 38 (Fall 1989): 295-312.

"Factors Related to Output Measures for Reference Services in Public Libraries."*Public Libraries* 29 (January-February 1990): 42-47.

"Introduction: The Man [Rothstein] and His Work." *The Reference Librarian* 25-26 (1990): 1-5.

1991-1997

"Ethics and the Reference Librarian." In: *Ethics and the Librarian: Papers Presented at the Allerton Park Institute, 1989.* Champaign: University of Illinois Graduate School of Library and Information Science, 1991.

"Gathering and Using Patron and Librarian Perceptions of Question-Answering Success." In: *Evaluation of Public Services and Public Services Personnel: Papers Presented at the Allerton Park Institute, 1990.* Champaign: University of Illinois Graduate School of Library and Information Science, 1991.

"CD-ROM Stress." *Library Journal* 116 (15 April 1991): 63-64.

"Accreditation." In: *Libraries and Information Services Today.* Chicago: American Library Association, 1991.

"Accreditation Standards Revision: Does it Matter?" *Wilson Library Bulletin* 65 (June 1991): 65-66.

"Stress and Burnout in the Library Workplace." *Encyclopedia of Library and Information Science*, vol. 49. New York: Marcel Dekker, 1992.

"An 'Alms-Basket' of 'Bric-a-Brac': Brewer's Dictionary of Phrase and Fable." In: *Distinguished Classics of Reference Publishing*, edited by J. Rettig. Phoenix: Oryx Press, 1992.

"The Philosophies and Objectives of Graduate Programs in Library and Information Studies." *Journal of Library Administration* 16 (1992): 13-18.

"Evaluating Reference Services and Reference Personnel." *The Reference Librarian* 43 (1994): 195-207.

"Doing Better: Reauthorizing the Library Services and Construction Act." *Public Libraries* 33 (January-February 1994): 15-20.

"Responsive Reference Service: Breaking Down Age Barriers." *School Library Journal* 40 (March 1994): 142-45.

(with C. Ferguson) "The Shape of Services to Come: Values-Based Reference Service for the Largely-Digital Library." *College and Research Libraries* 58 (May 1997): 252-65.

PART 1:
THE REFERENCE ENVIRONMENT

Select Bibliography and Overview of Bunge's Publications Related to the Reference Environment

Sarah B. Watstein

BIBLIOGRAPHY

"Beliefs, Attitudes, and Values of the Reference Librarian." *Musings* 5 (1980): 7-15.

"Strategies for Updating Knowledge of Reference Resources and Techniques." *RQ* 21 (Spring 1982): 228-32.

"Planning, Goals, and Objectives for the Reference Department." *RQ* 23 (Spring 1984): 306-14.

Sarah B. Watstein is Assistant Director for Academic Use Services, James Branch Cabell Library, Virginia Commonwealth University, Richmond, VA 23284 (E-mail: swatstei@ucc.edu).

[Haworth co-indexing entry note]: "Select Bibliography and Overview of Bunge's Publications Related to the Reference Environment." Watstein, Sarah B. Co-published simultaneously in *The Reference Librarian* (The Haworth Information Press, an imprint of The Haworth Press, Inc.) No. 66, 1999, pp. 9-11; and: *From Past-Present to Future-Perfect: A Tribute to Charles A. Bunge and the Challenges of Contemporary Reference Service* (ed: Chris D. Ferguson) The Haworth Information Press, an imprint of The Haworth Press, Inc., 1999, pp. 9-11. Single or multiple copies of this article are available for a fee from The Haworth Document Delivery Service [1-800-342-9678, 9:00 a.m. - 5:00 p.m. (EST). E-mail address: getinfo@haworthpressinc.com].

"Potential and Reality at the Reference Desk." *Journal of Academic Librarianship* 10 (July 1984): 128-32.

"Interpersonal Dimensions of the Reference Interview." *Drexel Library Quarterly* 20 (Spring 1984): 4-23.

"Stress in the Library Workplace." *Library Trends* 38 (Summer 1989): 92-102.

"Ethics and the Reference Librarian." In: *Ethics and the Librarian: Papers Presented at the Allerton Park Institute, 1989*. Champaign: University of Illinois Graduate School of Library and Information Science, 1991.

"Stress and Burnout in the Library Workplace." *Encyclopedia of Library and Information Science*, vol. 49. New York: Marcel Dekker, 1992.

OVERVIEW

Charles Bunge is most at home in the library workplace, and in particular in the reference environment. There is no question but that he finds reference librarianship to be a satisfying and rewarding pursuit. Indeed, in "Potential and Reality at the Reference Desk: Reflections on a 'Return to the Field,'" he comments: "I am impressed once again with what an exciting, challenging, and joy-filled calling reference librarianship can be." He is passionately interested in the many facets of reference service, and his writing reflects both this broad interest and his appreciation for the complexity of reference service.

Over the years, Bunge has tackled (and continues to tackle) timely–and timeless–subjects. Examples include the changes in reference and information resources; techniques and clients; planning, goals, and objectives for the reference department; the interpersonal dimensions of the reference interview; the challenges and frustrations of reference work in the 1980s; stress and burnout in the library workplace; and ethics and the reference librarian. He is careful to develop the conceptual framework for each article or paper as well as to define key terms and to provide a brief review of relevant literature before turning to discussion and debate. With a keen understanding of the "daily, hour-to-hour experience of a reference librarian," he strives in his writing to provide useful information to his colleagues in the reference workplace. Even his literature reviews, such as "Interpersonal Dimensions of the Reference Interview: A Historical Review of the Literature," are prepared with this purpose in mind.

Bunge's writings on the reference environment are insightful, provocative, and practical, especially for the application of planning principles and practices at the department level. He outlines and documents changes in focus and emphasis as authors through the years have discussed the reasons for, the nature of, the techniques used in, and the knowledge and skills useful to the reference interview. He reports on the situation of low morale among practicing reference librarians, and shares ideas for putting the joy back into reference work. He addresses the challenge of continual learning for reference librarians, and identifies strategies for updating knowledge and skills. He provides library employees with an understanding of stress and burnout in the library workplace, and shares organizational strategies for dealing with such phenomena. And in the end, Bunge helps reference librarians and others answer the questions, "What is ethical reference practice?" and "How should the librarian act or behave in providing reference service?"

Bunge has made and continues to make an exceptional contribution to the profession, in particular to front-line reference librarians. Bunge believes that a reference librarian will be more effective if s/he has "positive and accepting beliefs and attitudes toward reference librarianship as a job, toward the persons who are served, and toward himself or herself." There is no question but that Bunge's contributions in the area of the reference environment have had a positive impact on the development and maintenance of such beliefs, attitudes, and values.

Beliefs, Attitudes, and Values of the Reference Librarian

Charles A. Bunge

I am very happy and pleased to be invited to give the Beta Phi Mu lecture here at Michigan. I have a great deal of respect for the Library School at the University of Michigan. I think it ranks second perhaps only to another one in the Upper Midwest that I know well. I am especially respectful of your dean, Russ Bidlack, your assistant dean Ken Vance, and the rest of your fine faculty.

I would like to dedicate my talk today to Wallace Bonk, a friend and colleague, missed by all who knew him. Those of you who knew Wally and his feelings about reference librarianship may think it inappropriate that a talk on attitudes, beliefs, and values of reference librarians should be dedicated to a person who believed so strongly that the important thing for a reference librarian to have is thorough knowledge of reference *materials*, rather than a lot of training in reference process, the reference interview, attitudes, etc. In fact, Wally got himself engaged in a kind of silly confrontation in the literature on whether you needed to know materials or you needed to know process and the like. Wally came down on the side of materials. Thus, as I say, you may think it inappropriate to dedicate such a talk to his memory. And yet, Wally's articulate emphasis on the importance of reference materials in reference training challenged those of us who are inter-

---

Third Annual Mu Chapter/Beta Phi Mu Lecture–The University of Michigan.

Reprinted by permission of the University of Michigan School of Information from Charles A. Bunge, "Beliefs, Attitudes, and Values of the Reference Librarian," *Musings* 5:2 (June 1980): 7-15.

[Haworth co-indexing entry note]: "Beliefs, Attitudes, and Values of the Reference Librarian." Bunge, Charles A. Co-published simultaneously in *The Reference Librarian* (The Haworth Information Press, an imprint of The Haworth Press, Inc.) No. 66, 1999, pp. 13-24; and: *From Past-Present to Future-Perfect: A Tribute to Charles A. Bunge and the Challenges of Contemporary Reference Service* (ed: Chris D. Ferguson) The Haworth Information Press, an imprint of The Haworth Press, Inc., 1999, pp. 13-24.

ested in other aspects of reference training to be as substantive as possible and to make sure that our teaching about the reference process really contributes to the effectiveness of our students as reference librarians. And since this talk resulted from my own reflection and response to that challenge of Wally's, I think it is a fitting tribute to him and his ideas. I hope that you will agree.

As I was thinking about what I might do for the Beta Phi Mu talk today, and about what might be most valuable to the audience (as well as to myself), I thought I should do something in the area of reference services, because that is the area in which I have practiced, about which I feel I know the most, and which I might be able to share with you most meaningfully. I also thought that it might be useful for me to reflect and study a little bit on some of the things that had interested me with regard to reference service, but that I had not had time to pursue because of administrative duties or because I had not been able to get around to them in my teaching responsibility. So what you are going to get today is the result of my reflection and study on a couple of things that have interested me and that I hope will interest you.

I define reference service as personal assistance provided to someone who needs information–assistance in overcoming the various barriers that exist between that person and the information he or she needs. I think one of the key parts of that definition is the "personal assistance" that is provided. As I have thought about this personal service over the past several months, or even years, I have been interested in two strands of thinking and research and the implications they have for reference service. One of these I will characterize as the concept of 'helping relationships." You have probably heard counseling, social work, and other fields referred to as "helping professions," and I am interested in that concept and the relationship it might have to reference service. The other strand of thinking that I have been interested in I will characterize as "communication" or "communications research," and the new ideas coming from such research that are of relevance to reference service.

Taking the last first, just to give you a little more of an idea of what I have in mind, communications researchers have recently been telling us some very interesting things about people's use of information. Researchers like Brenda Dervin, for example, tell us that people are very individualistic about their information needs and uses. Indeed, our librarian's habit of categorizing people and information sources in order to make matches between them can become one of those barriers that I mentioned. Reference librarians, it seems, need to understand users in terms of the users' perceptions of the situation they are in–very individual situations–in order to know how they will use the information sought and in order to find appropriate information. Also, under this general rubric of communications and my interest in it, I have been increasingly aware of the importance of non-verbal communication in human interactions such as the reference encounter. We know, for example, that people take a great deal of meaning from non-verbal cues such as gestures, facial expressions, and voice tone, and that these cues can even contradict and undercut our verbal messages. Sometimes, I suppose often, this can happen without our even knowing it. So that is the sort of area of communication that has interested me, and on which I have wanted to follow up.

To elaborate a little bit on the concept of helping relationships, you are probably aware of the number of books that have come out in the '70's, even back into the '60's, that have explored the common elements of professions such as teaching, counseling, social work, and others. Often these are referred to as the helping professions, and the human interactions involved in them are characterized as "helping relationships." This is related to the so-called "client-centered" counseling, "client-centered" teaching, and the like, which draws heavily on some of Carl Rogers' ideas. Two things that have struck me as I have pursued some of this literature are that, first, the helping relationship is seen as a cooperative relationship, not one of "I, the professional, doing something *for* or *to* you, the client," but rather one of our cooperating to find a way for you to cope with your situation as you want to. Second, the technical skills and knowledge of the helping professional seem less important to effective practice than are the beliefs and attitudes held by the professional. This comes through in the literature often when you read about the successful helping professional.

As I was thinking, then, about what sort of talk I might prepare for the Beta Phi Mu lecture today, it occurred to me, "Why not explore the implications of these two areas of thinking, communications and helping relationships, to the practice of reference librarianship?" The more I studied the complexity of information needs and uses and the necessity for reference librarians to understand the unique situation and perceptions of each individual user, and the more I tried to understand how reference librarians can make their verbal and non-verbal cues reinforce each other, and the more I pondered how reference service can be built on effective helping relationships, the more I came to the conclusion that the beliefs, attitudes, and values of the reference librarian are of key importance. What then, I thought, are some of the beliefs, attitudes, and values that reference librarians should develop and cultivate, in order to enhance their effectiveness in assisting those who need information to overcome the barriers that exist between them and the information they need? I think it is useful to group these beliefs, attitudes, and values that are important for reference service into three categories: those concerning our job, those concerning the people we serve, and those concerning ourselves. I want to talk then about each of these groups in turn.

First, though, I should define very briefly what I mean by beliefs, attitudes, and values. A *belief* is a simple perception or proposition that one holds about an object or a situation. One may hold that something is true or false or that something is good or bad. For example, we may believe that smoking marijuana is harmful to health. We may believe that smoking marijuana leads to loss of motivation and loss of effectiveness as a student or a worker. Beliefs are based on what we perceive to be true or false, and beliefs can be changed by our getting more information or coming to hold a different view of what is true or false.

An *attitude* is a relatively enduring organization of beliefs around an object or situation which predisposes one to respond in some preferential manner. In other words, various things that we believe about something are organized together in a rather enduring pattern to cause us to be predisposed to act either positively toward it or negatively toward it. To carry my example about smoking marijuana further, various things we believe about smoking it become organized into a relatively enduring predisposition toward it and perhaps toward the people who engage in it. Attitudes can be changed by changing the beliefs upon which they are based or of which they consist. A *value* is a type of belief, a belief that is centrally located within one's total belief system, about some end state of existence. Such an end state of existence might be good health, or long life, or productivity. Our positive feeling toward health, or long life, or productivity, for example, will be associated with our attitude toward smoking marijuana. Values are deep-seated and difficult to change, except gradually and as we become aware of them and their relationship to each other and to our perceptions and beliefs about reality.

Going back then, I said that reference librarians need to develop certain beliefs, attitudes, and values about their jobs, the people they serve, and themselves. I want to talk quickly about beliefs and attitudes about our jobs that are important for reference librarians. First of all, we should believe that the job we are doing is important and worthwhile. If we feel our job as a reference librarian is trivial or of no importance to society, it will be difficult, if not impossible, to do well at it. Now you are probably thinking to yourselves that reference librarians should have no difficulty cultivating such a belief, the way we are bombarded these days with writings about the importance of information in the so-called post-industrial society, and I will agree with you. On the other hand, sometimes when you have spent the whole day answering puzzle questions and responding to questions you feel never should have arisen in the first place–people wanting you to do their term papers for them and the like–sometimes you need convincing that the job is of importance. So I think it is very important to reflect on, to think about, and to continue to believe in the importance and worthwhileness of your job.

I think, also, that a belief in the importance of our job can be enhanced by reflection on some of the basic values of librarianship as a profession and by relating reference service to these basic values of librarianship as a profession. We as librarians hold that being informed is the appropriate state of being. Being informed is a positive value for us, a positive professional value. We hold, or should hold, as a central belief that being informed is better than being ignorant. We hold that a fuller, richer life is based on education, information, and life-long learning, reading, and experience. Likewise, we hold that everyone has a right to the information he or she needs, and that the proper state of a democratic society is one where information flows freely and where access to it is equitable.

We reference librarians should believe firmly, then, that our job is very important to helping people be informed and to making access to information equitable. As a matter of fact, it is a firm belief of mine that one of the key functions of reference librarianship in the scheme of librarianship is to help guarantee this equitable access to information, which for various reasons is less than equitable, depending on the person's situation.

In addition to believing that our jobs are important, it is important that we hold certain beliefs about the purpose of our jobs as reference librarians. We must believe that the purpose of reference librarianship is to help people. This seems obvious, surely. And yet, over the weeks and months and years of day-to-day reference practice, there is an insidious tendency for us to come to believe that the real purpose of our task is to serve our own needs or those of the library. Rules and regulations, reference statistics, neatness and order become more important than individual people and their information needs in individual situations. We need to guard against the tendency that creeps in by which we think reference service really is for the purposes of the library and the library staff and to satisfy rules and regulations.

We must believe, furthermore, that the purpose of our service is to help the client realize his or her *own* goals, rather than what we think *should* be his or her goals. We should believe that our purpose is one of freeing and facilitating, rather than controlling or manipulating. How easy it is, and yet how detrimental to good service it is, to think we know what people really need. How tempting it is to take a question and turn it into one we can answer, rather than exploring what is really needed. We need to guard against that. In summary, then, we need to believe that our job as reference librarian is important and valuable, and we should believe that the needs and situations of the patrons are the touchstone of our service.

So, central to effective reference service are the clients we serve, and that is the second area of the three that I want to talk about. What are some of the beliefs, attitudes, and values about people that can enhance our effectiveness as reference librarians?

First of all, again to start with the obvious, we should like people and be interested in their well-being. If a reference librarian is not genuinely interested in people and does not like them, he or she should change jobs. (And probably should change jobs right out of librarianship!) Now it is easy to say that people should like people in order to be reference librarians, but what can we say about more specific bases for working with people effectively? First, I think we need to go back again to some of these central beliefs I defined as values. We need to hold a central and deep-seated commitment to the dignity of persons and their rights as individuals, for example, in the reference area, their right to privacy and confidentiality in relationships with the librarian and with information sources. Associated with this value of the dignity of persons and their rights as individuals are various beliefs and attitudes that can be strengthened in a reciprocal relationship with it. I want to talk about those briefly.

Reference librarians should believe that each person is a unique individual with his or her own goals and needs. One of the things I think is most detrimental to good library service, and to good reference service particularly, is thinking of people in stereotypes, of allowing ourselves to place people in boxes. We sometimes can even go so far as to come to think of people as just interruptions to the flow of the day, or interruptions to our task of selecting books or scheduling student assistants for desk duty or various other kinds of things that reference librarians have to do as the day progresses. Actually, there is a real dilemma here for reference librarians that one constantly has to work to mediate. On the one hand, it is very important that we treat people as individuals and avoid stereotyping. On the other hand, fundamental to the reference process is the matching of certain categories of users with certain categories of information sources; otherwise, we could make no sense at all of our task. To mediate between this task of treating persons as individuals on the one hand and trying to arrive at some judgment of categories and matching patterns between users and information systems on the other hand is one of the challenges of reference librarianship, day to day and hour to hour.

We need to be open to the differences among persons, especially the differences from ourselves. Another thing I think is very characteristic of human beings–of all of us–is to wish that everyone was like us. Then we could understand their talk, understand their values, and we could relate to them more easily. And yet, this kind of thinking is another form of stereotyping, of approaching people not as unique individuals, but wishing they were something other than they are, of wishing to change them, to change them in ways we think would be better for them, or better for society, or better for whatever. Rather than that, we need to be accepting of them as distinct persons and to seek to change them only in ways they themselves wish to change. We should seek to facilitate their changing their lot in ways they perceive are valuable rather than in ways we think would be helpful to them, or to society at large, or whatever.

The reference librarian needs to believe the client is capable of recognizing his or her own information need and of knowing when useful information has been found to serve it. One of the key concepts of client-centered helping, of the helping professions, is that the professional approaches the client as competent and able, rather than as incompetent and needing manipulation. I think that often we reference librarians get in the position of thinking we need to manipulate people, that when someone comes in with a reference question we have to go through a reference interview that tricks the client into telling us what is really wanted. Or that we have to go through a process that convinces them the information we have given them is what they want and is what is useful to them. This, it seems to me, undercuts the positive helping relationship we want to establish. The reference librarian needs to believe, then, that the client is capable of recognizing his or her information need and that our job is cooperatively exploring, articulating and bringing out that need. Then the information we find can be related to the client's perception and recognition of what is valuable to the client's situation.

Our attitude should not be one of judging or evaluating our clients and their information needs, but rather of seeking to understand them and to accept them. I think many of us who have practiced reference librarianship have had the experience of having someone ask a question and of thinking, "Oh-h-h, he wants to know about tha-a-at?!" Or someone asks a question and you have the attitude of "Why should he want to know about *that*?" This, also, is detrimental to effective reference service. In summary then, in this area of our attitudes toward persons and the clients we serve, an open, positive, supportive, and empathetic approach is the basis for the cooperation that is essential to the helping relationship and for coming to understand the unique information needs of each person we serve.

And what of our beliefs and attitudes toward the other half of the helping relationship, ourselves? You have heard the saying, almost a cliche by now, that you can't love others until you love yourself. Those who have studied human relationships know this to be true. We need to be basically happy and pleased with ourselves in order to interact with others effectively. I think there are several bases for such a feeling of self-worth. First of all, we must *know* ourselves. The reference librarian needs to know herself or himself as a unique individual, just as we need to approach our clients as unique individuals, with differences from others, with likes and dislikes, strengths and weaknesses, and all the rest. We should reflect on and know what we believe about other people, what values we hold, what attitudes we have about others, and the various kinds of things that I talked about earlier. We should know our strengths and weaknesses with regard to our knowledge of information sources and skills as reference librarians. So, the first step, I think, is to know ourselves.

Following from and building on such knowledge of ourselves, we need to be honest–honest with ourselves, and honest with others. If we honestly recognize our prejudices and biases, for example, we can deal with them, rather than denying and repressing them and having them manifest themselves in ways we cannot control. One of the faults, I think, that we sometimes make when we teach reference services, and especially when we teach collection development, is that we ask librarians to pretend they have no biases, that they are completely neutral. It seems to me a better approach is to ask librarians to explore, to reflect on, and to recognize their biases and then to take account of them in proper and appropriate ways in collection development and reference work. Those of you who have practiced reference service or have had other human interactions will find sometimes that you are accusing the people with whom you interact of having precisely the faults that you feel in yourself, or that you would rather you did not have yourself. This is what psychologists call 'scapegoating,' and it can happen in reference as it happens everywhere else. One of the ways to avoid this is to know your own biases, weaknesses, and things with which you are not satisfied in yourself, in order to keep from projecting them onto others. If we honestly reflect on our values, beliefs, and attitudes and on our strengths and weaknesses as reference librarians, we can change, strengthen, and develop them through learning and practice. You will recall that I said that the way to change beliefs is to learn more, to come to have a different perception of what is true and false, of what is a fact and what is not a fact. So, one way to change our beliefs and attitudes toward others, one way to change our strengths and weaknesses as reference librarians, is to become aware of them and then to set out to change those that need changing.

In addition to knowing ourselves and being honest about ourselves, we need to be confident in ourselves. We must believe we have knowledge and skills to offer, that we can be of help, that we can be effective as reference librarians. First of all, on the way to our feeling of confidence, is to be as competent as we can be. We should know as much as we can about information and information sources. Certainly, it seems to me, we cannot really feel proud of ourselves as competent reference librarians unless we are doing as much as we can in continuing to learn about information sources and information. We need to keep learning about people, their diversity, their individual uniqueness, and their information needs. We should be pleased and proud of the knowledge and skills we have. We should believe that we undoubtedly know more about information and its sources than does our client, and that we have skills that will be helpful in bringing together the client and the information that he or she needs. Oftentimes, we find this difficult in reference librarianship. As reference librarians we deal with a broad spectrum of people, and we sometimes find ourselves dealing in a subject area with someone who is a recognized scholar or expert. Sometimes we feel, "What do I have to offer?" in this situation, or "How can I be of help to someone who knows so much in this field?" I think often it is helpful to reflect on the fact that even though this person knows the subject field much better than we could, we probably know the literature of that field, or the literature structure of that field, or we know something about bibliographic structure or bibliography in general, that that person does not know and that can be helpful. We have skills in helping that person articulate and recognize an information need and then finding the information to serve it, skills that the person has never had the time to develop, or does not care to develop. So it seems to me that by reflecting on the skills we have and the knowledge we have, we can remain confident in our own competence. Certainly, we can if we continue to develop that competence.

Knowledge of ourselves, honesty with ourselves and others, and confidence in our ability to help will provide the basis for success in two important aspects of the reference relationship. On the one hand, this honesty with ourselves, knowledge of ourselves, and confidence in our ability will give us the personal strength to enter into relationships with others with empathy and sensitivity. We will be able to identify with our clients, their goals, and their information needs. Psychologists tell us that people who can enter most effectively into human interactions are those who have the most confidence in themselves. In order to offer yourself to someone else you need to be confident in yourself. On the other hand, such positive feelings about ourselves will help us maintain our own identity and keep us from being overwhelmed by our clients' problems. It will help us maintain the objectivity that is so important to the professional relationship. Here again, I think, is one of the dilemmas the reference librarian faces. On the one hand, you need to be empathetic, sympathetic, and sensitive to your clients, their information needs, and their problems, in order to understand them and to gain the confidence of the client in working them out. On the other hand, you need to maintain the proper kind of professional distance and objectivity in order to keep your own professional skills and judgments from being overwhelmed by your empathy and your relating to the client. To maintain that line between sensitivity and empathy on the one hand, and objectivity on the other hand is one of the important tasks of the professional in the helping relationship.

In summary, then, the reference librarian will be more effective if he or she has positive and accepting beliefs and attitudes toward reference librarianship as a job, toward the persons who are served, and toward himself or herself. How can we connect this with those two strands of thinking that I mentioned at the beginning of my talk? Well, if it is true, and I believe it is, that people will only use information they perceive to be relevant to their own situations, then the only way we are going to be able to find information for people that they will use and understand will be to understand each user's perception of his or her own situation to go quite beyond knowing such things as the subject of the question, the age and status of the user, and other such categories. Surely, the only way we can do this is through effective interpersonal communication and interaction. This requires that the user perceive us as supportive, empathetic, competent, and accepting of him or her as a worthwhile and capable individual. Such crucial perceptions by the client will be based on clues we give in our verbal and especially our nonverbal communication, clues that will spring from our beliefs, attitudes, and values. As I pondered on this matter of how a reference librarian can make sure his or her non-verbal cues are supportive to the verbal cues, it seemed obvious to me that our non-verbal communication is most often subconscious. We do it without thinking about it, and it springs from or is based on our beliefs, attitudes, and values. To the extent that the beliefs, attitudes, and values we hold are similar to the ones we are trying to verbalize, the non-verbal cues and the verbal cues will be consistent and supportive; to the extent that they are contradictory, the cues are going to be contradictory. It follows then, at least for me, that the way the reference librarian can best help those who need information to find and use that information is to approach them with empathy, sensitivity, openness, and authenticity. This is an approach in which the user shares his or her perceptions of the information need and the information situation and the reference librarian shares knowledge of information and its sources and skills in their exploitation, all aimed at helping the client achieve his or her own goals and aspirations. This cooperative relationship, as I understand it, is the essence of what is called the helping relationship.

Running through all of this is the importance of the individual. You will recall that I started by defining reference service as an individual person helping an individual person. I would like to close my talk today with a story I think emphasizes this idea of personal service and service to the individual nicely.

You may be familiar with the anthropologist, essayist, and philosopher, Loran Eiseley. Loran Eiseley has a story in his book, *The Unexpected Universe*, called "The Star Thrower." I want to share it with you. For our purposes here, I am changing the ending a little, to make it more explicit, but I do not think Eiseley would object.

The author of our story is walking on the beach one day and he discerns the figure of another man on the beach. As he comes closer, the author sees the man is bending down, picking something up, and throwing it into the ocean, again and again. The author becomes intrigued, and he asks the man, when he comes closer, what he is doing. The man says, "You see all these starfish here? They have been washed up by the ocean, and each time they seem to be about to be washed back down, a wave comes in and throws them farther up on the sand. They are going to stay up there, and when the sun comes out, it will bake them and kill them. I'm throwing them back into the ocean to save their lives, so they can continue to live." The author of our story becomes very agitated. He says, "Look at this beach. It's covered with starfish. The sun is going to kill hundreds, even thousands, of starfish. Your throwing back a few can't make any difference. Why do you do it? Why do you bother?" The man said, as he held up a single starfish, "It'll make a difference to this one!" and he threw it into the sea.

Ethics and the Reference Librarian

Charles A. Bunge

INTRODUCTION

The intent of this paper is to help reference librarians and others answer the question, "'What is ethical reference practice?'" or "How should the librarian act or behave in providing reference service?" The emphasis will be on the individual reference librarian's interactions with clients. Ethical concerns of the library as a whole or of librarians in general, such as fees for service and equitable availability of service will be left to other papers at this institute. The paper will set out a group of norms or obligations that should guide the reference librarian's service to clients. Guidelines for following these norms will be put forward, along with strategies for applying them.

Issues to be discussed in the paper, examples of situations that raise ethical concerns, and ideas for dealing with them have been drawn from the literature on reference ethics, especially the issue of *The Reference Librarian* that was devoted to the topic (Katz & Fraley, 1982). Statements in the American Library Association (ALA) 1981 "Statement on Professional Ethics" (ALA, 1981, pp. 63-64) that are particularly relevant to reference librarians are discussed, as are the norms articulated in the section on "Ethics of Service" in the guidelines of the Reference and Adult Services Division (RASD) of ALA (ALA, RASD, 1979).

Reprinted from "Ethics and the Reference Librarian" by Charles A. Bunge, In *F. W. Lancaster (Ed.), Ethics and the Librarian (*Papers Presented at the Allerton Park Institute No. 31) Urbana-Champaign IL: Graduate School of Library and Information Science, University of Illinois.

[Haworth co-indexing entry note]: "Ethics and the Reference Librarian." Bunge, Charles A. Co-published simultaneously in *The Reference Librarian* (The Haworth Information Press, an imprint of The Haworth Press, Inc.) No. 66, 1999, pp. 25-43; and: *From Past-Present to Future-Perfect: A Tribute to Charles A. Bunge and the Challenges of Contemporary Reference Service* (ed: Chris D. Ferguson) The Haworth Information Press, an imprint of The Haworth Press, Inc., 1999, pp. 25-43.

The conceptual framework for this paper relies heavily on Michael D. Bayles' (1981) work, *Professional Ethics*. Helpful insights on the complexities of public services practice and coping behaviors that public services professionals develop have come from Michael Lipsky's (1980) book, *Street-Level Bureaucracy*, and from Jane Robbins (1972). The emphasis in his paper on the importance of continual reflection by the reference librarian on his or her reference practice and how it can be made to conform to ethical norms has been influenced strongly by Donald A. Schön's (1983) *The Reflective Practitioner*. All these works would be useful reading for reference librarians who wish to understand and improve their reference practice, including its ethical dimension.

THE REFERENCE LIBRARIAN'S OBLIGATIONS TO CLIENTS

The Professional-Client Relationship

The distinctiveness of the ethical concerns of reference librarians derives from the reference librarian's distinctive role in library and information services, i.e., direct service to individual clients. What ethical obligations does the reference librarian have to clients? The following section will explore this question by discussing the professional-client relationship in general and then several specific obligations that derive from that relationship.

As Bayles says, "The central issue in the professional-client relationship is the allocation of responsibility and authority for decision making–who makes what decisions" (p. 61). Obviously, models of such allocation can range from one in which the client has the most authority and responsibility, through a relationship of equality, to one in which the professional has the most authority and responsibility.

For example, many of the articles on the reference interview are based on what Bayles calls the "paternalism" model, wherein the professional is in the superior position and is making decisions on behalf of the client for his or her well-being (pp. 65-68). One reason that is given for conducting a reference interview is that the client does not really know what he or she needs. Also, some of the articles on ethics in reference service pose dilemmas based on the assumption that reference librarians need to protect inquirers from obtaining information that would be harmful to them, whether information on committing suicide or "shortcut" materials that would undermine the learning intended by a teacher (Is It . . . Do, 1983; Delaney, 1955).

This conception of the reference librarian-client relationship is a poor one on which to base ethical decisions because it fails to recognize the knowledge of their own situation that clients bring to the reference desk, it fails to recognize the competence that clients have to recognize when their information needs are met, and it denies clients the freedom to direct their own lives. Dorothy Broderick (1982) writes that value judgments derived from this paternalistic view of clients put librarians in the same category as censors.

> They, too, are sure that if the potential for misuse of information exists, it will be misused. This is a very poor view of the human race, one that I do not share. I am convinced that most people, given access to all points of view, will choose for themselves that which is least destructive personally and for society. I worry far more about decisions based on ignorance than those based on information, . . . (p. 22)

If the paternalistic mode is not a satisfactory basis for settling ethical dilemmas, perhaps a better model is one wherein authority and responsibility are shared equally. Readers of reference literature will recognize this model as the one underlying arguments for client-centered or counseling approaches to reference service, as well as arguments for demystifying (or even deprofessionalizing) reference service. As Bayles points out, this concept of a professional-client relationship based on an agreement between equals, in which there are mutual obligations and rights (the "contract" model), "accords well with the liberal values of freedom and equality of opportunity" (p. 63).

However, for many reference transactions this model assumes an equality that does not fully pertain. Normally, the professional's knowledge and expertise in finding information exceed considerably that of the client. Also, to the extent that the information need of the client is an important one, the client has more at stake in the reference encounter than does the reference librarian, placing the client in a weaker position.

What is needed, then, is a conception of the reference librarian-client relationship that not only recognizes the professional's superior knowledge and expertise but also recognizes the importance of the client's competence, authority, and responsibility. Using a concept from the law, Bayles calls the appropriate model a "fiduciary relationship."

> In a fiduciary relationship, both parties are responsible and their judgments are given consideration. Because one party is in a more advantageous position, he or she has special obligations to the other. The weaker party depends upon the stronger in ways in which the other does not and so must trust the stronger party. (p. 68)

In a typical situation, the reference librarian is consulted by clients with a wide range of levels of competence and knowledge regarding the subject areas of their questions, available information sources, and strategies for using them. This means that in some (perhaps most) reference encounters, the relationship with the client will be close to a contract between equals, while in others the librarian will need to assume relatively more responsibility for making recommendations and even decisions on the client's behalf. This variation in the reference situation is one of the main reasons that ethical prescriptions designed to cover all cases are so unhelpful to the reference librarian. The fiduciary model accommodates this variety, allowing the client as much authority and responsibility as is warranted by his or her ability to make decisions. Normally, the reference librarian will have superior technical knowledge and expertise regarding information sources and their use, and it is appropriate that the librarian make judgments in these matters. However, the librarian does not have expertise in the inquirer's values, in how the information should be used, or in the inquirer's goals in life. These are areas in which the client should be allowed the fullest possible freedom to make judgments and decisions.

The fiduciary ethical model for the reference librarian-client relationship emphasizes the obligation the librarian has to be worthy of the client's trust. A useful way to explore ethical norms for librarians in their relationships with clients is to ask what obligations the librarian must meet in order to be worthy of the client's trust that reference service will be provided "in a manner that promotes the client's interest–including the freedom to make decisions regarding his or her life" (Bayles, 1981, p. 70). The next few paragraphs will discuss the obligations of competence, diligence, confidentiality, independence of judgment, honesty, and candor.

Competence

Competence is the most crucial obligation. No matter now hard reference librarians work at other ethical mandates, if they are incompetent, they are unworthy of their clients' trust. Both the ALA and RASD ethics statements require competent ("skillful," "accurate") responses to inquiries. This obligation has two important aspects: That the reference librarian not attempt to provide information of a sort he or she is not competent to provide and that the reference librarian be as competent as possible in providing the information that he or she and the employing agency purport to be able to provide.

The obligation not to practice in areas where one is not competent is the basis for the proscription against the reference librarian's providing medical or legal advice. Because the lengthy training periods required for doctors and lawyers are well known, the librarian's lack of competence to provide advice in these areas is quite obvious. However, the literature contains other examples, such as the provision of the librarian's evaluative opinions on consumer products and recommending particular service providers (Wood & Renford, 1982: Schick, 1979; Is it . . . Mechanic, 1983).

There are various guidelines that might be used to assist the reference librarian in acting ethically in this regard. One such guideline is to avoid providing information personally that cannot be documented or confirmed in information sources, except in limited circumstances where the reference librarian's special knowledge or training gives him or her competence to provide substantive information of the sort required. This was the tenor of most of the responses to the ALA Ethics Committee's question regarding the ethics of a librarian's recommending an auto mechanic to a patron (Is It . . . Mechanic, 1983). Another guideline is to try always to make a distinction between assisting the inquirer in finding information sources or using them to locate desired information, and interpreting the meaning of the information found or advising on a course of action based on the information found. The librarian has special knowledge and expertise (i.e., competence) in the former but not in the latter. Of course, this is simpler to say than to do in many instances because the line between explaining how to use a tool and interpreting what an entry in a tool means is often a fine one. Peter C. Schanck (1972) has some useful advice on how to avoid crossing this line (pp. 63-64).

A key factor in this matter is the client's perception of the situation. It is important that the reference librarian be honest and candid with the patron regarding the complexity of the information sought and its interpretation, the limitations on the information that is available, and the kind of assistance the reference librarian is providing. Schanck recommends avoiding giving the patron the impression that "This is the law" and advises attempting to get the patron to understand the complexity of the law (p. 53). Other authors offer similar advice for health-related information (Wood & Renford, pp. 78-79). In areas such as law and health, it is important that reference clients understand that, while the library attempts to obtain the most complete and current information feasible, there may well be more recent and more complete information and that consulting a competent health or legal professional may be advisable. It is also important that the reference librarian try to have the client understand the nature of the assistance that is being provided, i.e., assistance in finding and using information rather than in interpreting the information or deciding on a course of action based on it.

The other aspect of the obligation of competence, i.e., that the librarian be as competent as possible in assisting clients in obtaining and using the information they need, is an especially troublesome area. Every reference librarian is all too aware that the more one knows about information sources, whether in print or electronic formats, the more one has yet to learn. The same can be said of the librarian's knowledge and skill in the varying information needs of his or her clients and the complexities of interacting with them effectively.

Two obvious guidelines here are that the reference librarian continue learning and that colleagues with specialized knowledge be involved on questions that go beyond his or her competence. In practice, these guidelines can raise more dilemmas than they settle. As Samuel Rothstein (1982) points out, most reference librarians receive inadequate institutional support for pursuing continuing education (p. 4). The schedules of reference librarians often preclude getting assistance from a colleague except on a considerably delayed basis. However, at the least, the obligation of competence requires that reference librarians, individually and in staffing groups, reflect on the limits of their competence, pursue all feasible opportunities for maintaining and improving knowledge and skills, and attempt to make the best match possible between the needs of individual clients and the competencies of the staff members who assist them.

Honesty and candor with the client regarding the reference librarian's competence are important here as well. Potential disadvantage or even harm to the client due to assistance from a reference librarian who is not fully knowledgeable or skilled in the area of the client's question can be considerably lessened if the reference librarian explains the limitations on the assistance that he or she is able to provide, outlines alternatives (e.g., consulting a specialist colleague, referral to another source), and allows the client freedom of decision in the matter.

Diligence

Another obligation following from the requirement that the reference Librarian be worthy of the client's trust is that the professional exercise sufficient care and effort in responding to inquiries. A very high level of competence will be for naught if the reference librarian does not apply it to reference questions with diligence. Rothstein notes that "It has been pointed out that reference librarians are frequently less than assiduous in the information service they render . . .," citing failure to conduct adequate reference interviews and the findings of various reference evaluation studies as evidence (pp. 4-3).

Why should such seemingly unethical behavior by reference librarians be so prevalent? A great many such lapses from diligence result from habits and patterns of behavior borne of what Rothstein calls the "extraordinarily difficult circumstances" under which reference questions are answered.

> The reference librarians must serve anonymous clients whose needs and capabilities they cannot really know; they must be prepared to give instant answers to questions covering almost every conceivable subject; they must operate in full public view and under harassing requirements of speed. (p. 5)

Reference librarians develop coping mechanisms to deal with such circumstances, including truncated reference interviews, hurried use of information sources, and rationing time among users–sometimes treating different types of users or questions differentially.

Such coping behavior can represent a necessary balancing of obligations to various clients and can result in fuller and more equitable service to more people than would otherwise be the case. Unfortunately, without reflection and monitoring, this behavior can feed on itself and develop into habits of poor reference practice and discrimination among clients or questions on indefensible grounds.

How does the reference librarian work through the ethical dilemmas involved in the obligation to provide diligent service under difficult circumstances? Surely, an imprint step is to identify the characteristics and behaviors associated with effective reference service, to make such service the standard against which one compares one's practice, and to attempt to make such behaviors habitual. Seeking support and evaluation from reference colleagues can be helpful in this regard. When conflicting demands and time pressures seem to mandate providing less than ideal service, it can be helpful to concentrate on the client at hand (i.e., to honor to the fullest extent possible one's obligation of diligence to that client) and to try not to overcompromise, so as to provide poor service to many clients rather than at least adequate service to a reasonable number. Finally, if the situation seems to demand discrimination among types of patrons or questions in the allocation of time and effort (rather than using the principle of first come-first served), the reference librarian should make judgments based on principles of equality of access (e.g., offering more help to the naive or confused user than to the self-assured) or on the distinctive role and primary clientele of the library rather than on personal biases or preferences.

Confidentiality

Privacy is a central value in American society. Its crucial relationship to the free pursuit and use of information is recognized in both the ALA and RASD statements. Both statements require that reference librarians not reveal information about their clients, either about the information they seek or use, or information about the client gained from the reference interaction. Most dilemmas in this area of ethics involve the possibility of inadvertently revealing information that should be confidential and deciding when revealing confidential information might be permissible because it is in the client's best interest or in the best interest of society at large.

The potential for violating the client's privacy is the reason for the injunction that reference librarians not discuss with others their interactions with patrons, whether as interesting staff room conversation or with persons outside the library. Potential for betraying confidential information also arises from library recordkeeping systems, including those for interlibrary loan or online search services. M. Kathleen Cook and Mary K. Isbell (1986) have useful suggestions in this regard, including limiting access to such records, limiting the length of time the records are kept, limiting client identification on the records, and revealing information only with client approval.

The question of when information about a client and his or her use of library resources might ethically be revealed is a complex one. Surely, at times, service to the client would be improved if the question were discussed with a colleague. A useful guideline here is to seek the client's permission for such discussion. When this is not feasible, perhaps the best guide is the reference librarian's good faith assessment of what the client would approve, having assessed the necessity for sharing confidential information and the colleague's commitment to confidentiality.

In some circumstances the reference librarian becomes aware that two clients could benefit if each knew that the other was working on a particular problem. The work of each client or of the company that operates the information service could possibly be enhanced if one client knew of the other's work. Here again, obtaining the client's permission to discuss his or her information use with others is an obvious guideline.

Sometimes, the needs of other members of society or of society at large seem to suggest revealing information about a client's use of information. Mark Stover (1987) uses examples of clients who use the information for known or suspected criminal activity and of helping a teacher determine whether a student library user has committed plagiarism. A more general discussion of obligations to such third parties is the subject of another section of this paper. It is sufficient here to articulate the guideline of revealing confidential information only after very careful consideration, only when there is a high degree of certainty that serious negative consequences will result from maintaining confidence, or when required by competent legal authority.

Independence of Judgment

Both the ALA and RASD ethics statements specify that the service provided by the librarian should not be influenced by personal philosophies and attitudes and should not be compromised by conflicting financial interests of the librarian. If the reference librarian does not apply his or her special knowledge and skills to make judgments that will promote the client's best interests, the librarian is not worthy of the client's trust.

Judith Farley (1982) mentions the potential for unethical reference behavior that arises with requests for information on topics on which the reference librarian has a strongly held philosophical position, and Broderick (1982) discusses various biases of reference librarians that can influence reference practice. Obviously, a reference librarian who allows such personal philosophies and attitudes to influence the amount and quality of reference that is provided is unworthy of the client's trust and is acting unethically.

This is not to say that the reference librarian should be without personal beliefs and attitudes. In fact, the more fully aware the librarian is of his or her beliefs and attitudes, the more likely he or she is to be able to keep them from detrimentally influencing professional practice. The best approach is continual awareness and reflection so as to keep one's judgments from being clouded or colored by personal philosophies and biases.

Broderick points out that a written reference service policy can also help in reducing the influence of personal biases on reference practice (p. 19). If a library or its reference staff believes that restrictions are necessary in responding to certain types of questions or certain client groups in order to allocate resources and to serve the primary clientele appropriately, such policies should be arrived at carefully and should be made known to the public so that users and potential users can make choices and decisions with full information. Point 6.4 of the RASD statement makes this point along with the point that such rules and practices should be carried out impartially.

Financial conflicts of interest are another source of loss of independence of judgment. John C. Swan (1982) points out that one's judgments and information provision regarding information sources can be influenced by special relationships that one has with a particular tool or publisher, e.g., as a salesperson, consultant, or reviewer. Steps that

Swan recommends to minimize such conflicts include making clear to the client one's special relation with reference resources, refraining absolutely from allowing outside work to creep into regular reference work, and "careful, honest scrutiny of oneself . . . " in each reference situation (p. 109-110).

The growth of fee-based information services has been accompanied by an increased potential for conflicts of interest for the reference librarian. The freelance, for-fee reference librarian is involved in a conflict between obligations to the client and the need to make a living that cannot be entirely removed. Bayles writes that such conflicts are inherent in private practice professions. He points out that they can be minimized through firm agreements with clients as to what will be done and its total cost. Where the cost cannot reasonably be estimated in advance, the professional should try to develop alternative fee systems (e.g., standard fees for certain categories of service) that will reduce the potential for financial issues interfering with independent professional judgments regarding what will best serve the client's interests (p. 78).

When the reference librarian is employed both at a "free" reference desk and by a fee-based information service (whether within the same library or outside), obvious potential conflicts of interest arise. Here again, it is easier to write into ethics codes an injunction not to let such considerations cloud judgments than it is to tread the line between referrals to fee-based services that are truly in the client's best interest and decisions to refer that are based on the librarian's (perhaps unconscious) desire to keep the fee-based service's volume at a viable level. Sometimes, honest reflection will cause the reference librarian to conclude that avoiding unethical conflict of interest would be so difficult as to preclude holding both positions. In other situations, honesty and candor with clients along with continuous monitoring of one's judgments and behavior will result in ethical practice. Swan's advice, cited above, of honest scrutiny of oneself in each situation holds here as well.

Honesty and Candor

The importance of dealing with the reference client honestly and candidly has been mentioned a number of times above, so that only a summary treatment is needed here. As Bayles says, "By definition, a dishonest professional is not worthy of a client's trust" (p. 71). The ethical obligation not to lie to a client is clear and is probably seldom violated by reference librarians.

The obligation for candor is not so straightforward, though it is at the heart of the fiduciary relationship with one's clients. In this relationship, the reference librarian respects the judgment of the client and involves the client in decisions regarding the search for information. If the reference librarian withholds or manipulates information that would help the client participate fully in such decisions, the librarian is acting on his or her own judgments of what is good for the client, and the relationship is paternalistic.

Because candor involves the amount and kind of information to be shared with the client rather than simply its truth or falsity, meeting this obligation involves the reference librarian's continually making judgments regarding how much and what kinds of information regarding the situation and options that are open to the client should be shared with him or her. Examples of areas where the issue of candor arises that have been used elsewhere in this paper include sharing knowledge regarding the reference librarian's competence and the reference collection's completeness regarding a particular question, informing the client regarding options available such as taking the question to another source of information, and disclosing the reference librarian's financial interests that might cause conflicts of interest. Certainly, candor regarding fees for service and options available to the client in attempting to gain the best value for fees paid is very important.

Are there situations where full candor is not desirable or necessary? The most obvious one would be when candor with one client would violate confidentiality with another. Another is when honest reflection convinces the reference librarian that sharing of information would not affect the client's decisions and would only result in unnecessarily taking the time of the client and the librarian. The best overall guideline is for the reference librarian to ask in each situation, "How can I best help my client make judgments and decisions regarding the pursuit and use of information that will be in his or her best interest?"

OBLIGATIONS TO THIRD PARTIES

The ethical dilemmas that receive the most attention in the literature of reference ethics concern conflicts between the reference librarian's obligations to a client and obligations to others, including society at large. Perhaps the best-known example is Robert Hauptman's (1976) experiment, wherein he asked reference librarians for information on constructing a small bomb that would blow up a home (pp. 626-627). Other examples include requests for information from city directories that could result in invasion of the privacy of those listed, requests for information that might result in or facilitate illegal activities, and requests that the reference librarian commit dishonest or illegal acts in the pursuit of information (Prokop & McClure, 1982; O'Brien, 1982).

Such conflicts raise some of the most difficult problems of professional ethics. Because librarianship has a special role and function in society and because the professional-client relationship is crucial to that function, the reference librarian must give special attention to clients that is not given to others. Thus, such obligations as diligence in serving the client's needs, confidentiality, and use of judgment independent of influence by social or political considerations are of primary importance.

On the other hand, the special function of librarianship and its authority to devise and follow special ethical obligations are for the good of society as a whole. That is, reference librarians, by carrying out their obligations to their clients, enhance the functioning of a democratic society without which the client would not be able to use the information provided. It does not make sense, then, that professional ethics would require actions that would be contrary to the values of a democratic society or that would undermine its operation or viability. When conflicts arise between the reference librarian's obligations to clients and to others, the issue is whether or not the special obligations to the client should be limited by general obligations to others and to the values of a democratic society.

Hauptman (1976) frames the issue incorrectly when he describes the dilemma as a conflict between professional ethics and personal ethics and accuses reference librarians who provided "bomb" information of failure to make personal ethical judgments and of simplistically or unthinkingly following professional ethics. Surely, purely personal ethical norms, such as those based on religious or political beliefs that are not part of the laws and values of a democratic society, cannot restrict professional obligations in the librarian's practice. Conflicts between obligations to the reference client and personal religious beliefs (e.g., aversion to certain religious practices or birth control methods) must be resolved in favor of the obligation to assist the client diligently and with independence of judgment. On the other hand, in order to assure ethical behavior, the reference librarian must make a personal commitment to the norms of professional ethics and to the values of a democratic society to which professional norms must bear a functional relationship. Thus, the conflict is not between professional ethics and personal ethics but is between special obligations to clients and general obligations to third parties within society as a whole. Acting ethically in particular instances is a matter of weighing responsibilities so as to produce a balance that most fully enhances the values of a democratic society.

Bayles (1981) further points out that the problem of conflicts between obligations to clients and to third parties is especially acute for employee professionals (as opposed to those in private practice) because such professionals can be caught between the demands of the employer and what they consider best for the client (p. 23). Reference librarians sometimes experience such conflicts between policies and practices of the library and what would best serve the needs of an individual client. An additional concern is the fact that the library in which the reference librarian works has been set up and is funded to serve the functions of a parent institution or organization (e.g., an educational institution or a corporation), adding other possible areas of conflict between obligations to the client and to others. Robert M. Pierson (1967), for example, says that reference librarians in libraries committed to the support of education should take this into account when students ask for help in shortcutting school assignments.

What general obligations to others might limit the reference librarian's obligations to the client? Because governance by law and truthfulness (if not full candor) are basic values in a democratic society, the professional should not act illegally or dishonestly even if the client's access to information would seem to be enhanced thereby. Compliance with copyright laws and honoring agreements with vendors of information sources are examples of areas where the potential for acting illegally on behalf of clients is said to be especially high. The same general obligation or principle would make it unethical to assist a patron to commit an illegal act or one that is immoral according to the values of society.

The obligation of honesty and for honoring agreements into which one has entered might also underlie the reference librarian's obligations to the employing library and to the larger institution that the library serves. To the extent that the reference librarian has made an explicit or implied agreement to carry out the policies of the library, or to the extent that the library's existence and support is understood to derive from it's agreement to serve the objectives of a parent institution (e.g., the educational goals of an educational institution), obligations to the policies and functions of the library and its parent institution might restrict the librarian's obligations to assist the client in obtaining the information he or she requests.

Another fundamental value of a democratic society is the protection of people from injury by others. This means that the reference librarian's obligation to clients to act with diligence and confidentiality in assisting them to find and use the information they request is limited by the obligation that such actions not result in injury to third persons. Hauptman (1988) argues that this is the limitation that the reference librarians in his experiment should have applied (pp. 42-46).

Stating these areas of possible restrictions on the reference librarian's obligations to the client provides little help in the question-by-question attempt to balance special obligations to the client and general obligations to others. What guidelines might the reference librarian follow in attempting to weigh and balance these obligations and to act ethically? It is useful to reflect on the fiduciary model of the professional-client relationship. This model considers clients to be competent, responsible persons. As Swan puts it, we "put our faith in the connection between knowledge and responsible action" (Wiener, 1987, p. 162). An important guideline, then, is to consider the probability (or the reference librarian's certainty) that violation of the values of society or injury to third parties will actually occur. Swan points out that "Reading about bomb building is not the same as bombing; reading about suicide is not the same as committing it . . . " (p. 162). Surely, merely the potential that the information might be used for illegal purposes or to injure someone, or even the vague suspicion that this will be the case, is not sufficient reason to limit one's obligation to one's client to assist in finding requested information. However, faced with reasonably clear and certain knowledge that the client intends to use the requested information for illegal or injurious purposes, the reference librarian could ethically refuse to provide requested assistance.

Another guideline is to consider the seriousness of the potential harm to third parties. Reference librarians argue, for example, that the invasion of privacy and harassment incurred by persons whose names and addresses are obtained from directories in the library are not serious enough to balance limiting their obligation to provide access to information in published sources. Faced with the use of information for clearly illegal purposes or for violence toward other persons, the same librarians would strike a different balance.

Another useful way to look at this balance is to consider the result that might come from limiting the librarian's obligations to the client. For example, students who cannot rely on the confidentiality of their interactions with reference librarians (as would be the case should the librarian report to teachers suspected plagiarism or "shortcuts" on assignments) are likely to avoid using the reference librarian's service and perhaps libraries generally. The detrimental effects that this could have on the students' well-being would more than offset obligations to society or to the educational objectives of the library and the school it serves.

As an overall aid to finding the proper balance among obligations, Bayles proposes that the professional ask what balance a reasonable person with liberal values would conclude best promotes the values of a democratic society. In this process one asks whether one would rather live in a society where the balance is struck in favor of one obligation or another (pp. 99-100). Surely, such a person would conclude that he or she would not want to live in a society where access to information and privacy in its use are restricted because the information *might* be put to a use that is harmful to the user or to others. On the other hand, a reasonable person would recognize that governance by law is fundamental to a democratic society and would not want to live in a society where reference librarians were obligated to use any means, legal or not, to serve their clients' needs, or where professional norms required librarians knowingly to assist clients in the performance of acts of violence toward others.

Bayles and Hauptman, following Kant's categorical imperative, suggest that ethical decisions be tested as to whether or not the actions that would follow from them can be universalized, i.e., whether the same action would be taken in a later similar case (Bayles, 1981, p. 100; Hauptman, 1988, p. 2). Such consideration can keep the reference librarian's judgments from being unduly influenced by unique aspects of the present situation and can remind the librarian to seek basic principles to guide individual decisions and actions.

Finally, the reference librarian should always keep in mind Hauptman's advice to follow Kant's dictum that we "always treat human beings as ends and never merely as means. In other words, always consider the dignity and human worth of each individual" (Hauptman, 1988, p. 2). Such consideration will help give the reference librarian's special obligations to the client proper weight in balancing apparently conflicting ethical demands. Even if the librarian decides that special obligations to the client must be limited by obligations to others or to society, the client should be treated with the honesty, courtesy, and respect that will affirm his or her worth as a human individual.

CONCLUSION

This paper has attempted to provide a philosophical or conceptual framework for considering the ethical concerns of the reference librarian. It has argued that central to the professional-client relationship is the trust in the reference librarian that the client must have in order to be worthy of this trust. The reference librarian is obligated to act with competence, diligence, confidentiality, independence of judgment, honesty, and candor.

The paper has also tried to show that the obligations of the reference librarian to the client bear a functional relationship to the values of a democratic society and to obligations to third parties that derive from these values. Some of the most complex ethical dilemmas of reference librarians arise from the need to balance special obligations to clients and ordinary obligations to others and to society as a whole.

The paper has provided guidelines and principles that can be used to address ethical issues and dilemmas that arise in reference work, along with strategies for applying the guidelines in particular situations. Central to applying these strategies is the realization that reference service is a very complex undertaking and that it is often practiced under very difficult circumstances of limited resources and almost unlimited expectations. The development of coping behaviors to make the reference situation more manageable and less stressful is a very human response; but without monitoring, these behaviors can become habits of response to clients and their information needs that do not serve librarians' ethical obligations to their clients or to the values of society such as governance by law, freedom, equality of opportunity, prevention of harm, welfare, and privacy.

In order to act ethically in reference practice, the reference librarian must continually be in a reflective dialogue with the situation as it unfolds. As each encounter with a client develops and the librarian becomes familiar with the client's information need, the reference librarian must ask, "How should I act so as to be worthy of the trust of this client and to support and enhance the values of our democratic society?" The answer will not always be obvious or easy to implement. But if the question is not asked and the answer is not confronted, the chances of the reference librarian's acting ethically will be smaller than they should be.

REFERENCES

American Library Association. (1981). The ALA's statement on professional ethics. In Jonathan A. Lindsey and Ann E. Prentice (Eds.), *Professional ethics and librarians* (pp. 63-64). Phoenix, AZ: Oryx.

American Library Association, Reference and Adult Services Division, Standards Committee. (1979). A commitment to information services: Developmental guidelines. *RQ*, 18(3), 275-278.

Bayles, M. D. (1981). *Professional ethics*. Belmont, CA: Wadsworth.

Broderick, D. (1982). Value laden barriers to information dissemination. *The Reference Librarian*, 4(Summer), 19-23.

Cook, K. M., & Isbell, M. K. (1986). Confidentiality of online bibliographic searches: Attitudes and practices. *RQ* 25(4), 483-487.

Delaney, J. J. (1955). Questions to hedge. *Library Journal*, 80(1), 48-50.

Farley, J. (1982). Reference ethics: A true confession. *The Reference Librarian*, 4(Summer), 13-17.

Hauptman, R. (1976). Professionalism or culpability? An experiment in ethics. *Wilson Library Bulletin*, 50(April), 626-627.

Hauptman, R. (1988). *Ethical challenges in librarianship*. Phoenix, AZ: Oryx.

Is it ethical for a librarian to recommend a mechanic? (1983). *American Libraries*, 14(May), 270.

Is it ethical to help a student find a how-to-commit-suicide manual and is that all you do? (1983). *American Libraries*, 4(November), 643.

Katz, B., & Fraley, R. A. (Eds.). (1982). Ethics and reference service. (Issue theme). *The Reference Librarian*, 4(Summer).

Lipsky, M. (1980). Street level bureaucracy: Dilemmas of the individual in public service. New York: Russell Sage Foundation.

O'Brien, P. M. (1982). Some ethical problems of reference service. *The Reference Librarian*, 4(Summer), 123-127.

Pierson, P. M. (1967). Is Moby Dick the whale or the captain? *RQ* 7(1), 21-24.

Prokop, M., & McClure, C. R. (1982). The public librarian and service ethics: A dilemma. *Public Library Quarterly*, 3(4), 69-82.

Robbins, J. (1972). The reference librarian: A street-level bureaucrat? *Library Journal*, 97(8), 1389-1392.

Rothstein, S. (1982). Where does it hurt? Identifying the real concerns in the ethics of reference service. *The Reference Librarian*, 4(Summer), 1-12.

Schanck, P. C. (1979). Unauthorized practice of law and the legal librarian. *Law Library Journal*, 72(Winter), 57-64.

Schön, D. A. (1983). *The reflective practitioner: How professionals think in action.* New York: Basic Books.

Stover, M. (1987). Confidentiality and privacy in reference service. *RQ*, 27(Winter), 240-244.

Swan, J. C. (1982). Ethics at the reference desk: Comfortable theories and tricky practices. *The Reference Librarian*, 4 (Summer), 99-116.

Wiener, P. B. (1987). Mad bombers and ethical librarians: A dialog with Robert Hauptman and John Swan. *Catholic Library World*, 58(4), 161-163.

Wood, S. M., & Renford, B. L. (1982). Ethical aspects of medical reference. *The Reference Librarian*, 4(Summer), 75-87.

Reference Librarians/Educators: Vision of the Future

Ilene F. Rockman
Sarah B. Watstein

SUMMARY. Reference librarian roles are evolving in today's rapidly changing environment. Values that have shaped and guided our profession thus far are discussed, and the rigors of working at a general reference desk are portrayed. Information overload, the demands of the information age, general societal trends, and new technologies are credited with shaping service directions. Strategies for maintaining professional competence and currency are presented, and emerging roles are profiled. *[Article copies available for a fee from The Haworth Document Delivery Service: 1-800-342-9678. E-mail address: getinfo@haworthpressinc.com <Website: http://www.haworthpressinc.com>]*

BACK TO THE FUTURE: VALUES AND VISIONS

As reference librarians approach the millennium, we are reminded of the values and vision that have shaped and guided our profession thus far. We are a service profession, dedicated to creating environ-

---

Ilene F. Rockman is Deputy Director and Head of Interpretive Services, University Library, California State University, Hayward, CA 94542 (E-mail: irockman@csuhayward.edu). Sarah B. Watstein is Assistant Director for Academic User Services, James Branch Cabell Library, Virginia Commonwealth University, Richmond, VA 23284 (E-mail: swatstei@vcu.edu).

[Haworth co-indexing entry note]: "Reference Librarians/Educators: Vision of the Future." Rockman, Ilene F., and Sarah B. Watstein. Co-published simultaneously in *The Reference Librarian* (The Haworth Information Press, an imprint of The Haworth Press, Inc.) No. 66, 1999, pp. 45-59; and: *From Past-Present to Future-Perfect: A Tribute to Charles A. Bunge and the Challenges of Contemporary Reference Service* (ed: Chris D. Ferguson) The Haworth Information Press, an imprint of The Haworth Press, Inc., 1999, pp. 45-59. Single or multiple copies of this article are available for a fee from The Haworth Document Delivery Service [1-800-342-9678, 9:00 a.m. - 5:00 p.m. (EST). E-mail address: getinfo@haworthpressinc.com].

ments and collections conducive to discovery and self learning; providing reader advisory and reference desk services that equitably and efficiently match information sources to a specific user at the point of need while helping users find the information they need; developing collections using subject expertise; and providing outreach services that promote library services and collections to current and future constituencies. Tyckoson elaborates upon the commonalties of reference from its inception to the current day, suggesting that we must retain those core founding principles when rethinking or redesigning reference services for today's users.[1] Ferguson and Bunge consider evolving models for reference services and service values for the largely digital library. They also identity "constants or enduring basics (that) might be used as touchstones or guides to shape this process (the evolution of new models for reference services and their applications in the largely digital library)."[2]

Within the contemporary cultural environment of reference services, reference personnel do, indeed, want to hold onto the core values of the profession. They also want to develop creative and flexible methods for the timely and expeditious delivery of information, assist users wherever they are physically located, and develop tools to educate users about the appropriate use of information sources, whether based in paper, electronic, or emerging technologies; to help users find archived information and recorded knowledge; and collaborate with others in the teaching-learning process. They want, in the words of a recent publication, to create the library of the future without diminishing the library of the past.[3]

RIGORS OF WORKING AT A GENERAL REFERENCE DESK TODAY

No doubt about it: While the librarian-patron philosophy of reference service is alive and well, traditional reference service has changed. This is due to at least four factors: (1) the advent and explosion of information technology; (2) economic, political, and social conditions within the United States that have significantly influenced the collection, organization, and delivery of information; (3) changes in the technology associated with information; and (4) the heightened importance information plays in twentieth-century society. The challenge of working at a general reference desk today can best be described as *multifaceted*.

Today's reference department is often defined by its array of both technology services and enabling technologies, in much the same way as reference departments used to be defined by the breadth and depth of their reference collections. The absence of standards for equipment, software, and the protocols to access information associated with reference service has resulted in a complex automated environment. The inclusion of new technology services and resources has placed additional stress on reference librarians; maintaining previous levels of service requires reference librarians to keep abreast of both network and resource developments.

Reference librarians today are witnessing an increased demand for customer service and for teaching people how to access information sources using current technology. Berger notes "they must also possess the knowledge necessary to not only teach users how to access remote online catalogs and fulltext resources, but also the procedures for accessing electronic discussion groups; subscribing to internet LISTSERVS; locating desired electronic bulletin board services; and successfully using File Transfer Protocols (FTP) and software navigational tools."[4]

Today reference librarians also face the challenges associated with serving patrons from a multitude of cultures and socio-economic backgrounds. Working at a general reference desk now involves working with a growing and "still largely silent user group"[5]–the educationally disadvantaged. Some users may experience information anxiety differently than their peers, who may have had more experience learning how to learn and who may be differently prepared for lifelong learning. Coping with information load and information overload requires the acquisition of numerous skills: the ability to recognize when information is needed; the ability to locate information; the ability to evaluate information through analysis and synthesis; and the ability to use information effectively. One of the more significant challenges facing today's–and tomorrow's–reference librarians, then, is helping users from an increasing variety of cultural and socio-economic backgrounds to find their ways through the complex world of information.

An active awareness of trends currently affecting libraries and a willingness to adapt and restructure our services to accommodate economic, technological, and demographic trends are assets that will equip today's reference librarian for success. Re-thinking reference remains a common topic at professional meetings and in much of the current professional literature. The evolution of new models for reference service continues in academic libraries nation-wide. As the next millennium approaches, new opportunities for reference librarians will continue to present themselves, and reference librarians will witness the continual enhancement of their roles and image.

Information Overload and the Demands of the Information Age

Does the problem of information overload in society have direct relevance for the role of the librarian both now and in the future? Hopkins contends that it does: Users will continue to be faced with both a daunting number of publications and with a challenging variety of forms or formats. He states, "The librarian or information worker of the future will need to help the user find his or her way through this complex world of information."[6] He goes on to say that the ways and methods of accomplishing this enhanced role will (1) most likely involve a combination of print and electronic sources of information, and (2) clearly involve a combination of technological and human approaches to the problem of information overload. Hopkins believes that what is called for in the future is "a spirit of teamwork or cooperation, where librarians will assist users to locate as many sources of information on a subject as possible, will further assist them by providing clear indicators of the key or quality documents, and then will leave these trained and knowledgeable users to make final relevance judgements for themselves."[7]

Surviving and thriving in our expanding information world requires that reference librarians develop and maintain high-level skills, including expert technology skills; build partnerships with key constituents, such as computer center staffs, telecommunication experts, programmers, and publishers; and clarify service philosophies. Faries stresses the importance of possessing the skills both to use and to manage emerging technologies, and the importance of possessing expert communication skills. Communications skills are needed in order to work with a more diverse and sophisticated population, but also to sell the value and purpose of the library. Faries envisions the reference librarian as consultant and problem-solver, and predicts that "as libraries become more and more complex with information existing in many formats and through many avenues, reference librarians will have to provide maximum service to users of the future. Reference librarians will need to decipher complex information requests, and quickly find and provide this information to users. Most users will have neither the time, desire or motivation to look for their own information, so they will go to others to do this, hopefully reference librarians."[8]

Societal Trends and Service Directions

Several authors have chosen to examine current economic, technological, and demographic trends that will have an impact upon libraries and librarians in the future. Dawson and McCook cite economic, technological, and demographic developments as general societal trends that most often determine organizational structure and work-roles of knowledge workers. Low examines a number of current economic trends which are expected to continue in the future, e.g., the continual increase in the cost of materials; the decrease in public funding for libraries; and an increased demand for existing resources. We know, she states, that these trends will affect the jobs of reference librarians in numerous ways, and that the effect will depend upon individual positions, libraries, and organizations. She posits that these trends will alter the role of reference librarians in the future. For example, the trends could result in "reference librarians having to devote more time to scrutinizing the selection and content of library materials as well as other sources for the information. Reference librarians might find themselves instructed to devote significant amounts of time to developing and conducting community needs assessments. And the trends could also alter how and by what means librarians provide reference services."[9]

Technological trends, such as the entrance of commercial online services and the Internet, and the production and use of CD-ROM products, into the realm of general public consumer goods also shape the future. Here Low notes "these trends will bring about a metamorphosis in the manner in which reference librarians respond to queries and provide patrons with information."[10] She continues: "These trends will bring information direct to the end user, and will decrease the amount of some types of requests. But we also know that considerable amounts of information are not available in any electronic format. And we know that librarians possess knowledge which can aid individuals in selecting the best and most reliable electronic resources for the information they seek."[11] She notes that the role of reference librarians is to help people find the information they seek, a role that will not be altered by either economic or technological trends.

Lastly, Low considers demographic trends, including the growing number of immigrants arriving in the United States. Reference librarians will face the challenges associated with "serving patrons from a multitude of cultures, many with limited or no command of the English language."[12] She predicts that "reference librarians will have to be more culturally sensitive and more adept at providing service to individuals with different linguistic and cultural backgrounds. And they may answer a larger volume of questions dealing with survival skills, acculturation, and citizenship."[13] Once again, however, she arrives at the conclusion that the basic role of reference librarians will not change.

New Technologies Shape Service Directions

More so than any other factor, the advent and explosion of information technology have challenged and changed traditional reference service. Libraries are in a period of transition as new technologies influence and shape service directions. Several libraries have taken leadership roles within their organizations and the profession to mount virtual reference services. These services include using email to receive and answer reference questions, the development of web-based tours and instructional tutorials, the creation of interactive CD-ROM learning materials, and the implementation of synchronous (real-time) electronic reference services using video and computer conferencing and two-way communications technologies.

As reported on a recent electronic library listserv, the University of Iowa reported plans to introduce a CUSeeMe/Netscape Conferencing real-time interactive service between a library reference desk and a campus residence hall, which will connect students and reference librarians using a video camera and personal computer; the University of Arkansas and Southeastern Louisiana University are beginning to implement real-time remote reference services using MOO technologies; Jackson State Community College is offering limited reference service via e-mail, with the goal of combining reference services via the web with the use of a toll-free (1-800) telephone number to provide a "human voice" to talk to for those patrons in remote locations.[14]

As libraries adopt *value-added* services to meet the changing needs of their internal and external (remote) patrons, the service ethos remains intact, albeit a bit redefined–to support the need for information anywhere, anytime, anyplace, and in any fashion that satisfies an information need.

Training

In today's rapidly changing environment, it is imperative that reference librarians maintain professional competence and currency. Weingand contends that it is important to recognize that the profession has entered into a new paradigm, and, "as the twenty-first century approaches, the knowledge, skills, and attitudes necessary to remain a significant 'player' in the information industry will require a continual updating."[15] She asserts that the quality of information service is based in large part on the competence of personnel. Strategies for assisting movement into the new paradigm include defining and developing baseline competency guides, certification and licensure, and participation in continuing education.

As implemented at Texas A&M, the baseline competency concept furnishes the library with a tool to regulate consistent, competent, basic reference service no matter what the format. Baseline competencies are defined as "a body of knowledge every person staffing the reference desk should master in order to provide a consistent level of service."[16] Benefiel and others recognize that, while the "shape" of reference service points and access to information may shift with the new paradigms, all staff need baseline subject knowledge for dealing with the public in an information-sharing capacity. They acknowledge initiatives to rethink reference, and insist that baseline subject competencies become vital should some or all of these projected models of the future of reference service become reality.

Are all reference librarians "sold" on the competency model? Hardly. Sherrer, for example, does not think that meeting established competencies are all that is necessary to move individual libraries forward in a continually evolving information environment. He comments: "We need to look for people who excel beyond basic competencies and we need people who will challenge existing ones."[17] He insists that now more than ever, "it is necessary to emphasize the service aspect of reference work."[18] The importance of interpersonal skills and abilities is stressed, as are analytic and creative thinking skills, personal traits or attributes, and a commitment to service. Sherrer believes that all reference competencies, however defined, must be centered on the service component.

Role Reconsideration

As new information technologies make finding information quicker and easier, many reference and bibliographic instruction librarians are reconsidering their long-standing belief that their primary role in undergraduate teaching is that of teaching students how to find information. Many reference librarians at the front line question whether they will, indeed, have a role. Still others believe that academic reference and bibliographic instruction librarians will have a role, albeit an enhanced role, as teaching colleagues in the years ahead. Farber points out the critical role reference and bibliographic instruction librarians play in helping students learn how to sift through and evaluate information. He understands the importance of personal touch, and the reference librarian's ability to make a "small but significant contribution,"[19] to a student's education. According to Farber, while both reference and bibliographic instruction will change, their thrusts will remain very much the same.

EMERGING ROLES: SOME OLD, SOME NEW

Just as desk services are reflective of an environment characterized by a high level of change, so is the traditional role of the reference librarian. In many institutions today, as in the past, librarians have multiple roles. Sloan summarizes a number of these roles: teacher, knowledge manager, organizer of print and networked information, advocate for information policy development, community partner, collaborator with technology resource provider, technician, and information consultant.[20] Another role that has been suggested is that of an information intermediary. Berger contends that the traditional philosophical foundation of reference service is still relevant and that reference librarians continue to be vital and valued. He challenges reference librarians to be information intermediaries, "but not in the traditional sense of linking clients to appropriate sources. Rather, the emphasis will be in connecting clients to the content from multiple sources which can then be used to create new information."[21] All of these roles speak well to the personal characteristics of reference librarians: intellectual curiosity, flexibility and adaptability to change, risk-taker, comfortable with technology, assertive teacher, and empathetic, confident communicator. Three specific roles are described: role of the librarian/teacher, role of the librarian? information provider, and role of the librarian/consultant, facilitator, organizer.

Role of the Librarian/Teacher

As technologies become more complex, the role of the librarian-teacher grows in importance, particularly in academic institutions where librarians hold faculty status. Partnerships with college-based faculty to teach and design workshops, credit courses, and instructional programs are becoming more important. A regional accrediting official recently described the change in the traditional role of the reference librarian to one of an educational leader this way:

> Forging faculty/library partnerships will require new roles for librarians and a level of leadership and initiative that has not been traditionally asserted or recognized within the institution beyond the orb of the library itself. Librarians will need to become and be seen by members of the faculty and administration as educational leaders and innovators, and not just as custodians of the institution's print media.
>
> *Ralph A. Wolff*
> *Executive Director*
> *Accrediting Commission for Senior Colleges and Universities*
> *Western Association of Schools and Colleges*

Many librarians have responded to the challenges created by the information age by taking responsibility for *information literacy*, the skills of finding, evaluating, and using data. At the University of Washington's Bothell campus, assistant campus librarian Esther Daniels helped professors incorporate information literacy into a business writing seminar. At York College of Pennsylvania, Library Director Susan Campbell trains students in PowerPoint, Microsoft Word, and the Pine e-mail system as part of a required course in mastering electronic data. At Virginia's James Madison University, librarians have created a virtual tutorial called "Go for the Gold," which features on-line tests for instant feedback and teaches students how to format their citations and distinguish reliable information from unreliable information.

Within the 23-campus California State University system, the systemwide Information Competence initiative[22] has specifically encouraged such faculty partnerships[23] to develop credit courses, or course-integrated instruction within a specific major. The results become part of the general education program,[24] first year or capstone experience,[25] or discipline-based curricular offerings of the institution.[26] In addition, workshops and outreach efforts build relationships and articulation agreements with K-14 entities. Other states have similar initiatives, although not all experiences are the same.[27]

Concomitant with the changing role of the reference librarian has come a conceptual rethinking in the definition of teaching and learning for undergraduate education.[28] Librarians have come to recognize that not all teaching is learning, and not all instructional activity needs to take place across the physical reference desk. Instructional sessions can occur one-on-one in discipline-based faculty offices, in residence halls, and in librarian offices for specialized research consultation by appointment. This change in thinking has been the focus of debate and discussion, and is well-documented in the reference literature.[29]

Support for the changing role of academic librarians and strengthening librarian/teaching partnerships has also come from the Association of College and Research Libraries in its discussion group, "Alliances for New Directions in Teaching and Learning."[30] The discussion group was established to provide a venue for librarians to exchange ideas and to promote the role of the library within such organizations as the American Association of Higher Education, the Coalition for Networked Information, and The Higher Educational Technology Association (formed by the merger of EDUCOM and CAUSE). Presentations by librarians to these groups help to advance the agenda of the teaching librarian as a collaborative partner within the broader university learning community.

Role of the Librarian/Information Provider

In 1985, Mary Ann Griffin made some predictions concerning the changing role of librarians as information providers. She suggests that the key to the future of scholarly communication, research, and information dissemination lies in the ability of librarians to provide effective access to information regardless of the format.[31] Three years later, David Lewis considers the invention of the electronic university and describes the new roles of librarians as information providers and facilitators.[32] In the 1990's, the academic librarian's *new role* as information provider continues to be of interest. For example, Jackson-Brown claims that a "key role of the librarian of the future in a democratic society will be to provide every member in society an avenue for free access and exchange of information."[33] Jackson-Brown observes that the type of instruction which librarians are called upon to conduct as a result of the demands of electronic resources is complex. She predicts that instruction and teaching by librarians will become a greater part of the role of librarians as they are called upon to facilitate the use of information technology among researchers.

Roles of the Librarian/Consultant, Facilitator, Organizer

An interesting perspective on our evolving roles as information providers/consultants is provided by Sutton in his consideration of the ramifications on reference service processes of the movement from traditional to digital library, from site-based to geographically disperse resources. Sutton looks at developments in computing power, telecommunication technologies and their fusion with computing, and complex new information structures in the form of multi- and hyper-media. He then presents a preliminary typology of library types, ranging from the traditional to the automated, to the hybrid, to the digital and discusses the service models associated with each type of library. The service model of the traditional and automated libraries is one of resource-dispensing. The goal is the provision of resources from which the user manages all of the processes of engagement with the actual information. An increased level of human intermediation is a significant component of the service model of the hybrid library. In these facilities a shift away from the simpler resource-dispensing model of service toward a consultative, value-added model where librarians are actively engaged in the processes of direct information access and assessment is observed. The networked environment of the digital library consists of an abundance and complexity of information structures. Sutton predicts that the digital library will bring to full fruition the service model which he sees transitioning from its beginning as simple resource-dispensing in the traditional library to a more consultative, value-added model in the hybrid library. In the digital library, reference librarians will most likely provide such consultative services exclusively–"client-centered services which deliver the right information, to the right person, at the right time, in the right form, in the right place, and for the right price."[34]

Sutton also posits that the interface component has been the primary function of reference and will remain so in the future. He predicts, however, that the nature of the interface function will change as we move across the library continuum, taking its largest leap with the digital library. He also observes that the issues raised for education of reference librarians by the movement of libraries on the continuum from traditional to automated, to hybrid, to digital–from library as place to library as logical entity–are manifold.

What will library reference services of the future be like? Kelly and Robbins predict that reference librarians may use their skills in both organization of information and sensitivity to user needs to work on the development of more powerful navigation tools. They also predict that librarians will be more involved with computer specialists and support staff, and more active in outreach to users no longer obligated to come to the library to use its resources. They speculate that teaching, both formally and informally, may become more of an emphasis for librarians of the future and that consumer analysis (asking users about their needs) will be one of the new roles for reference librarians. In their conclusion, they share the opinion of one author that "'the business we are in is consultation, facilitation, and organization, although the tools and products may change over time."[35]

CONCLUSION, WITH A NOD TO CHARLES BUNGE

It is particularly relevant to explore the evolving roles of reference librarians in today's rapidly changing environment in a volume that pays tribute to Charles Bunge. As expressed in countless publications, Bunge's interest in reference services and reference personnel benefits all of us who serve, or have served, at the front lines. A strong proponent of the evaluation of reference services, Bunge challenges reference personnel to do their best at helping their patrons to be their best. He has a keen understanding of the values that have shaped and guided our profession thus far, and he appreciates the difficult area of standards for reference service. Does he grasp the rigors of working at a general reference desk? Absolutely. Can he identity with the factors that today are credited with shaping service directions, including information overload, the demands of the information age, general societal trends, and new technologies? Why, certainly! Does he understand the importance of keeping up-to-date on reference materials and information sources and on reference techniques? Yes, there is no doubt that he shares our emphasis on the importance of maintaining professional competence and currency.

In this piece, finally, we have profiled emerging roles for reference librarians. We are confident that Bunge would applaud the roles suggested–the librarian/teacher, librarian/information provider, and librarian/consultant, facilitator, organizer. Bunge champions the importance of the individual and the idea of personal service to the individual; he believes reference librarians should develop a cooperative and helping relationship with their users. As we strain our eyes to glimpse the future, and find that service directions demand the assumption and integration of new roles, it is comforting to know that Bunge still walks side-by-side with us.

REFERENCES

1. David Tyckoson, "What We Do: Reaffirming the Founding Principles of Reference Services," *The Reference Librarian* 59 (1997): 3.

2. Chris D. Ferguson and Charles A. Bunge, "The Shape of Services to Come: Values-Based Reference Service for the Largely-Digital Library," *College and Research Libraries* 58 (May 1997): 262.

3. Cheryl LaGuardia and Barbara A. Mitchell, eds., *Creating the Library of the Future without Diminishing the Library of the Past* (New York: Neal-Schuman, 1998).

4. Christopher Berger, "Reference Service: A Thing of the Past?" *The Reference Librarian* 54(1996): 118.

5. See discussion in Susana Hinojosa, "Re-Thinking Reference–A True Change?" *The Reference Librarian* 54(1996), 98-101.

6. Richard L. Hopkins, "Countering Information Overload: The Role of the Librarian," *The Reference Librarian* 49-50(1995): 330.

7. Ibid., 331.

8. Cindy Faries, "Reference Librarians in the Information Age: Learning from the Past to Control the Future," *The Reference Librarian* 43(1994): 25.

9. Kathleen Low, "The Future Role of Reference Librarians: Will It Change?" *The Reference Librarian* 54(1996): 148.

10. Ibid., 149.

11. Ibid.

12. Ibid., 150.

13. Ibid.

14. Sue Swanson, "Virtual Reference: Examples of Current Practices," DIGLIB listserv, 1 April 1998.

15. Darlene Weingand, "Competence and the New Paradigm: Continuing Education of the Reference Staff," *The Reference Librarian* 43(1994): 173.

16. Candace R. Benefiel et al., "Baseline Subject Competencies for the Academic Reference Desk," *RSR: Reference Services Review* 25:1(1997): 84.

17. Johannah Sherrer, "Thriving in Changing Times: Competencies for Today's Reference Librarians," *The Reference Librarian* 54(1996): 13.

18. Ibid.

19. Evan Ira Farber, "*Plus ça change . . .*" *Library Trends* 44:2 (Fall 1995): 43.

20. Bernie Sloan, "Service Perspectives for the Digital Library," http://alexia.lis.uiuc.edu/-sloan/e-ref.html (December 1997), page 5.

21. Berger, 117.

22. Http://www.lib.calpoly.edu/infocomp (May 1998).

23. *The Academic Library in the Information Age: Changing Roles* (Seal Beach, CA: Consortium for Educational Technology for University Systems (California State University, State University of New York, City University of New York, 1977), 3. Also http://www.cetus.org (May 1998).

24. Gabriela Sonntag and Donna M. Ohr, "The Development of a Lower Division, General Education, Course-Integrated Information Literary Program," *College and Research Libraries* 57:4 (July 1996): 331-337.

25. Joan Parks and Dana Hendrix, "Integrating Library Instruction into the Curriculum through Freshman Symposium," *RSR Reference Services Review* 24 (Spring 1996): 65-71.

26. Carla List, "Branching Out: A Required Library Research Course Targets Discipline and Programs," *The Reference Librarian* 51-52(1995): 385-398.

27. Loanne Snaveley and Natasha Cooper, "Competing Agendas in Higher Education: Finding A Place for Information Literacy," *Reference and User Services Quarterly* 37:1 (Fall 1997): 53-62.

28. Robert Barr and John Tagg, "From Teaching to Learning–A New Paradigm for Undergraduate Education," *Change: The Magazine for Higher Education* 27:6 (November-December 1995): 12-25.

29. Jackie Mardikian and Martin Kesselman, "Beyond the Desk: Enhanced Reference Staffing for the Electronic Library," *RSR: Reference Services Review* 23:1 (1995): 21-28, 93.

30. "Strengthening Librarian Teaching/Learning Partnerships," *College and Research Libraries News* 59:3 (March 1998): 177-179.

31. Mary Ann Griffin, "Collection Development to Information Access: The Role of Public Service Librarians," *RQ* 24 (Spring 1985): 286.

32. David W. Lewis, "Inventing the Electronic University," *College and Research Libraries* 49 (July 1988): 299.

33. Grace Jackson-Brown, "The Academic Librarian's New Role as Information Provider," *The Reference Librarian* 39(1993): 79.

34. Stuart A. Sutton, "Future Service Models and the Convergence of Functions: The Reference Librarian as Technician, Author and Consultant," *The Reference Librarian* 54(1996): 141.

35. Julia Kelly and Kathryn Robbins, "Changing Roles for Reference Librarians," *Journal of Library Administration* 22(1996): 120.

Peer Reflection: Collegial Coaching and Reference Effectiveness

Nancy Huling

SUMMARY. Greater attention needs to be paid to communication behaviors comprising the reference interview. As a prelude to the formal evaluation of reference services, the technique of peer coaching can be used to raise self- and collegial-awareness of behaviors specific to the reference interview, and can serve as a way of continually evaluating how well users are served. This article reflects on the application of peer coaching to the reference environment, suggests strategies for implementation, and relates peer coaching to the evaluation of reference effectiveness. *[Article copies available for a fee from The Haworth Document Delivery Service: 1-800-342-9678. E-mail address: getinfo@haworthpressinc.com <Website: http://www.haworthpressinc.com>]*

An old *Peanuts* cartoon depicts Peppermint Patty explaining to Marcie that there seem to be more questions than there are answers. Marcie responds, "So?" and Patty replies, "So try to be the one who asks the questions." Reference librarians are on the receiving end of those questions, and the literature is replete with how well they do in supplying what users want and whether or not the answers are correct.

Nancy Huling is Division Head, Reference and Research Services, University of Washington Libraries, Seattle, WA 98195 (E-mail: hulingn@u.washington.edu). The author thanks Karen A. Liston for suggesting peer coaching as a tool applicable to the reference environment and for her guidance and comments throughout the writing process.

[Haworth co-indexing entry note]: "Peer Reflection: Collegial Coaching and Reference Effectiveness." Huling, Nancy. Co-published simultaneously in *The Reference Librarian* (The Haworth Information Press, an imprint of The Haworth Press, Inc.) No. 66, 1999, pp. 61-74; and: *From Past-Present to Future-Perfect: A Tribute to Charles A. Bunge and the Challenges of Contemporary Reference Service* (ed: Chris D. Ferguson) The Haworth Information Press, an imprint of The Haworth Press, Inc., 1999, pp. 61-74. Single or multiple copies of this article are available for a fee from The Haworth Document Delivery Service [1-800-342-9678, 9:00 a.m. - 5:00 p.m. (EST). E-mail address: getinfo@haworthpressinc.com].

But in order to improve service, reference librarians must also ask questions of their users during the reference transaction. The reference interview is the communication vehicle employed to gather information from the user regarding the specific need. It is two-way communication, involving the user in the process, conveying both verbally and with non-verbal signs interest in the need, and listening carefully to user response. Peer coaching is a technique that encourages reference librarians to ask questions of one another and provide meaningful and specific feedback. As a developmental and diagnostic tool applied to the different facets of the reference interview, peer coaching can result in improved reference service. By its nature, the reference culture is one of collegiality and teamwork; peer coaching lends itself to this environment.

EVALUATIONS OF REFERENCE EFFECTIVENESS

Over his long career, Charles Bunge has reflected on both the evaluation of reference in general and on the performance of reference librarians. He has written extensively on aspects of evaluation and on the tools developed to measure effectiveness. With Marjorie Murfin and Gary Gugelchuk, he developed the Reference Transaction Assessment Instrument (RTAI), which collects information from both users and librarians on the success of the entire reference transaction, from interview to completion. A description of this and other evaluation tools are covered in the *Reference Assessment Manual.*[1]

Information on the effectiveness of reference services is gathered in several ways. The library-wide user survey is the most common, but also the least helpful. Reference is usually covered in only one question. Tracy Bicknell notes that these surveys do not attempt to discover reasons for user satisfaction or dissatisfaction, nor do they usually measure user expectations, which may be low.[2] Library-wide surveys at the University of Washington in 1993 and 1995 asked users how often they used specific services and how satisfied they were with those services. As in most libraries, there was a high level of satisfaction with reference services. Because this information is non-specific and proved over two surveys to be fairly useless, the 1998 survey did not include this question. Instead, users in the Fine Arts and the Biosciences were asked to rate and comment on services for their areas. The information gathered will be analyzed to see if this method might be applied more broadly in the future. Information from general library surveys can be used, however, to establish baseline data against which to measure general improvement.

Murfin has noted that behavioral guidelines cannot substitute for user perception, but nevertheless they are a critical part of the evaluation process.[3] A statewide survey of public libraries in Maryland "(1) to determine what degree a user is likely to receive a correct answer to moderately difficult questions and (2) what levels of resources and kinds of activities are most likely to lead to desired levels of performance" reveals that 55% of the users received correct answers, and that the major reason for incorrect answers was the lack of attention to communication behaviors and their application to the reference situation.[4] Other factors, such as the size of the reference collection, the number of staff, and the availability of time, did not seem to be associated with performance. Joan Durrance devised an instrument for unobtrusive evaluation of the reference interview, focusing on behaviors and measuring effectiveness by the willingness of the user to return to the same librarian for assistance.[5] On the basis of her findings, Durrance concludes that greater effort needs to be taken to improve the interviewing skills of librarians. A survey of reference users at the University of Albany found that satisfaction depends upon more than the accuracy of the answers and includes behavioral characteristics.[6] Helen Gothberg provides an overview of assessments of interpersonal communication in reference.[7] Jennerich offers examples of techniques that have been used to evaluate the reference interview.[8] Some of these methods, such as videotaping, are generally neither practical nor popular because they are so obtrusive. Rao Aluri emphasizes that reference evaluation has to be done continuously, with one or more measures used to monitor quality. He argues that the key measures of reference service need to reflect what is important to the users and focus on quality.[9]

The ability to communicate effectively with library users, both verbally and non-verbally, is critical to the outcome of the reference interaction. Failure to exhibit such behaviors as eye contact, open questioning, active listening, empathy, and paraphrasing may result in misinterpreting the user's question and ultimately in the failure of the reference transaction. Although the profession now recognizes the components of the model reference interview, more attention needs to be paid to training and ongoing evaluation methods. Jennerich notes that "It has taken much longer to evaluate any reference services, because it is not easy to evaluate human interaction."[10]

BEHAVIORS AND THE REFERENCE PROCESS

The importance of behaviors to the reference process has been discussed often in the literature over a period of years, and some libraries developed their own guidelines by which to measure the performance of reference librarians. But it was not until the early 1990s that the profession as a whole recognized the importance of such guidelines. As President of the Reference and Adult Services Division (RASD, now RUSA) in 1992, James Rettig appointed an ad hoc committee to draft guidelines for the behavioral performance of reference and information staff. Noting that studies measuring reference accuracy "do not take into account the complex librarian/patron interaction during the reference process" and that "reference performance cannot be measured solely by the accuracy of an answer to a factual question," the committee published the "Guidelines for Behavioral Performance of Reference and Information Services Professionals in 1996."[11] These guidelines address the major components of those behaviors deemed necessary to successful reference encounters. In composing the Guidelines, the Ad Hoc Committee on Behavioral Guidelines for Reference and Information Services drew on the work of a number of librarians, including one who implemented a peer coaching program.

Behavioral guidelines can and should be used to evaluate the performance of individual librarians. A combination of the collegial environment and the impossibility of the reference manager to spend the requisite number of hours observing each reference librarian at the desk make evaluation particularly challenging. Because reference librarians are encouraged to work as a team, a program that allows peer observation should assist them to hone their skills. Peer coaching is an ideal method in that reference librarians are often unable to view objectively the quality of their interactions with users. It is naturally difficult for individuals to judge how their facial expressions, body language, tone of voice, and other personal characteristics affect the user. Having one's peers provide feedback on specific behaviors in a non-judgmental, constructive environment can contribute to an improvement in the reference process.

PEER COACHING

Peer coaching is a collaborative process in which two or more people at the same level observe, provide feedback, and coach one another on specific and agreed upon performance issues. Peer coaching is a widely used technique in business and in education, although its application in each differs. A broad examination of the business literature indicates that peer coaching is most often used in situations involving substandard and problematic performance.[12] Supervisory rather than peer coaching is the norm, although more attention is being paid to the application of coaching techniques in team environments. Such recent books as *The Tao of Coaching*[13] discuss coaching techniques that can easily be used by peer and manager alike, and are applicable to any environment. The goal of coaching in business is to improve the productivity of the employee and ultimately customer service.

Peer coaching in education has been implemented primarily as a staff development tool. Educators have discovered that teachers have a low transference of skills learned in workshops to the classroom environment and school setting. Incorporating time for practice in workshops does not seem to improve the situation. Beverly Showers and Bruce Joyce, early researchers on peer coaching, discovered in the 1980s that weekly seminars enable teachers to practice, discuss, and apply the new techniques gained in workshops.[14] Eventually this results in the formation of peer coaching groups. In addition to assisting teachers in transferring new skills to the classroom, colleagues may also work collaboratively with issues unrelated to a shared training event. Regardless of how it is applied, peer coaching is a collaborative effort to refine, expand, and enhance knowledge about the teaching profession.[15]

Educators cite the advantage of peer coaching in encouraging collaboration and collegiality. School reform author Roland Barth notes that "by embedding adult, mutual visibility and learning into the fabric of the schoolhouse, peer coaching can transform the very nature of the school culture from a place where some are transmitting learning to others to a place where everyone engages in the most important enterprise of the schoolhouse–learning."[16] The goal of peer coaching in education is to improve student learning and enhance performance through more effective teaching techniques.

Tenets of Peer Coaching

Zemke has identified the following conditions as conducive to implementing a peer coaching program: a supportive culture/environment; awareness of the limits–and strengths–of peer coaching; training in the skills of giving and receiving feedback; and practice in the art of accepting peer coaching.[17] He stresses that peer coaching is a two-way, voluntary event providing balanced feedback and support. Peer coaching is not judgmental, nor is it therapy. Peer coaching is also not a peer evaluation process. Gers notes that coaching may be viewed as a form of behavior modification.[18] Interactions between the coach and the coached must be confidential. Some of the "dos" of peer coaching include: listen actively; pause and make reflective statements; insert neutral probing questions to get the peer to continue reflection; let the coachee talk; let the coachee fill the silent gaps; and focus on the agreed-upon areas for the particular coaching session.[19] Other important guidelines include helping the coachee with specific tasks, being businesslike and frank, checking to see that the real issue is being addressed, and moderating the amount and depth of coaching.[20] (See Table 1.)

PEER COACHING IN REFERENCE

Little has been written regarding the application of peer coaching to the reference process. Two articles have addressed its use in library instruction,[21] but only three have substantively discussed peer coaching in the provision of reference desk service.

Gers describes the implementation of a peer coaching program in Maryland public libraries following a statewide survey of reference response accuracy. Although librarians were receiving training in communication techniques, discomfort and awkwardness with new skills prohibited them from fully applying them on the job. As in the field of education, coaching was viewed as a way to reinforce skills. Gers discusses the importance of feedback, specifically technical feed-

TABLE 1. Implementing Peer Coaching: A Quick Guide

Acquire basic information by reading seminal articles in the fields of business and education
Investigate applications to the reference environment by reading articles from the library literature
Ensure that an environment of trust, respect, and collegiality exists in the Reference Department
Agree upon and establish behavioral guidelines for reference performance
Brainstorm behavior areas on which to concentrate in peer coaching
Ask for volunteers to participate in a pilot program
Provide training, with an emphasis on feedback skills
Implement program as a pilot for a minimum of three months
Evaluate the benefit of the program to the coaches and the reference process

back. This, he states, has the following characteristics: it is solicited, it is timely, it is directed toward modifiable behavior, it is specific, and it is descriptive. He provides a number of helpful examples of the difference between evaluative and technical feedback.[22]

Isenstein offers an example of peer coaching at the Baltimore County Public Library using Gers's technical feedback,[23] and Arthur describes an experience with peer coaching in Temple University's Reference and Information Department.[24] Temple had an ongoing and active staff development program focusing on behaviors and skills pertinent to the reference interview. Wanting to expand their program, they decided that "coaching might be useful to our reference staff, not only assisting them in their transfer of new skills or information to on-the-job situations, but also providing them with support for fine-tuning and maintaining positive reference desk behaviors."[25] Arthur notes that peer coaching works especially well in the academic environment, in which librarians generally have a modicum of professional autonomy and work collegially. The program was deemed a success, benefiting reference service as well as increasing the self-awareness of communication style and behaviors.

Why is peer coaching apparently not used more widely in the reference environment? Lack of knowledge about the process is one major reason. One must read outside the library literature to learn more about coaching. Another factor may be that although librarians are encouraged to consult often with their colleagues on reference questions, there is a natural tendency to hang onto questions, to let ego get in the way, and to feel that requesting assistance is an admission of failure. In this case, coaching may be viewed as threatening and as interference. Time is another major factor. Desk service is now only one of the many responsibilities of reference librarians, and it is often the most comfortable. Other duties, such as teaching, consulting, and learning and advising on new technologies away from the reference desk take considerable effort.

Finally, there may be a perception that by and large the individual reference librarian copes adequately with the reference interview and displays appropriate behaviors most of the time, resulting in success. This tends to be supported by those general user surveys reporting a high rate of satisfaction with reference, and by a lack of complaints about service. A colleague once noted, in expressing concern about the adoption of behavioral guidelines, that "we weren't raised by wolves." A certain air of complacency and confidence, combined with a belief that a knowledge of the sources is all that is necessary for good service, creates a decided lack of interest in any kind of ongoing program focused on the reference interview.

Implementing Peer Coaching in Reference

Libraries interested in implementing a peer coaching program in reference can turn to the plethora of literature in the business and education fields, along with the few excellent articles in librarianship. Libraries share some important traits with both business and education: we are a customer-oriented service and we are committed to learning, regardless of the type of library. Because libraries are learning environments, we ourselves need to be committed to our own learning and sharing our knowledge with our colleagues. Peer coaching provides one opportunity for this; in general, those libraries that tried it feel that it improved reference performance.[26]

A peer coaching program may be formal or informal. Those in schools tend to be highly prescriptive and formal. Schools and teachers who participate in peer coaching programs devote considerable time to training. These programs are often implemented on a school-wide basis. This formality may be neither necessary nor desirable in a reference setting given time constraints and a less structured environment for observation and feedback. An informal program drawing upon the main characteristics of peer coaching may prove an effective alternative. Although training is still essential, it need not be extensive. The Temple University model is a good example of organizing and training for peer coaching. Reference departments can draw extensively from such books as *The Tao of Coaching* for guidance on incorporating peer coaching into everyday work life. Whereas teachers in schools are formally paired (although they usually choose their own partners), reference departments may wish to work more loosely by having everyone participate at one time or another as librarians are assigned together at the desk. For peer coaching to work, there must be an atmosphere of trust and respect in the reference department. The majority of the librarians should work well together. Once it is determined that the environment is conducive to peer coaching, department members need to agree upon a set of behavioral guidelines. Several published lists will assist this process, including the RUSA Guidelines for Behavioral Performance of Reference and Information Services Professionals, and the University of Nebraska at Omaha's Reference Desk Performance Standards.[27] Both can be tailored to meet the individual reference department's needs and goals.

Once behavioral guidelines have been agreed upon, the department can develop a list of goals on which to focus. Reference librarians should brainstorm those behavioral areas perceived to be in need of attention. All areas should eventually be addressed over time, but it is necessary to select specific behaviors on which to concentrate. To assist in selecting behaviors, department members should consider taking a self-assessment test. An excellent interviewing test appears in *The Reference Interview as a Creative Art*,[28] with such questions as, "Do I make eye contact with each patron? Do I have any distracting habits and what are they? Do I tend to make too many assumptions about a patron right away? Do I interrupt patrons to hurry them along?" The purpose of this test is to assist reference librarians in honestly assessing their approach to the reference interview. Later in the peer coaching process, the coaches can use this same list to provide feedback on some of these interviewing behaviors. Another useful resource is David Tyckoson's list of positive and negative attributes for each behavior.[29] For example, under the behavior "availability," a positive attribute would be "the librarian makes eye contact with potential patrons," and a negative attribute is "the librarian works on paperwork while at the desk."

At this point, training for peer coaching can begin. Although it is recommended that peer coaching be voluntary, it is important that all members of the department participate in the training. A discussion of what constitutes peer coaching should be discussed, based on the reading of several articles. Probably the most important facet of training is feedback. Most reference librarians, even those who have been managers, are not practiced in the art of providing feedback. Feedback is usually viewed in a pejorative sense because it is most often associated with the negative. In the peer coaching realm, feedback is supportive and professional, neither positive or negative. Technical feedback as practiced in the Maryland libraries is probably the most helpful.[30] The ability to accept feedback is as important as learning how to provide it.[31]

The training also needs to allow time for practice in a controlled environment. Arthur recommends that the video *Coaching: Practice Makes Perfect* be viewed as part of the training.[32] A staff training office can assist in organizing and offering the training. Lack of such a resource, however, does not preclude instituting a program. Zemke offers suggestions on how to proceed in the absence of formal resources.

Reference librarians who decide to participate in a peer coaching program should select a colleague they respect and with whom they work well. Following the formal training, coaches need to meet together to work out their coaching plan. A written agreement between the coaches may be useful in establishing ground rules. This agreement addresses which specific behaviors are to be observed, and determines what is and is not allowable coach behavior. One participant, for example, may want feedback on the initial interaction with the user, specifying that the coach not follow movement away from the desk. The coaches will also find it easier to work from a checklist of behaviors, using those developed in the self-assessment process and tied to the guidelines accepted by the department. Over an agreed-upon period, coaches begin observing each other at the reference desk. Depending upon how busy the desk is, the partners may be assigned to work together or may agree to select hours during which to observe. Follow-up sessions between coaches, as soon as possible after the observation, need to occur to make the feedback meaningful. At a prescribed time, the entire department should meet to review the program, discuss benefits and concerns, and to determine whether to continue or what to change.

Advantages of Peer Coaching

The advantages of peer coaching in the reference environment are many. It is an agreement between colleagues based on identified behaviors and goals, encouraging collaboration and cooperation. Peer coaching also contributes to teamwork, which in turn can improve the reference process as librarians are more willing to turn to their colleagues for advice and assistance and incorporate a broad range of possible solutions that out-of-the-box brainstorming among several individuals can generate. Since many libraries now practice peer evaluation, who better than peers to provide supportive feedback outside the formal evaluation process on how a librarian is meeting shared goals? Reference desk staff at all experience levels can participate.

Peer coaching can be particularly effective in the area of non-verbal communication; most individuals have no idea how their facial expressions and body language affect those with whom they are communicating. They may be quite surprised to learn that users react negatively to behaviors they feel are neutral. For example, some librarians tend to question users during the reference interview to the extent that the user is made to feel that the inquiry is somehow questionable. There is also the "pm/am" factor: is the librarian in a preoccupied mode or an available mode?[33] A recent poster session at ALA noted that availability is an important non-verbal signal, contributing to the user's first impression of the reference librarian.[34] The librarian, however, may have no clue as to what the user is perceiving. Peer coaching can detect such nuances in non-verbal communication.

At some point, the entire department may want to discuss issues related to attentiveness, which can be indicative of heavy workloads. Although users responding to University of Washington surveys expressed satisfaction with reference service, several commented that reference librarians seemed preoccupied because lines were long. Peer coaching promotes self-awareness and self-evaluation; during observations, the coaches may think about their own behavioral responses. But most important, a peer coaching program can contribute to improved reference service, which may ultimately be reflected in user evaluations.

Disadvantages of Peer Coaching

Time is certainly a barrier to peer coaching. The changing and broadening roles of librarians means that the time and inclination available to learn yet another technique is limited. Reference librarians may be reluctant to buy into yet another "new" management tool. Another drawback is the observation environment. It is often difficult to observe a colleague when the desk is busy, and some users may feel overwhelmed by a second librarian tagging along for observation purposes. It is a challenge for the coach to remain outside the interview as an impartial observer. And although coaches may represent all levels of staff and experience, some may be less suited to the process than others, particularly if for whatever reason they do not comprehend or agree with the behavioral objectives adopted by the majority of the department.

CONCLUSION

Peer coaching in this article refers to the user-librarian interaction within the physical library setting. How peer coaching can be applied as reference expands to the online environment–assisting users via email, video conferencing, and other technological means–needs to be examined. It may provide a greater opportunity for unobtrusive sharing and discussion since the user is not present. It also presents challenges in communication and interpretation.

Peer coaching focused on the reference interview can improve the reference process by making reference librarians more aware of their verbal and non-verbal communication behaviors, thus resulting in a higher quality of service and greater effectiveness. As Charles Bunge notes in talking about the evaluation of reference service and reference personnel, ". . . as so often happens with our favorite patrons, the informing, learning, and improving process never ends; it just keeps evolving and challenging us to do our best at helping our patrons be their best."[35] Peer coaching is not an evaluative process, but it is an improvement process that can directly contribute to the betterment of service to users. And it encourages self-questioning and colleague questioning as a way of continually evaluating how well users are served.

REFERENCES

1. American Library Association, *The Reference Assessment Manual* (Ann Arbor: Pierian Press, 1980).

2. Tracy Bicknell, "Focusing on Quality Reference Service," *Journal of Academic Librarianship* 20 (May 1994): 77-81.

3. Marjorie E. Murfin, "Evaluation of Reference Service by User Report of Success," *The Reference Librarian* 49-50(1995): 229-41.

4. Ralph Gers and Lillie J. Seward, "'I Heard You Say . . . ': Peer Coaching for More Effective Reference Service," *The Reference Librarian* 22(1988): 245-60.

5. Joan C. Durrance, "Reference Success: Does the 55 Percent Rule Tell the Whole Story?" *Library Journal* 114 (15 April 1989): 31-36.

6. Carolyn W. Jardine, "Maybe the 55 Percent Rule Doesn't Tell the Whole Story: A User-Satisfaction Survey," *College and Research Libraries* 56 (November 1995): 455-85.

7. Helen M. Gothberg, "Communication and the Reference Interface," in *The Reference Assessment Manual* (Ann Arbor: Pierian Press, 1995), 76-81.

8. Elaine Z. Jennerich and Edward J. Jennerich, *The Reference Interview as a Creative Art* (Englewood, CO: Libraries Unlimited, 1997).

9. Rao Aluri, "Improving Reference Service: The Case for Using a Continuous Quality Improvement Method," *RQ* 33 (Winter 1993): 220-36.

10. Jennerich, 95.

11. Reference and User Services Association, "RUSA Guidelines for Behavioral Performance of Reference and Information Services Professionals," *RQ* 36 (Winter 1996): 200-03.

12. Ron Zemke and Kristin Anderson, *Coaching Knock Your Socks off Service* (New York: AMACOM, 1997).

13. Max Landsberg, *The Tao of Coaching: Boost your Effectiveness at Work by Inspiring Those Around You* (Santa Monica, CA: Knowledge Exchange, 1997).

14. Beverly Showers and Bruce Joyce, "The Evolution of Peer Coaching," *Educational Leadership* 53 (March 1996): 12-16.

15. Pam Robbins, *How to Plan and Implement a Peer Coaching Program* (Alexandria, VA: Association for Supervision and Curriculum Development, 1991). Reproduced in Educational Resources Information Clearinghouse, ERIC Document 337881.

16. Roland S. Barth, "Introduction," in Barbara Little Gottesman and James O. Jennings, *Peer Coaching for Educators* (Lancaster, PA: Technomic Publishing, 1994), x.

17. Zemke, 130.

18. Gers, 249.

19. Gottesman and Jennings, 44.

20. Landsberg, 105.

21. Lee-Allison Levene, "Peer Coaching: Professional Growth and Development for Instruction Librarians," *Reference Services Review* 21(1993): 35-42; and Paul Burnham, "Fine-Tuning Classroom Technique: A Peer Coaching Experience," *Research Strategies* 11 (Winter 1993): 42-46.

22. Gers, 251-52.

23. Laura J. Isenstein, "On the Road to STARdom: Improving Reference Accuracy," *Illinois Libraries* 73 (February 1991): 146-51.

24. Gwen Arthur, "Peer Coaching in a University Reference Department," *College and Research Libraries* 51 (July 1990): 367-73.

25. Ibid., 368.

26. Gers, Arthur, Isenstein.

27. Carole A. Larson and Laura K. Dickson, "Developing Behavioral Reference Desk Performance Standards," *RQ* 33 (Spring 1994): 349-57.

28. Jennerich, 19.

29. David A. Tyckoson, "Wrong Questions, Wrong Answers: Behavioral vs. Factual Evaluation of Reference Service," *The Reference Librarian* 38(1992): 151-73.

30. Gers, 250-51.

31. Zemke, 135.

32. American Library Association, *Coaching: Practice Makes Perfect* (Baltimore: Library Video Network, 1986). Video.

33. Virginia Boucher, "Nonverbal Communication and the Reference Interview," *RQ* 16 (Fall 1976): 31.

34. Paula M. Ganyard and Lori Ott, "Do You Know What You Are Really Saying? Nonverbal Communication & Reference Librarianship," ALA Poster Session 11-2,27 June 1998, Washington, D.C.

35. Charles A. Bunge, "Evaluating Reference Services and Reference Personnel," *The Reference Librarian* 43(1994): 204.

PART 2: REFERENCE SOURCES

Select Bibliography and Overview of Bunge's Publications Related to Reference Sources

Julia Gelfand

BIBLIOGRAPHY

"Current Reference Books." *Wilson Library Bulletin* 1972-81. Column.

"The Reviewing of Adult Reference Materials for General Libraries." *The Reference Librarian* 1-2 (Fall-Winter 1981): 21-29.

"If I Had to Choose." *RSR: Reference Services Review* 10 (Fall 1982): 11-13.

Julia Gelfand is Applied Sciences Librarian, Science Library, University of California, Irvine, Irvine, Ca 92623-9556 (E-mail: jgelfand@lib.uci.edu).

[Haworth co-indexing entry note]: "Select Bibliography and Overview of Bunge's Publications Related to Reference Sources." Gelfand, Julia. Co-published simultaneously in *The Reference Librarian* (The Haworth Information Press, an imprint of The Haworth Press, Inc.) No. 66, 1999, pp. 75-77; and: *From Past-Present to Future-Perfect: A Tribute to Charles A. Bunge and the Challenges of Contemporary Reference Service* (ed: Chris D. Ferguson) The Haworth Information Press, an imprint of The Haworth Press, Inc., 1999, pp. 75-77. Single or multiple copies of this article are available for a fee from The Haworth Document Delivery Service [1-800-342-9678, 9:00 a.m. - 5:00 p.m. (EST). E-mail address: getinfo@haworthpressinc.com].

"The Publishing of Heavily Illustrated Reference Books." *RSR: Reference Services Review*, 11 (Spring 1983): 89-98.

"An 'Alms-Basket' of 'Bric-a-Brac': Brewer's Dictionary of Phrase and Fable." In: *Distinguished Classics of Reference Publishing*, edited by J. Rettig. Phoenix: Oryx Press, 1992.

OVERVIEW

Charles Bunge's prolific body of work concentrates on service issues and patterns as they have been affected by new information readiness, users' expectations, changing functions of libraries outside of reference, methods of communication, available technology, and the work environment of libraries. It is clear that the activities associated with reference work and information products that are the foundation for reference collections are a bloodline for him. His is a surpassing method of scholarship and inquiry into reference work, a style of teaching, and legacy of experience. Bunge's writings typically provide a context for the situation and then develop a thesis that contains insight, revelation, and new ideas. His passion for service principles is as hard to conceal as his innate ability to see a variety of library environments and their implications for reference. With respect to reference sources in particular, Bunge has pondered, studied, and then written about how librarians become familiar with resources and how they are always preparing to become better at what they do.

When asked, "If you were stranded on a desert island and had to create a reference-information service with only ten sources, which ten would you choose?" Bunge took a content-rich approach in "If I Had to Choose" by concentrating on the "ten sources with the most information." This allowed him to think exactly how he would offer a list of balance, richness in scope, and breadth with different kinds of information–pictorial, statistical, textual. He concentrates on books dense with factual information, directions for survival (cookbook and *Merck Manual*), or how to communicate clearly (dictionary and book of quotations).

When we think about the *perfect* reference work, the list of what it must contain almost always includes images and illustrative material. Bunge devotes an entire article in 1983 ("The Publishing of Heavily Illustrated Reference Books") to this very notion, affirming both how technology has advanced and how we continue to struggle with some of the issues of preserving the plates and images found in reference works.

In "The Reviewing of Adult Reference Materials for General Libraries," readers learn how Bunge approaches collection development activities for small- and medium-size general libraries. Bunge speaks especially to the value of the mixed and somewhat varied reviewing tools. He is cautious so as to be fair in his assessment and, by his own words, is more descriptive than critical. The activity of reviewing, he notes, is not done as a single function by librarians but is part of a larger workflow. He positions the major themes of timeliness, evaluative content, and what librarians expect from the reviewing process as key elements of the survey he conducted to gain first-hand information.

An "Alms-Basket" of "Bric-a-Brac": *Brewer's Dictionary of Phrase and Fable*

Charles A. Bunge

DEVELOPMENT AND HISTORY

The first edition of *Brewer's Dictionary of Phrase and Fable* was published in the year that Charles Dickens died. It was as firmly rooted in and reflective of the literary, intellectual, and social concerns of Victorian England as were the novels of Dickens, and, like them, *Brewer's Dictionary* has entertained and informed successive generations to the present day. Both Dickens and Brewer addressed social problems–in Brewer's case the need to make the fruits of nineteenth-century scholarship accessible to an ever widening range of readers–but they were also willing to respond to the Victorian hunger for diversion and entertainment, a formula that has stood them both in good stead for over a century.

Ebenezer Cobham Brewer was born in 1810 into the family of a Norwich schoolmaster. He worked his way through college at Trinity Hall, Cambridge, graduating with first-class honors in 1836. In 1848 he was awarded the LL.D. He entered the priesthood in 1838, probably hoping this would be an entrée into a university or scholarly career. However, after graduating from college, he assisted his father at the family's boarding school, becoming its headmaster when his father retired. He traveled extensively on the Continent and lived for awhile in Paris. He read very widely and had excellent facility with languages.[1]

[Haworth co-indexing entry note]: "An 'Alms-Basket' of 'Bric-a-Brac': *Brewer's Dictionary of Phrase and Fable*." Bunge, Charles A. Co-published simultaneously in *The Reference Librarian* (The Haworth Information Press, an imprint of The Haworth Press, Inc.) No. 66, 1999, pp. 79-89; and: *From Past-Present to Future-Perfect: A Tribute to Charles A. Bunge and the Challenges of Contemporary Reference Service* (ed: Chris D. Ferguson) The Haworth Information Press, an imprint of The Haworth Press, Inc., 1999, pp. 79-89.

Around 1840, Brewer's *Guide to Science* (London: Jerrold) launched a successful career of writing informational and instructional materials for a popular audience. The *Guide* sold several hundred thousand copies and was translated into numerous languages. In the early 1860s Brewer started what would be a long and fruitful association with the publishing house of John Cassell. By then, Cassell, social reformer and former temperance lecturer, had firmly established his publishing company and its policy of publishing good educational and recreational reading for the working man.[2]

Undoubtedly, Brewer's experience as a schoolmaster and his proven ability as an educational writer were particularly attractive to the publisher. Brewer had an office at Cassell's La Bell Sauvage quarters, where he wrote and edited many of the firm's popular works for adults and children.[3] He was the compiler of such reference books as the *Reader's Handbook of Famous Names in Fiction* (London: Chatto & Windus) and the *Historic Notebook* (London: Smith, Elder), which were considered standard sources for many years.

THE DICTIONARY'S ANTECEDENTS

Brewer's grandson, P.M.C. Hayman, writes that Brewer himself attributed the genesis of the *Dictionary of Phrase and Fable* to "his boyhood habit of notetaking, which he continued all his life."[4] This habit of making and saving notes from one's reading, along with correspondence between authors and their readers, seems to have been common in Brewer's day. Brewer wrote that the popularity of his Guide to Science "brought me a large number of questions on all imaginary matters." He accumulated the answers to these questions, along with other notes and references, in AZ pigeonholes, and they became the nucleus of the *Dictionary.*[5]

The *Dictionary of Phrase and Fable* also had roots in antiquarianism and the miscellanies of folk custom, beliefs, and curiosities it produced, including Hone's *Every-Day Book* (London: Hunt & Clarke, 1825-26), John Timbs' *Things Not Generally Known* (London: David Borgue, 1856) and other works, and Robert Chambers' *Book of Days* (Edinburgh: W. & R. Chambers, 1862-64). Brewer called his miscellany "bric-a-brac" and said that his entries drew in the "curious . . ., historical trifles . . ., and references to Scandinavian and other mythology."[6] If the *Dictionary* had a tap root, it surely fed on the nineteenth-century philology that produced many etymological dictionaries in Brewer's day, culminating in the *Oxford English Dictionary.* He wrote that etymology "forms a staple of the book," especially etymologies and explanations of familiar phrases, allusions that would puzzle the common reader, and "words that have a tale to tell."[7] And there was the Victorian impulse toward self-improvement and Brewer's concern for making knowledge and literature accessible to the increasingly literate working class. He called his work an "alms-basket," alms being gifts for the less fortunate, and said that he selected from his mass of notes those items that he thought were "best suited for popular purposes."[8] The second ("New") edition was published in 13 installments (hence, the frequent references to it as the 1894-95 edition), a common nineteenth-century strategy for making books affordable to working-class people.

John Buchanan-Brown, former manager of Cassell's Reference Department, points out that a more immediate inspiration for Brewer was William Adolphus Wheeler's *Noted Names in Fiction* (Boston: Ticknor and Fields).[9] Buchanan-Brown believes that Wheeler was not only the source for some of Brewer's entries, but that he challenged Brewer to provide information on such things as "celebrated customs and phrases" that represented what Wheeler called "too vast a field of enquiry" for him to have undertaken. Indeed, Brewer's first edition does contain entries for phrases that Wheeler used as examples of his exclusions, such as "flap-dragon" and "to carry coals to Newcastle."[10]

Brewer's, in turn, has influenced other reference works, especially literary handbooks. For example, Henrietta Gerwig, in the preface to Crowell's Handbook for Readers and Writers, acknowledged her debt to the Dictionary, and a number of her entries were taken directly from it.[11] William Rose Benét, in his preface to the Handbook's successor, The Reader's Encyclopedia, expressed his pleasure with this association, noting that Brewer's was among the reference books in his father's library.[12]

CRITICAL RECEPTION

Reference book reviewers have treated *Brewer's* well over the years. Early printings contained a page of "Selections from Notices of the Press" that quoted complimentary notes from newspapers and periodicals of the day. These notes pointed out features that would be mentioned again and again for the next 120 years. The writer in *The Daily Telegraph* noted that the *Dictionary* offered "the rare attraction in a book of reference of being thoroughly readable," and others noted that it would provide much pleasure and amusement. The *West Sussex Gazette* and *The Manchester Examiner* recommended the work to students, speakers, writers, and general readers who needed explanations of allusions or "who are in want of pertinent illustrations," while another reviewer characterized the knowledge in the volume as "one of the very best means of effecting a pleasant diversion from the dull level of commonplace small-talk in ordinary company." From the first printing onward, reviewers agreed that Brewer's should "find a place in every library, whether public or private."[13]

Reviewers greeted each successive major revision with notes of from one to several paragraphs. The *London Quarterly* review of the 1894-95 edition is typical among these. It notes *Brewer's* "enormous popularity," its improvement through updating and correction of old entries and the addition of new ones, its delights for lovers of the curious, and its general usefulness to other readers.[14] The *Reference Books Bulletin* note on the 1989 edition strikes a similar tone.[15] In between these, reviewers took special note of the 1970 centenary edition. For example, B. Hunter Smeaton, writing in *Library Journal*, reflected on Brewer's particular usefulness for items that are likely to be absent from other reference books,[16] and the reviewer in *The Times Literary Supplement* wished that the new edition had concentrated on such items, leaving "all the other terms to works which cover them more fully and knowledgeably . . ."[17]

Such reviews both reflected and confined *Brewer's* early-won status as a standard reference book. The same is true of its treatment in lists of recommended reference works. As early as 1877, Justin Winsor included it on a list of reference books for small libraries, albeit with note of its borrowings from Wheeler mentioned above.[18] Alice B. Kroeger included it in her 1902 *Guide to the Study and Use of Reference Books*, (Boston: American Library Association) as has every edition of "Mudge" (or "Winchell" or "Sheehy" depending on one's generation). Likewise, Bessie Graham included it in the first edition of her *Bookman's Manual* (New York: Bowker, 1921), and it is still listed in the latest edition of *The Reader's Adviser* (New York: Bowker, 1986-88). British guides have been equally consistent in listing it.

Not surprisingly, *Brewer's* is included among the tools that are taught in courses on reference materials in library schools, and is among the tools considered "vital" for all types and sizes of libraries in a study conducted by Wallace Bonk to see what sources all library school students should be taught.[19] And John C. Larsen found that most library schools included *Brewer's* among the "tried-and-true" titles in their humanities literature or bibliography courses.[20] Various reference course textbooks, from Shores to Katz, have also included *Brewer's*.

EVOLUTION AND EDITIONS

No sooner was the first printing of the *Dictionary* off the press than Brewer was noting needed corrections and addenda. While the pagination and most of the entries remained constant through the 1870 version's numerous printings (called "editions" through at least 26), some corrections and additions were made on the pages, and many printings had one or more pages of "addenda et corrigenda." Many of these had been suggested in letters from readers of the volume, whom Brewer acknowledged in additions to the preface. Alter several printings, the publisher added a "Bibliographic Appendix," which was a listing of English authors and their works, based on W. Davenport Adams' *Dictionary of English Literature* (2nd ed., London: Cassell, Petter, & Galpin, 1878). This appendix was discontinued with the 1923 edition.

By 1894, the needed correction and additions were beyond what could be done "with such clipping and verbal changes as can be made in stereotyped plates," and a completely reset "New Edition" was published.[21] By this time, the publishers claimed that 100,000 copies of the volume had been produced, and the title page of printings of the new edition indicated increases in this number (e.g., "110th Thousand" in 1899, "129th Thousand" in 1905).

Brewer expanded the size of his dictionary by a third in the second edition. He also corrected many entries and substituted new items for less useful ones. His preface to the new edition credits two sources for these corrections and expansions. First, there were "many hundreds of correspondents," some of whom seem to have gone through the first edition painstakingly, suggesting corrections, quotations, and other changes. The other source was the wealth of material coming out of what Brewer dubbed "The Era of English Philology." He wrote that he took advantage of "this great literary movement from every available source," very probably including the early installments of the *New English Dictionary.*[22]

The 1894-95 edition was reprinted numerous times up through World War I. Another "New Edition" was published in 1923. Buchanan-Brown says that Lawrence H. Dawson edited this version, though he is not mentioned on the title page or elsewhere in the volume.[23] Revisions consisted mainly of dropping numerous terms and allusions that had fallen out of use since the 1890s, and the addition of new terms and phrases.

By the end of World War II, *Brewer's* was much in need of revision again, and it was the first of the Cassell reference books to receive attention after the turmoil of the war period subsided.[24] Cassell's chairman, Desmond Flower, took personal interest in the revision, and a "Revised & Enlarged" edition came out in 1952.[25] The unnamed editor wrote in the volume's "Editor's Note" that the new edition had been "brought up to date by the inclusion of many forms of expression that have arisen during the past years," including phrases that came into use during the war, such as "blood, toil, tears, and sweat" and the V-for-victory symbol.

With the 1952 edition, the publishers again adopted the practice of referring to printings as editions. The "fifth edition" of 1959 contained minor revisions within the same page set-up, and in 1963 a "Revised Edition" (also referred to as the eighth edition) was published "in order to keep pace with the coinage of new phrases."[26]

In 1963 Desmond Flower appointed Ivor H. Evans editor of what was to be the 1970 "Centenary Edition." Evans was recommended by S. H. Steinberg, Cassell's editor in charge of dictionaries, with whom Evans had worked on the *Dictionary of British History* (New York: St. Martin's).[27] Evans, like Brewer, was a school teacher. He was educated at King's College, London, and the University of London Institute of Education.

Evans completely revised the *Dictionary.* He discarded many entries that seemed inappropriate to Brewer's original conception, especially technical expressions and other terms for which one would be likely to consult a general dictionary or encyclopedia.[28] Many remaining entries were rewritten for accuracy, clarity, and conciseness. Some 2,000 new entries for recent and current phrases were added, and an improved system of cross-referencing was used.

Ivor Evans has remained editor through two subsequent editions, the 1981 "Revised Edition" and the 1989 "Fourteenth Edition." His methods of collecting materials for the *Dictionary* are strikingly similar to those used by Brewer himself. "I have always read extensively and have been blessed with a good memory and always register anything that might be worth space in *Brewer's*, either as an entry or a worthwhile quotation. I work on the principle of Captain Cuttle in Dickens's *Dombey and Son*, When found make a note of ". . ." He also picks up expressions from conversation, newspapers, periodicals, and correspondence. Each potential new entry is carefully checked in several sources and weighed as to its appropriateness for *Brewer's*. Entries that pass the test are placed in Evans' equivalent of Brewer's pigeonholes to await the next revision.[29]

American publishers have published editions and printings of *Brewer's* parallel to those of Cassell. Except for the title pages, these versions have been exactly the same as Cassell's. The firm of Claxton, Remsen and Heffelfinger was the American publisher into the 1880s, and Lippincott published the volume through the 1923 edition. In 1952 George W. Jones added the *Dictionary* to Harper & Row's list of "staples," where it has more than met the criteria of being practical and informative and having long-term sales potential.[30] Various publishers have also found *Brewer's* an attractive title to reprint. The 1894-95 edition appeared as one of Henry Altemus' cheap reprint editions in 1898, and Avenel Books published a reprint of the same edition in 1978 (both with a curious extraneous quotation mark in their printed transcriptions of Brewer's handwritten preface that was in early printings of the 1894-95 edition as a facsimile).

THE CURRENT EDITION

The 1989 edition of Brewer's is quite similar to that of 1870. Several small sections of the alphabet (100 entries) in the 1989 edition were examined by this author, as were the same sections of the 1870 edition (97 entries). Fifty-six entries are in both editions, 37 of them largely the same in content and wording. Reflections of successive generations of scholarship and changes in usage can be found by tracing such entries as "Stonehenge," "Barbecue," and those under "Oil" through various editions. The first edition contains 41 entries that have not survived into the "fourteenth" edition, e.g., "Hegemony," "Newfangled," "Papa," and "Swiss Family Robinson." The latest edition contains 44 entries not found in the first edition, e.g., "Blurb," "Heidelberg Man," "In the Swim," and "Switched on." The 1989 edition adds a 20-page index that will supplement the volume's cross-references.

ITS ENDURING VALUE

Why has a work that was so much a product of its age survived to serve eras that have been so different in characteristics and needs? The answer lies in its combination of two features that were pointed out by reviewers of the first edition. First, Brewer emphasized practical reference usefulness. Through the years, the volume has helped a broad range of readers and writers, from the student or the self-educated reader who wished to understand literary allusions and to share the culture they represent, to the scholar or the well-educated writer who needed to verify a half-remembered phrase or its source. The *Dictionary* has been especially useful for phrases and adages that often get left out of, general dictionaries and for lists of such phenomena as patron saints, national anthems, or dogs of note. Certainly, a key to the volume's continued usefulness has been Cassell's willingness to support revisions, so that users could find recently coined phrases, along with now obscure allusions found in literature from the past.

The second feature that has accounted for *Brewer's* remarkable success over the years is its delights for the browser. It is a disciplined user, indeed, who can look up one phrase in the *Dictionary* and put the book down immediately. Curiosity is a timeless human trait, whether in the Victorian antiquarian or in the trivia buff of the 1990s, and Brewer's has always spoken to it. Librarians who have bought the book for reference collections, readers who have perused it in libraries, and those who have it on their shelves at home will admit, with only a little hesitation, that the book may have been bought for its reference value but that it is loved for its hours (or moments, however fleeting) of browsing enjoyment.

To keep "Brewer's" from the fate of "Webster's" and "Roget's," Cassell's has registered the name as a British trademark. On the other hand, the publisher would like to take advantage of the widespread familiarity with "Brewer's" as a name, perhaps using it to enhance the acceptance of a similar reference tool for young people and another with a political emphasis.[31] Since the latest edition of the *Dictionary* has come out very recently, it is too early for the publisher to have formulated definite plans for yet another revision. However, allusions to fables of the past and the coinage of phrases will surely continue apace. Just as surely, *Brewer's Dictionary of Phrase and Fable* will continue to offer alms to readers (and listeners and viewers) of the twenty-first century who need help in sorting out the bric-a-brac of their past and present.

PUBLICATION HISTORY

Dictionary of Phrase and Fable, Giving the Derivation, Source, or Origin of Common Phrases, Allusions, and Words that have a Tale to Tell, by E. Cobham Brewer. London: Cassell, Petter, & Galpin, 1870. 976p.

Dictionary of Phrase and Fable, Giving the Derivation, Source, or Origin of Common Phrases, Allusions, and Words that have a Tale to Tell, by E. Cobham Brewer, New Edition, Revised, Corrected, and Enlarged, to which is added A Concise Bibliography of English Literature. London: Cassell, 1895. 1,440p.

A Dictionary of Phrase and Fable, by E. Cobham Brewer. New Edition. London: Cassell, 1923. 1,157p.

Brewer's Dictionary of Phrase & Fable. Revised & Enlarged. London: Cassell, 1952. 977p.

Brewer's Dictionary of Phrase & Fable. Revised Edition. London: Cassell, 1963. 970p.

Brewer's Dictionary of Phrase and Fable. Centenary Edition, revised by Ivor H. Evans. London: Cassell, 1970. 1,175p.

Brewer's Dictionary of Phrase and Fable. Revised Edition, by Ivor H. Evans. London: Cassell, 1981. 1,213p.

Brewer's Dictionary of Phrase and Fable. Fourteenth edition, by Ivor H. Evans. London: Cassell, 1989. 1,220p.

BIBLIOGRAPHY

Neither primary nor secondary sources regarding E. Cobham Brewer and his *Dictionary* are plentiful. Most of the relevant Cassell archives were destroyed in the air raid that destroyed La Belle Sauvage in 1941. The only easily accessible biography is the "brief memoir" by his grandson, P. M. C. Hayman, that is part of the introductory material in the 1970 Centenary Edition of the *Dictionary*. John Buchanan-Brown, former manager of Cassell's Reference Department, has provided a useful introduction to the 1981 and 1989 editions that places the work in its cultural context. Ivor H. Evans' editor's preface to the 1970, 1981, and 1989 editions provides brief information on the history of *Brewer's* and on his revisions. An understanding of John Cassell's background and activities in publishing informational and educational materials for working-class people is important to understanding the cultural context of *Brewer's*, and Newell-Smith's book on Cassell's publishing house will provide useful and interesting insights in this regard. Likewise, good treatments of education and reading in the Victorian era, such as those by Richard Altick, will provide context very helpful to understanding Brewer and his works.

Altick, Richard D. *The English Common Reader: A Social History of the Mass Reading Public 1800-1900*. Chicago: University of Chicago Press, 1957.

Buchanan-Brown, John. "Introduction." In *Brewer's Dictionary of Phrase and Fable*, edited by Ivor H. Evans, ix-xvi. 14th ed. London: Cassell, 1989.

Collison, Robert. *Encyclopedias: Their History Throughout the Ages*. New York: Hafner, 1966.

Hayman, P.M.C. "E. Cobham Brewer LL.D.: A Brief Memoir by His Grandson." In *Brewer's Dictionary of Phrase and Fable*, edited by Ivor H. Evans, vii-xii. Centenary ed. London: Cassell, 1970.

McArthur, Tom. *Worlds of Reference: Lexicography, Learning and Language from the Clay Tablet to the Computer*. Cambridge: Cambridge University Press, 1986.

Nowell-Smith, Simon. *The House of Cassell, 1848-1958*. London: Cassell, 1958.

NOTES

1. P.M.C. Hayman, "E. Cobham Brewer LL.D.: A Brief Memoir by His Grandson," in *Brewer's Dictionary of Phrase and Fable*, Centenary ed., ed. by Ivor H. Evans (London: Cassell, 1970), vii-xii.

2. Simon Nowell-Smith, *The House of Cassell*, 1848-1958 (London: Cassell, 1958), 36-49.

3. John Buchanan-Brown, "Introduction," in *Brewer's Dictionary of Phrase and Fable*, 14th ed., ed. by Ivor H. Evans (London: Cassell. 1989), xii.

4. Hayman, ix-x.

5. Ibid.

6. E. Cobham Brewer, "Preface," in *Dictionary of Phrase and Fable* (London: Cassell, Petter, & Galpin, 1870), v-viii.

7. Ibid.

8. Ibid.

9. Buchanan-Brown, xi-xii.

10. William A. Wheeler, *An Explanatory and Pronouncing Dictionary of the Noted Names of Fiction* (Boston: Ticknor and Fields, 1866), v-vi.

11. Henrietta Gerwig, *Crowell's Handbook for Readers and Writers* (New York: Crowell, 1925), v. See, for example, entries for 'Abigail," and "Abracadabra."

12. William Rose Benét, "Preface to the First Edition," *in The Reader's Encyclopedia*, 2nd ed. (New York: Crowell, 1965), unpaged.

13. Selections from "Notices of the Press," in *Dictionary of Phrase and Fable*, 3rd ed., by E. Cobham Brewer (London: Cassell, Petter, & Galpin, 1872), unpaged.

14. Review *of Dictionary of Phrase & Fable, London Quarterly and Holborn Review* 86 (July 1896): 389-90.

15. Review of *Brewer's Dictionary of Phrase and Fable, Booklist* 86 (1 March 1990): 1380-81.

16. B. Hunter Smeaton, Review of *Brewer's Dictionary of Phrase and Fable, Library Journal* 97 (15 March 1972): 1002.

17. "As They Brew . . .", *The Times Literary Supplement* no. 3581 (16 October 1970): 7.

18. Justin Winsor, "Reference Books in English," *Library Journal* 1 (31 March 1877): 247-49.

19. Wallace J. Bonk, *Use of Basic Reference Sources in Libraries* (Ann Arbor: University of Michigan, 1963), 116-28.

20. John C. Larsen, 'Titles Currently Studied in Humanities Courses," *Journal of Education for Librarianship* 10 (Fall 1969): 120-28.

21. E. Cobham Brewer, "Preface," in *Dictionary of Phrase and Fable*, New ed. (London: Cassell, 1895), unpaged.

22. Ibid.

23. Buchanan-Brown, xv.

24. Nowell-Smith, 243.

25. Buchanan-Brown, xv.

26. "Preface," in Rev. ed. (London: Cassell, 1963), v.

27. Ivor H. Evans, letter to the author, 17 February 1990.

28. Ivor H. Evans, "Editor's Preface," in *Brewer's Dictionary of Phrase and Fable*, Centenary ed. (London: Cassell, 1970), v-vi.

29. Evans, letter to author, 17 February 1990.

30. Eugene Exman, *The House of Harper* (New York: Harper & Row, 1967), 240, 283.

31. Steven Cook, Assistant Editor, Reference, Cassell Publishers, Ltd., telephone conversation with author, 2 February 1990.

The Omnipaedia Is Here, But Where Is It?

James Rettig

SUMMARY. Electronic access to information is transforming both the vision of future libraries and the way in which librarians today deliver information services. In reference service, especially in academic libraries, the wide availability of electronic access to periodical indexes and full-text periodical databases has raised speculation about the possibility of relying on purely electronic reference collections. A field test indicates that this is not yet a viable option and points to the continued vital role of the reference librarian as guide, interpreter, and integrator of print and electronic information sources. In the tradition exemplified by Charles Bunge's "Potential and Reality at the Reference Desk: Reflections on a 'Return to the Field,'" this article rests on field experience and testing, and is written in part in the first person. *[Article copies available for a fee from The Haworth Document Delivery Service: 1-800-342-9678. E-mail address: getinfo@haworthpressinc.com <Website: http://www.haworthpressinc.com>]*

The year 2000 problem is a highly-hyped technical problem of unknown proportions. Experts pontificate about it, reports explore it, prophets predict it will bring apocalyptic doom, and entrepreneurs hope to get rich quick (before 2000, surely) with their software solutions.

James Rettig is University Librarian at the University of Richmond, Richmond, VA 23173 (E-mail: jrettig@richmond.edu).

This article is a somewhat longer version of a paper presented at the Southern California Online Users Group's "Rethinking Reference and Research" workshop in Industry, CA, April 29, 1998.

[Haworth co-indexing entry note]: "The Omnipaedia Is Here, But Where Is It?" Rettig, James. Co-published simultaneously in *The Reference Librarian* (The Haworth Information Press, an imprint of The Haworth Press, Inc.) No. 66, 1999, pp. 91-109; and: *From Past-Present to Future-Perfect: A Tribute to Charles A. Bunge and the Challenges of Contemporary Reference Service* (ed: Chris D. Ferguson) The Haworth Information Press, an imprint of The Haworth Press, Inc., 1999, pp. 91-109. Single or multiple copies of this article are available for a fee from The Haworth Document Delivery Service [1-800-342-9678, 9:00 a.m. - 5:00 p.m. (EST). E-mail address: getinfo@haworthpressinc.com].

Reference service also has a year 2000 problem, but nothing will crash if it isn't solved in the next four months. In 1993 Judy Myers of the University of Houston sketched a vision of reference service in the year 2000.[1] In that vision, cast as epistolary exchanges with library users, she writes that in 2000 libraries "still buy plenty of books, [both] in electronic form and in paper."[2] She also writes that, "The book is a marvelous technology for telling extended stories and mailing overarching statements. Books will be around for a long time."[3] The context of her letters makes it doubtful that she includes reference works among those "books," a category that implies print on paper even though she mentions books in electronic media as well. The evidence that Myers sees no long-range future for printed reference books is inferential. She writes to one of her correspondents: "I work more at night and on weekends because there's lots of demand then, but usually I don't come to the library on those days. I do most of my night and weekend work by email at home."[4] Unless she has a phenomenally diverse collection of printed reference books at home, Myers in her year 2000 vision delivers reference service relying exclusively on electronic information resources.

Others have intimated the imminent demise of the reference book, even if they have not been as precise about the brevity of the medium's life expectancy. In 1995 Nicholas Negroponte felt compelled to justify publishing his *Being Digital* in the retrograde printed codex format.[5] He bluntly asked of himself rhetorically, "So why an old-fashioned book, Negroponte, especially one without a single illustration?" Among the reasons he cited, one stands out. He wrote, "First, there are just not enough digital media in the hands of executives, politicians, parents, and all those who most need to understand this radically new culture. Even where computers are omnipresent, the current interface is primitive–clumsy at best, and hardly something with which you might wish to curl up in bed."[6] Yet while turning his pages one senses his insistent yearning to transcend his chosen medium in which his words are "forever fixed by the confines of three physical dimensions."[7]

Myers's vision and Negroponte's regret reflect public sentiment, at least among one or more generations. Ask any reference librarian today who works with young people such as college students and that librarian will tell you that (once all of their "likes" and "you knows" are edited out) many students ask specifically for Web sites or other electronic resources that will answer their questions. When a suitable electronic resource is not available some will simply walk out of the reference room rather than use a specialized printed periodical index. Or they will sit down at a computer–any computer–and go into a database that is not at all suited to their needs just to try to do their work electronically. Such students don't wonder at Myers's vision or Negroponte's wishes; they wonder what is taking so long! They don't want to have to wait until 2000.

The year 2000 is not far off. Will Myers' vision end Negroponte's yearnings come true by then? Will reference librarians be able to do their work from afar using nothing but electronic information sources rather than, as we do it today, by working within a library building using a rich mix of printed reference books, locally owned CD-ROM databases, licensed remote online databases, and quality resources made available free on the World Wide Web? These questions bear assessment through a field test.

On a modest scale I recently conducted such a test, recording reference questions I received in person at the reference desk of the Earl Gregg Swem Library, the main library serving the College of William and Mary in Williamsburg, Virginia. Founded in 1693 and the second-oldest university in the United States, the College of William and Mary is a primarily undergraduate institution with a large on-campus residential population. It enrolls 5,500 undergraduates and 2,200 graduate and professional students. Most are enrolled in programs in the College of Arts and Sciences, the remainder in programs in the Schools of Education, Business, Marine Science, and Law. It offers master's degrees in six fields that do not also offer doctoral programs and the doctorate in nine fields, including American studies, history, and the sciences.

Questions used in the field test described below were gathered during several evening and weekend stints at the reference desk just after mid-point of the spring 1998 semester. All were gathered by me. The questions exhibit some expected repetitiveness due to the immanence of course assignment deadlines, usually the day after a particular data collection period. Since all of these data collection periods were during evening or weekend hours, nearly every question was asked by a William and Mary student. Directional questions and questions regarding specific local library holdings have been excluded from consideration. With rare exception, only questions in which the patron requested assistance in locating information about a topic are included. Within the circumstances described, the questions below allow a reasonably reliable real-life test of the extent to which, in early 1998, reference service in an academic library can rely on electronic information resources.

All of the questions gathered appear in the Appendix, listed in order received, along with notation of the source(s) used to respond to each one. Summaries of these questions are rendered in Tables 1-3 below.

This field test, involving a small sample at only one library, cannot be considered definitive. I believe it is, however, indicative of the relative reliance on print and electronic reference sources in an academic library in 1998. One statistic not explicit in the tables above is the percentage of all questions that involve newspaper or periodical

TABLE 1. Medium of Resources Used

	All Printed	All Electronic	Electronic and Printed Combined
Question Numbers	4, 9, 10, 11, 12, 14, 16, 17, 19, 26, 28, 29, 31, 32, 37, 38, 40	1, 5, 6, 7, 8, 13, 15, 20, 22, 23, 24, 25, 27, 33, 34, 35, 39	2, 3, 18, 21, 30, 36
Total and Percentage	17 Questions 42.5%	17 Questions 42.5%	6 Questions 15%

TABLE 2. Types of Resources Used*

	Electronic Periodical/ Newspaper Indexes	Printed Periodical/ Newspaper Indexes	Other Types of Electronic Resources	Other Types of Printed Resources
Question Numbers	1, 5, 6, 7, 8, 13, 15, 29, 22, 23, 24, 25, 30, 34, 36, 39	2, 9, 12, 17, 19, 28, 29, 30, 31, 33, 36	2, 18, 21, 27	2, 3, 4, 10, 11, 14, 16, 18, 21, 26, 32, 35, 36, 37, 38, 40
Total and Percentage	16 Questions 40%	11 Questions 27.5%	4 Questions 10%	16 Questions 40%

*Total is greater than 40 since in answering some questions more than one type of source was used.

TABLE 3. Distribution of Electronic Media

Questions in Which Response Used Electronic Media Exclusively			
	CD-ROM Only	World Wide Web Only	CD-ROM and WWW
Question Numbers	5, 6, 7, 13, 15, 20, 25, 33, 34, 39	1, 8, 22, 23, 24, 27, 35	30
Total and Percentage	10 Questions 25% of Total	7 Questions 17.5% of Total	1 Question 2.5% of Total

indexes–fully 60 percent (only three of which required use of such indexes in both print and electronic media). This demonstrates the nature of academic library reference work, especially at mid-semester when many students are beginning to work on research papers.

The test demonstrates that printed sources are still very important. Indeed, a great many extraordinary changes will have to occur in the next eighteen months if Myers's vision of reference service in the year 2000 is to come true.

In the forty questions analyzed above, electronic sources played their strongest role as periodical indexes (some of which sometimes also provide full-text and/or full image of an article). Certainly librarians have seen the effects, first on a small scale of mediated online searching in the 1970s, then the greater effect of CD-ROM access to periodical indexes in the 1980s, and the avalanche effect of online access to periodical indexes and full-text journal databases in the 1990s. Freed of the tedium of transcribing citations from printed indexes, library users have happily printed page after page of citations and abstracts and demanded access to articles from an ever increasing range of periodicals. The national growth in interlibrary loan traffic is a testament to the ease with which patrons have been able to identify items on their own.

In my little sample, print resources were the only sources consulted in 42.5 percent of all instances and figured in a total of 57.5 percent of all instances. In a few cases, I could have used electronic sources instead of print sources. The medium itself, however, should not be a prime factor in choosing information sources to answer reference questions in face-to-face encounters. In an email-based reference service, clearly electronic sources from which needed information can be cut and pasted and emailed to the person asking a question is the preferred medium. Not so, though, when librarian and patron can consult a source together in the same physical location.

For example, I could have guessed at the Web site URL for Brigham Young University (I would have guessed <http//www.brighamyoung.edu> rather than reach back to the ready reference shelf two feet away to consult the *Higher Education Directory* to look up the university's mailing address. Had I done so, I would have been wrong. (The correct URL, it turns out, is <http://www.byu.edu>; the university's mailing address appears at the foot of its home page.) I could also have worked my way through the Swem Library home page's "Reference" section to the subsection for "Colleges & Universities" and then worked my way through one of the directories of college Web sites available there. And I would have taken more time than by answering this question using the printed source readily at hand.

Another example–I could have answered the question about the meaning of "irony" as a literary term by checking a CD-ROM station through which Swem Library provides access to a number of stand-alone, non-networked CD-ROM reference databases. Chances are the CD-ROM magazine containing the disk for the *Scribner Writers Series* would not have been in the drive. I would have had to load it, then wait for the *Scribner Writers Series* database to load. Then I could have looked up the term in the on-disc *Handbook to Literature* (a useful enhancement to the lengthy author bio-bibliographies, thoroughly integrated through judiciously chosen hyperlinks).

And another example–I could have gone through the Swem home page to the *Statistical Abstract* on the Web and found the table providing the statistics for educational attainment of the residents of Tennessee. And that would have taken longer than turning to the printed copy, like the *Higher Education Directory*, on the ready reference shelf just two feet away.

As these three examples show, I could have relied less on print and more on electronic resources. For me to have done so, however, would have served little purpose other than perhaps ostentatious display of reference librarian electronic wizardry. One of the principles that ought always to guide good reference service is Ranganathan's Fourth Law: "Save the time of the reader." By using the printed sources that I could retrieve quickly, I was able to provide answers quickly, in most cases from a print duplicate of the source I could have used online or on CD-ROM. To serve the users well, I chose the more quickly accessible print sources.

The relative accessibility of these print resources compared to electronic sources for the same information may vary from library to library and may even be reversed in some. It may also be that librarians with fewer years of experience working in the bygone all-print reference collections that were the norm when I started my career in the mid-1970s are quicker with the electronic sources than middle-aged (albeit technologically adept) relics like me. Furthermore, in time the situation will change; and it may change radically. Instead of layers of flat menus to work through to get from a library's home page to a needed table in the *Statistical Abstract*, maybe three-dimension holographic virtual reality environments will evolve that will allow experienced reference librarians, fully at ease in such an environment and able to customize it to suit their habits of mind and working strategies, to reach out and touch an electronic source with the same speed and ease with which I reached out and consulted the printed *Statistical Abstract* or the *Higher Education Directory*. Not, however, by the year 2000! Nevertheless, such an environment would be very effective and very exciting to work in. If that complex environment could be economically replicated outside the library building, then reference librarians could practice their craft from home as fully as they can today in the library. That would surely benefit information seekers, but it may be a mixed blessing for reference librarians if the reference staff of a single institution tries to do it on its own! Cooperative reference arrangements in which libraries team together to provide answers to difficult questions has not been one of the profession's strongest programs. Technology allows greater flexibility and real-time (or something close to real-time) interaction across distance and time zones. The environment presents opportunities to examine anew the possibilities of developing a cooperative reference service along the lines sketched by Anne Lipow in her "21st Century Job Description."[8]

Field testing of the sort described and analyzed above needs to be done on a much larger scale in many libraries of various types serving varied populations at various times of year, in testing conducted by an investigator who is strictly an observer and not a participant. Surely data for reference service in academic and public libraries needs to be both isolated for comparative purposes and pooled for overall purposes before broad conclusions can be drawn about the relative roles of electronic and print reference sources. Furthermore, such studies need to be carried out and replicated over time to discern trends.

ADDITIONAL EVIDENCE

While some students do pose their reference questions in terms of the medium through which they want their needs fulfilled (i.e., a computer system of one sort or another), there is evidence that library users heartily agree with the importance and wisdom of Ranganathan's Fourth Law and want information services that save their time.

In April 1997 *PC Novice* magazine ran an article describing how the author devised a simple comparative test between the library and the Internet to determine which service would provide answers to a set of questions in the shorter time.[9] The test consisted of just eight questions, most of them factual in nature:

1. What kinds of dishes go best with white wine?
2. How does the Internet work?
3. Who won the second battle of Bull Run?
4. What is the chemical composition of gunpowder?
5. How do you get out grass stains?
6. How do you repair a Kenmore washing machine?
7. Who won the (local political issue) yesterday?
8. What is the third stanza of Lewis Caroll's "The Jabberwocky?"

The library proved faster in five instances, the Internet proved faster in two, and one ("How does the internet work?") was a draw. Average time for the Web was seven minutes versus four for the library. The greatest time difference in either direction was eighteen minutes (twenty-one versus three minutes). The Web was definitely not the better place to look for information about repairing a Kenmore washing machine. The greatest temporal advantage the Web had over the library was on the grass stain question, an advantage of nine minutes; the Web produced an answer to that one in one minute whereas at the library it took ten minutes. The author conducted this test at the Lincoln, Nebraska, Public Library. He also noted that "The hassle of visiting the library has to be figured in . . . The downtown library we visited doesn't have its own parking lot. With two inches of snow on the ground, it took us 10 minutes to find a parking space within a reasonable walking distance."[10]

Accuracy and precision of information retrieved also count. This past February, *Washington Post* staff writer John Schwartz wrote about how he and his wife, an archivist who is very adept at using paper-based information retrieval systems such as card catalogs, used different approaches to help their 10-year-old daughter find needed information for a school assignment.[11] The girl and a study partner had to learn about a dance popular during the colonial era in North America and then perform it in costume for their classmates. Schwartz's wife headed to the library to find the book the teacher recommended, only to learn that no book by that title exists in the Montgomery County Public Library collections. Schwartz surfed the Web for several hours. While his time-consuming Web surfing helped smoke out names of some specific dances, it did not provide the information needed. Supplied with this additional information, Schwartz's wife was able to return to the library and, although he implies she would have preferred a card catalog to the Montgomery County Public Library's OPAC, she found just the right record album-cum-book for the girls to complete their assignment successfully and on time. The Schwartz family would have appreciated a less time-consuming information search-and-retrieval experience.

ELECTRONIC REFERENCE SOURCES

As the PC Novice article illustrates, at this point in its development the Web is a more reliable source for factual information than for interpretive information. Thus far electronic information sources adopted by libraries fall into two very broad categories:

- Those that replicate sources that existed in the print world or that resemble such works
- New sources that allow libraries to provide information that the limitations (especially the temporal limitations) of printed sources did not allow for

In this first category are the electronic sources that figured very prominently in my field test–newspaper and periodical indexes. Only recently have these begun to grow into something beyond the replication of their print forebears by providing access to the full text and/or full image of the journal articles they index. This is a significant advance, albeit very incomplete.

Some reference sources, especially encyclopedias and statistical compendia, are also migrating to electronic media. Editors of these sources are learning lessons from the second broad category of electronic information sources, about which more anon, by incorporating frequent updating as well as links to external third-party electronic sources. *Britannica Online, Encarta, World Book*, the *Grolier Interactive Encyclopedia*, and others, in both Web-based and CD-ROM releases, have exploited these opportunities effectively. These modifications have benefited their users.

The second broad category includes those sources not formerly available in libraries. Among these are sources developed specifically for the Web, sources such as Checkfree Investment Services' stock quotes,[12] the United States Census Bureau's POPclock,[13] the Universal Currency Converter,[14] current weather information, news flashes, InterLotto's reports on state lottery results and jackpot projections,[15] up-to-the-second time from the United States Naval Observatory,[16] comparative interest rates from the Bank Rate Monitor,[17] interactive mapping of a specific address and its environs such as Big Book[18] and Big Yellow[19] allow, and more. All of this, of course, needs to be identified and organized.

HOW LIBRARIES ARE ORGANIZING ELECTRONIC REFERENCE SOURCES

Two approaches to organizing these resources are reflected in two Web sites–The Swem Library "Reference" section,[20] already alluded to, and the Internet Public Library[21] (see Figures 1 and 2). These differ in some important ways but are identical in one significant respect–their spirit. First, the differences.

The Swem site combines free Web sites offered principally by businesses and government agencies along with licensed resources for which an annual fee is paid as a part of the library's membership in the statewide Virtual Library of Virginia (VNA) project. Another salient characteristic of the "Reference" section of the Swem Web site is that it largely limits itself to sources that provide factual information. It does not list sources that provide speculative or advocacy information.

FIGURE 1. The Swem Library Reference Page

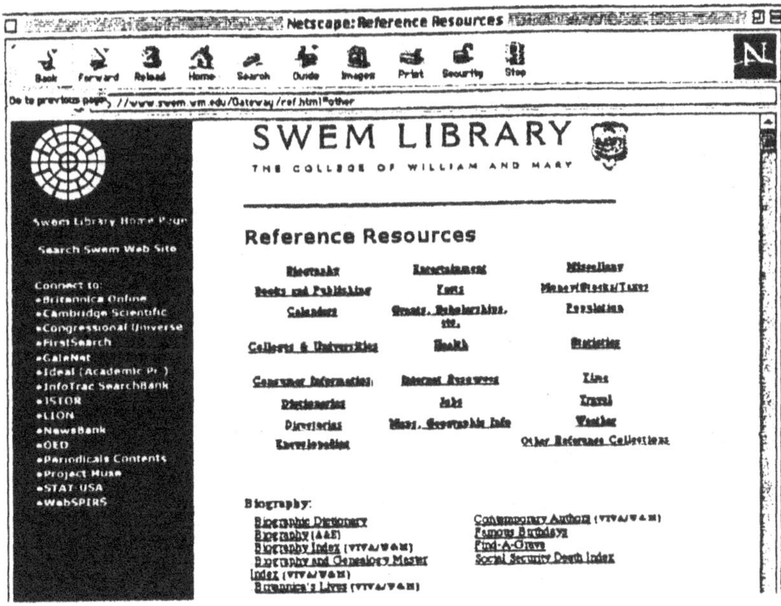

In both respects the Swem site differs from the Internet Public Library. The latter's "Reference" section lacks licensed sites, but does largely limit itself to non-speculative factual resources. Its topical sections, however, range widely.

Both of these sites exhibit our long-felt, deeply-felt, very human desire for simplicity. All of us–librarians and library users alike–would like to be able to obtain all of our information in one convenient place. Indeed, when online services such as Prodigy and America Online were new and offered much less than they do today (and even before there was the World Wide Web for them to link to and exploit), they wooed prospective customers with claims that theirs was the only information service a person would ever need. The impulse is as old as the written record. Call it the desire for an omnipaedia–an information resource easy to use, ubiquitous, and capable of answering just about any information query. The omnipaedia has gone by various names, including Vanever Bush's Memex machine, envisioned in 1945, [22] and John Sculley's Knowledge Navigator, unveiled at the 1987 EDUCOM

FIGURE 2. The Internet Public Library Home Page

conference. The omnipaedia is here today–or, at least as close as it is ever likely to come to be. But where is it?

HISTORY OF THE OMNIPAEDIA

The omnipaedia has a long history. Bill Katz has recently provided a short survey of the history of the encyclopedia, one of the few reference sources, along with the phone directory and the dictionary, nearly every American of school age and up seems to know about.[23] So well known is the encyclopedia as a genre that some library users seem to impute to it mythic powers of being the one and only information source anyone needs. They are amazed to learn about the plethora of specialized encyclopedias available in most reference collections.

Katz traces the encyclopedia's antecedents back to ancient Greece and its origins to Pliny the Elder of first-century Rome.

The desire for simplicity and for having everything needed readily accessible in one source is, apparently, self-renewing in every generation. It is implicit in Myers's vision of reference service in the year 2000. Indeed, in her 1993 article, Myers writes little about the nature of the resources she would use while providing reference service electronically from home. Again, inference plays a part in divining the particulars of her general vision, just as it does in concluding that her envisioned world will rely very little if at all on print resources. One possibility is that the notion of distinct genres among information sources will disappear by 2000 and that reference librarians will use a single all-purpose information system capable of answering all sorts of information queries.

In the traditional all-print reference world, the distinctions among genre have been very important. Reference librarians, when developing a strategy to answer a reference question, have thought in the nexus of subject discipline and genre–in other words, what subject does this question deal with and what sources of a particular type, or in a particular genre, exist that can supply the needed information? As links among electronic reference sources grow, as the scope of electronic reference sources expands, as electronic reference tools encompass multiple genres, the desire for an omnipaedia will grow and grow and grow. John Schwartz of the *Washington Post* and his wife each thought they knew where to turn for the omnipaedia–he to the World Wide Web and she to the public library. Each found something of what they were looking for. Schwartz's article does not reveal whether or not his wife, when she went to the Montgomery County Public Library, asked for reference assistance. Had she, Schwartz's wife would have been employing the omnipaedia, or at least as close as we are going to come to having an omnipaedia. Even a pair as breathlessly taken by technology as Arthur and Marilousie Kroker recognize this, at least implicitly. They note that "Human beings always go faster than technology because people have always been hypertext: fully linked, netted, downloaded, parallel processed, and interfaced."[24] In a world in which print resources still play a significant role, the omnipaedia is the guide and interpreter who knows both the print and electronic realms and who can synthesize them. The omnipaedia is the reference librarian.

No reference librarian knows every source and its potential and its limits. No reference librarian performs flawlessly. Yet the superiority of an experienced, dedicated, knowledgeable reference librarian with strong public service skills over any electronic information system or source or any classification or organization scheme, is, if not self-evident, demonstrable through experience of both library patrons and reference librarians. As remarkable as the capabilities of reference librarians are, that is not reason to become lax about improving the utility, unity, and reliability of electronic information systems any more than the estimable capabilities of pilots would be reason to become lax about improving avionic systems. Keeping up with the growth and variety of resources in multiple formats available to reference librarians is an ever increasing challenge for reference practitioners. Our ability to remain walking, talking, serving omnipaedias depends, in part, upon improvements in the systems and information resources we use. We have–for example, back in those days when I began my career in the 1970s–managed to provide good information service without automated systems; we unquestionably provide, however, better service with them. Yet without us to help users choose among the myriad options they face on the Web and in our print and CD-ROM reference collections, those sources and systems will not be able to serve their purposes fully. They, along with our users, often need us to help them optimize use of their time and to help them select authoritative, up-to-date information sources. Reference librarians, with their knowledge of information systems and sources in all media, integrate those sources and media for ease of use; reference librarians will continue to serve as the omnipaedia.

REFERENCES

1. Judy E. Myers, "Reference Services in the Virtual Library," *American Libraries* 25 (July/August 1994): 634-8.
2. Ibid., 638.
3. Ibid.
4. Ibid.
5. Nicholas Negroponte, *Being Digital* (New York: Alfred A. Knopf, 1995).
6. Ibid., 7.
7. Ibid., 67.
8. Anne G. Lipow, "21st Century Job Description," in *Rethinking Reference in Academic Libraries*, ed. Anne G. Lipow (Berkeley, CA: Library Solutions Press, 1993), 201-05.

9. Joel Strauch, "The Web vs. The Library: An Information Showdown," *PC Novice* 8 (April 1997): 80-2.

10. Ibid., 80.

11. John Schwartz, "They Took 2 Directions on the Path of Knowledge and Had a Ball," *Washington Post*, 16 February 1998, "Washington Business" section, 20.

12. http://www.secapl.com/ (April 1998).

13. http://www.census.gov/cgi-bin/popclock (April 1998).

14. http://www.census.gov/cgi-bin/popclock (April 1998).

15. http://www.interlotto.com/ (April 1998).

16. http://tycho.usno.navy.mil/what.html (April 1998).

17. http://www.bankrate.com/brm/ (April 1998).

18. http://www.bigbook.com/ (April 1998).

19. http://wwwl.bigyellow.com/ (April 1998).

20. http://www.swem.wm.edu/Gateway/ref.html (April 1998).

21. http://www.ipl.org/ref/ (April 1998).

22. Vannevar Bush, "As We May Think," *Atlantic Monthly* 176 (July 1945): 101-08.

23. Bill Katz, "Encyclopedias," in *Cuneiform to Computer: A History of Reference Sources* (Lanham, MD: Scarecrow Press, 1998), 19-52.

24. Arthur and Marilouise Kroker, *Hacking the Future: Stories for the Flesh-Eating 90s* (New York: St. Martin's Press, 1996), 137.

APPENDIX

THE REFERENCE QUESTIONS

#1- Question topic: Journal articles on the origins of *homo horribilus*
Source(s) consulted: *Cambridge Scientific Abstracts*
Medium of source(s): Electronic index on the WWW

#2- Question topic: President Clinton's welfare reform bill veto in 1996
Source(s) consulted: *Congressional Quarterly Almanac* for text of the veto message; *Congressional Compass* online on the WWW for legislative history; *National Newspaper* Index on CD-ROM and *Periodical Abstracts* on CD-ROM for articles about it
Medium of source(s): Printed reference book, supplemented by electronic indexes on the WWW and CD-ROM

#3- Question topic: Names of principals of two high schools in North Carolina
Source(s) consulted: *Patterson's American Education* in print, because it gave initials for one of the names and the student also wanted to know whether to address a job application letter' "Ms." or "Mr." We also checked the North Carolina Depart-

APPENDIX (continued)

ment of Education Web site and its directory of North Carolina school district Web sites, but neither of these schools' districts has a Web site.

Medium of source(s): Print, supplemented unsuccessfully by the World Wide Web

#4– Question topic: Plot summaries and characters in one of Shakespeare's plays
Source(s) consulted: *The Reader's Encyclopedia of Shakespeare, Shakespeare A to Z*
Medium of source(s): Printed reference book

#5– Question topic: Neanderthals, for an assignment in an archaeology course
Source(s) consulted: *Repertoire d'Art et d 'Archeologie*
Medium of source(s): Electronic index on CD-ROM

#6– Question topic: Faunal assemblages, for the same assignment
Source(s) consulted: *Repertoire d'Art et d'Archeologie*
Medium of source(s): Electronic index on CD-ROM

#7– Question topic: Stonehenge, for the same assignment
Source(s) consulted: *Repertoire d'Art et d 'Archeologie*
Medium of source(s): Electronic index on CD-ROM

#8– Question topic: The King William reservoir, a local water project
Source(s) consulted: Newport *News Daily* Press newspaper index on the World Wide Web
Medium of source(s): World Wide Web and the newspaper backfile on microfilm (The student could have chosen to pay for online access to each article identified through the free index, but opted instead for reading them from microfilm in the library.)

#9– Question topic: *Virginia genealogy*
Source(s) consulted: Virginia Historical Index
Medium of source(s): Printed periodical index (Because of its next-door proximity to Colonial Williamsburg, Swem Library attracts numerous genealogists looking for information on Virginia families. This index, compiled decades ago by the library's namesake, is a standard starting point for these queries.)

#10– Question topic: Biographical information on Daniel Dulaney
Source(s) consulted: *Dictionary of American Biography*
Medium of source(s): Printed reference book

#11– Question topic: What is the equivalent to the Congressional Record for the 1799 session of the Congress

Source(s) consulted: Balay's *Guide to Reference Books* to learn that the desired source is *Annals of the Congress*
Medium of source(s): Printed reference book

#12- Question topic: Virginia genealogy
Source(s) consulted: *Virginia Historical Index*
Medium of source(s): Printed periodical index

#13- Question topic: Articles on adolescent suicide
Source(s) consulted: *Sociofile* and *PsycLit* on CD-ROM
Medium of source(s): Electronic index on CD-ROM

#14- Question topic: Address of Brigham Young University
Source(s) consulted: 1998 edition of the *Higher Education Directory*
Medium of source(s): Printed reference book

#15- Question topic: Cluster grouping and racial identity
Source(s) consulted: ERIC database on CD-ROM
Medium of source(s): Electronic index on CD-ROM

#16- Question topic: Address of a William and Mary alumnus
Source(s) consulted: *The Society of the Alumni 1996 Directory*
Medium of source(s): Printed reference book

#17- Question topic: Explain citation from the printed *New York Times Index*
Source(s) consulted: Front matter to the *New York Times Index*
Medium of source(s): Printed newspaper index

#18- Question topic: A play tilled *Midsummer Night's Dream* by Peter Brooks (name turns out to be "Brook," with no "s" on the end)
Source(s) consulted: FirstSearch *WorldCat* database online on the WWW, *Books in Print* online on the WWW, *Play Index* in print
Medium of source(s): Electronic, supplemented by print

#19- Question topic: Meaning of "J Cell Physiol"
Source(s) consulted: *List of Journals Indexed in Index Medicus*
Medium of source(s): Printed reference book

#20- Question topic: Articles on gifted education and underachievers
Source(s) consulted: ERIC database
Medium of source(s): Electronic index on CD-ROM

#21- Question topic: Biographical information on Elizabeth Frey
Source(s) consulted: *Biography and Genealogy Master Index* on GaleNet online on the WWW; *Directory of American Scholars* in print
Medium of source(s): Electronic, leading to print

#22- Question topic: DNA or the human genome and its relation to criminal justice

APPENDIX (continued)

Source(s) consulted: *Cambridge Scientific Abstracts*
Medium of source(s): Electronic index on the WWW

#23- Question topic: Menopause and old age
Source(s) consulted: *Cambridge Scientific Abstracts*
Medium of source(s): Electronic index on the WWW

#24- Question topic: Rift Valley fever
Source(s) consulted: *Cambridge Scientific Abstracts*
Medium of source(s): Electronic index on the WWW

#25- Question topic: *The Wide Sargasso* Sea by Jean Rhys
Source(s) consulted: *MLA International Bibliography*
Medium of source(s): Electronic index on CD-ROM

#26- Question topic: Interpretation of a number of periodical title abbreviations
Source(s) consulted: *Periodical Title Abbreviations*
Medium of source(s): Printed reference book

#27- Question topic: An IRS form needed to meet special circumstances of a foreign student
Source(s) consulted: IRS Web site <http://www.irs.ustreas. gov/>
Medium of source(s): Electronic WWW resource

#28- Question topic: Newspaper article on Wyatt Earp from his lifetime (1848-1924)
Source(s) consulted: *New York Times Index, Poole's Index to Periodical Literature, 19th Century Readers' Guide to Periodical Literature, Readers' Guide to Periodical Literature*
Medium of source(s): Printed indexes

#29- Question topic: Meaning of "Art N"
Source(s) consulted: List of journal title abbreviations used in *Art Index* in print
Medium of source(s): Printed index

#30- Question topic: Women in the Mining Industry in Bolivia
Source(s) consulted: *Hispanic American Periodicals Index, Sociofile,* and *Econlit* on CD-ROM; *PAIS International* through OCLC FirstSearch on the WWW
Medium of source(s): Printed periodical index and electronic periodical indexes on CD-ROM and the WWW

#31- Question topic: Obituary for musician Roger "Pigpen" McKernan, died March 1973

Source(s) consulted: *New York Times Index, Reader's Guide to Periodical Literature, Music Index*
Medium of source(s): Printed indexes

#32– Question topic: The definition of irony in literature
Source(s) consulted: C. Hugh Holman, *Handbook to Literature*, 7th ed.
Medium of source(s): Printed reference book

#33– Question topic: 1860s newspaper articles on Charles Darwin
Source(s) consulted: *Palmer's Index to the Times*
Medium of source(s): Electronic newspaper index on CD-ROM

#34– Question topic: Contemporary French feminism
Source(s) consulted: *Women's Studies*
Medium of source(s): Electronic index on CD-ROM

#35– Question topic: Locate a library with holdings of *Alcheringa*, a paleontology journal published by the Geological Society of Australia
Source(s) consulted: FirstSearch *WorldCat* database online on the WWW
Medium of source(s): Electronic database on the WWW

#36– Question topic: *Thirty-Two Short Films about Glenn Gould*
Source(s) consulted: Internet Movie Database on the WW to verify release date of 1993; *Film Literature Index* in print–disappointing; *Periodical Abstracts* on CD-ROM– nothing; *National Newspaper Index* on CDROM–one citation to an article two column inches long; *Reader's Guide to Periodical Literature* in print–numerous citations to reviews
Medium of source(s): Electronic indexes on the WWW and CD-ROM and printed periodical indexes

#37– Question topic: Educational attainment of residents of Tennessee
Source(s) consulted: *Statistical Abstract of the United States*
Medium of source(s): Printed reference book

#38– Question topic: What was everyday life like in the United States during the 1930s?
Source(s) consulted: *American Decades* volume for the 1930s
Medium of source(s): Printed reference book

#39– Question topic: Literary criticism on Edward Lear
Source(s) consulted: *MLA International Bibliography*
Medium of source(s): Electronic index on CD-ROM

#40– Question topic: Ainu people of Japan
Source(s) consulted: *Kodansha Encyclopedia of Japan*
Medium of source(s): Printed reference book

PART 3: MEASURING EFFECTIVENESS

Select Bibliography and Overview of Bunge's Publications Related to the Measurement of Reference Effectiveness

Sarah B. Watstein

BIBLIOGRAPHY

"Approaches to the Evaluation of Library Reference Services." In: *Evaluation and Scientific Management of Libraries*, edited by F.W. Lancaster & C.W. Cleverdon. Leyden: Noordhoff, 1977.

"The Measurement and Evaluation of Reference and Adult Services." *RQ* 22 (Spring 1983): 251-54.

Sarah B. Watstein is Assistant Director for Academic Use Services, James Branch Cabell Library, Virginia Commonwealth University, Richmond, VA 23284.

[Haworth co-indexing entry note]: "Select Bibliography and Overview of Bunge's Publications Related to the Measurement of Reference Effectiveness." Watstein, Sarah B. Co-published simultaneously in *The Reference Librarian* (The Haworth Information Press, an imprint of The Haworth Press, Inc.) No. 66, 1999, pp. 111-113; and: *From Past-Present to Future-Perfect: A Tribute to Charles A. Bunge and the Challenges of Contemporary Reference Service* (ed: Chris D. Ferguson) The Haworth Information Press, an imprint of The Haworth Press, Inc., 1999, pp. 111-113. Single or multiple copies of this article are available for a fee from The Haworth Document Delivery Service [1-800-342-9678, 9:00 a.m. - 5:00 p.m. (EST). E-mail address: getinfo@haworthpressinc.com].

(with M. Murfin) "Evaluating Reference Service from the Patron Point of View." *The Reference Librarian* 11 (Fall-Winter 1984): 175-82.

"Factors Related to Reference Question Answering Success." *RQ*, 24 (Summer 1985): 482-86.

(with M. Murfin) "Responsible Standards for Reference Service in Ohio Public Libraries." *Ohio Libraries* 1 (March-April 1988): 11-13.

"Factors Related to Output Measures for Reference Services in Public Libraries." *Public Libraries* 29 (January-February 1990): 42-47.

"Gathering and Using Patron and Librarian Perceptions of Question Success. In: *Evaluation of Public Services and Public Services Personnel: Papers Presented at the Allerton Park Institute, 1990.* Champaign: University of Illinois Graduate School of Library and Information Science, 1991.

"Evaluating Reference Services and Reference Personnel." *The Reference Librarian* 43(1994): 195-207.

OVERVIEW

Charles Bunge has been an effective advocate for evaluating reference services, and in particular a spokesperson for evaluation programs that are built-in, continuing, and varied. Leadership activities in this capacity, including chair of the Evaluation of Reference and Adult Services Committee of RASD, and several articles on measurement effectiveness reveal that Bunge thinks of evaluation as including the following components: determining program goals, translating goals into measurable indicators or goal achievement, collecting data on these indicators, and comparing the data with goal criteria. Bunge asserts that the evaluation of reference service should consist of the determination of the level of goal achievement, and he believes that the first step to successful evaluation is the accurate statement of the objectives and goals of the activity to be developed. In his article, "Approaches to the Evaluation of Library Reference Services," he grapples with measurement issues that are involved in the evaluation of reference service. He discusses various approaches to gathering data on the effectiveness with which questions or requests for assistance have been satisfied. Studies that have attempted to assess reference output are reviewed, and attention is given to attempts at examining the parts of the reference system and their contribution to effectiveness. Evaluation through costs and benefits is discussed, as is micro-evaluation (evaluation of the components of reference service).

In other articles, "Factors Related to Output Measures for Reference Services in Public Libraries: Data from Thirty-Six Libraries" and "Factors Related to Reference Question Answering Success: The Development of a Data-Gathering Form," Bunge reports on the development of a computer-scannable form that gathers data from both reference librarians and their patrons on answering success and various factors in the reference situation. In "Gathering and Using Patron and Librarian Perceptions of Question-Answering Success" he shows that the reference librarian and the patron can both be valuable sources of data on which to base evaluation of question answering effectiveness if appropriate care is taken in gathering and interpreting this data.

Bunge's interest in evaluation fueled his interest in reference standards where familiarity with the literature on the evaluation of reference services and reference personnel is demonstrated in several bibliographic essays. "Evaluating Reference Services and Reference Personnel: Questions and Answers from the Literature" serves both this bibliographic review purpose as well as provides a series of questions that might be considered a model for the reference evaluation process.

Gathering and Using Patron and Librarian Perceptions of Question-Answering Success

Charles A. Bunge

SUMMARY. This paper discusses the strengths and weaknesses of patrons and reference librarians as sources of data for the evaluation of reference question-answering effectiveness, along with ways to enhance the usefulness of data from each source. It describes the Wisconsin-Ohio Reference Evaluation Program and discusses some illustrative statistics from the project, including data on relationships between patron-perceived answering success and factors such as staffing patterns, effort spent on answering questions, types and sources of questions, and collection size. *[Article copies available for a fee from The Haworth Document Delivery Service: 1-800-342-9678. E-mail address: getinfo@haworthpressinc.com <Website: http://www.haworthpressinc.com>]*

INTRODUCTION

The two most frequently used sources of data on reference question-answering success are the librarian who answers the question and the patron who asks it. Both *Output Measures for Public Libraries*

Reprinted from "Gathering and Using Patron and Librarian Perceptions of Question-Answering Success," by Charles A. Bunge. In *B. Allen* (Ed.), *Evaluation of Public Services and Public Services Personnel* (Papers presented at the Allerton Park Institute No. 32) (pp. 59-83). Urbana-Champaign, IL: Graduate School of Library and Information Science, University of Illinois.

[Haworth co-indexing entry note]: "Gathering and Using Patron and Librarian Perceptions of Question-Answering Success." Bunge, Charles A. Co-published simultaneously in *The Reference Librarian* (The Haworth Information Press, an imprint of The Haworth Press, Inc.) No. 66, 1999, pp. 115-140; and: *From Past-Present to Future-Perfect: A Tribute to Charles A. Bunge and the Challenges of Contemporary Reference Service* (ed: Chris D. Ferguson) The Haworth Information Press, an imprint of The Haworth Press, Inc., 1999, pp. 115-140.

(Van House et al., 1987, pp. 65-71) and *Measuring Academic Library Performance* (Van House et al., 1990, pp. 95-108) suggest these as basic sources. This paper will discuss briefly the strengths and weaknesses of each of these sources, as well as ways to enhance the usefulness of each. Within this context, the Wisconsin-Ohio Reference Evaluation Program will be described, and some illustrative statistics from the project will be discussed.

THE REFERENCE LIBRARIAN AS DATA SOURCE

Undoubtedly, the most widely used measure of reference effectiveness is the librarian's perception of how successfully questions are answered. Many reference staffs record such perceptions, albeit often quite informally. Public libraries that follow the recommendations of *Output Measures for Public Libraries* (pp. 69-71) record the number of questions for which the users receive requested information on the same day they are asked, and staffs in various types of libraries record unanswered reference questions in one way or another.

One advantage of librarians as a source of data for reference evaluation is ease of data collection. Recording librarian perceptions of answering success can be fit into the normal work flow of the reference desk, without the additional staffing or special efforts required for patron surveys and other approaches. Using staff perceptions can be considerably less costly than hiring outside observers or proxy patrons. Staff motivation to provide full and accurate data can be higher than that of patrons, due to the staff's desire to improve service, or to pressure from peers and administrators.

Librarians can be a unique or especially valuable source of certain types of data. For example, librarians can provide information on factors that might be related to question-answering success, such as the number and type of sources consulted or collection weaknesses.

On the other hand, serious reservations have been raised regarding data from reference librarians. Librarians usually report a higher success rate than do independent observers or researchers. It is difficult for a librarian to report a reference encounter as unsuccessful when he or she has given it the best possible effort and when the information produced seems at least partially responsive to the question. Also, the librarian may not understand the real information need represented by the question and may feel that this need has been met when it has not.

Gathering data on reference transactions can be intrusive to the reference process, causing reference librarians to be selective regarding the questions on which data is gathered, thereby raising concerns about the reliability and validity of the data produced.

Rather than reject the reference librarian as a source of data on question-answering success because of such reservations, reference evaluators should attempt to overcome or reduce the problems while taking advantage of the strengths. For example, one way to reduce the inflation of reported success is to avoid forcing a choice between "answered" and "not answered." Librarians are more likely to report less-than-complete success if they are allowed to choose options such as "partially answered" and "don't know." Librarians are also more likely to report less-than-successful results if they are given an opportunity to record reasons for lack of success. Providing such an opportunity also lakes advantage of one of the potential strengths of the librarian as data source and provides fuller information for use in evaluation. The problems caused by the intrusiveness of data gathering can be addressed through sampling and by simplifying the data recording process.

THE REFERENCE PATRON AS DATA SOURCE

Like the librarian, the patron as a source of data on answering effectiveness has both strengths and weaknesses. Obviously, patrons are the most important source of data on their satisfaction with the information and service they receive. Because patron perceptions play a crucial role in their decision to use the information they receive and their inclination to use the reference service again, data on their perceptions are of great importance to reference evaluation.

On the other hand, patrons, too, have a tendency to report higher levels of satisfaction than the success rates found using outside observers or unobtrusive approaches. Conventional wisdom holds that, because patrons appreciate any attention and help they receive, they will report satisfaction even when the information they receive is less than completely useful. Also, patrons often are not knowledgeable about the information that could and should be provided to answer their questions and will report satisfaction with information that is inaccurate, incomplete, or out-of-date.

While reference patrons are an easily available source of data, they are frequently in a hurry and may be unwilling to be interviewed or to fill out survey forms to record their perceptions. Patrons who feel most strongly might be most likely to take the time and effort to respond, raising concerns about the reliability of the data gathered in this approach.

Patrons are too valuable as a source of evaluative data to reject because of potential reliability and validity problems, and steps can be taken to reduce these problems. For example, the problem of low response rate and patron reluctance to report perceptions can be addressed by making the survey forms as simple and quick to complete as possible. Patron response rate can be improved by having reference staff members exhibit a positive, upbeat attitude as the forms are handed to patrons, by emphasizing the survey's potential for improving service, and by using attractive signs to remind patrons to complete and return forms.

Patrons' tendency to overrate answering success can be addressed in a number of ways (Murfin & Gugelchuk, 1987, pp. 317-19). First, not forcing a choice between "answered" and "not answered" (or some equivalent dichotomy) is important. Patrons, like librarians, are more likely to report less than completely useful answers if options like "partially" are provided. Also, allowing patrons to report their reactions to particular aspects of the answer can increase validity and the richness of the data. Examples include the amount of information provided, the depth or complexity of the information, and the point of view or approach of the information in relation to the patron's need.

The conventional wisdom regarding reference patrons' inability to distinguish between the usefulness of the information they receive and the quality and extent of the service they receive is not necessarily true. If these two important aspects are carefully separated and addressed with focus, users can report one level of satisfaction with the information or materials received and another for the extent and nature of the service provided by staff members.

To summarize, reference librarians and their clients can provide valuable and unique data for the evaluation of question-answering effectiveness. It is important that evaluators take advantage of the strengths of such data, while recognizing their limitations and the need to take care to reduce problems with validity and reliability. It is most important to recognize that librarians and patrons can provide only their perceptions. The degree to which these perceptions accurately reflect reality is an issue to be addressed in the design and use of data-gathering instruments and in the interpretation of data. One way to address this issue is to use data from a variety of sources, including both librarians and patrons, to check, balance, and reinforce each other.

THE WISCONSIN OHIO REFERENCE EVALUATION PROGRAM

Concerns such as these led Marjorie Murfin and this author to develop forms and associated computer programs for gathering and analyzing data from reference librarians and their patrons. The researchers' intent was to develop and provide a service that could be used by reference staffs to evaluate their question-answering effectiveness and to provide information that would suggest ways in which such effectiveness could be improved. It was also expected that the data gathered by participating libraries would accumulate into a national database that could be used for research and for the establishment of national norms that would be useful for various purposes. The result of these efforts is the Wisconsin-Ohio Reference Evaluation Program.

Several objectives guided the development of the data-gathering forms for the program. The first was to provide a means by which reference staffs could gather reliable and valid data from librarians and patrons regarding the degree to which reference questions are answered effectively. Second, data should be gathered from patrons and librarians on various environmental or situational factors that might be related to or used to explain answering success. Third, data from the two sources should relate to each other at the question-by-question level. Fourth, the data should be gathered and analyzed in the least intrusive and time-consuming manner possible.

The result of addressing these objectives is a set of forms that are called Reference Transaction Assessment Instruments (RTAI) (see Appendices A-F). Basic to the accomplishment of several of the researchers' objectives is a set of forms that are computer readable and the generation of data that can be analyzed by computer. The forms can be completed by librarians and patrons by simply filing in small circles with a pencil, thereby making them easy and quick to complete. Librarian and patron data can be related question-by-question through the use of computer-readable coding that allows the data from the patron's form and the librarian's form for each question to be brought together by the computer for comparison and analysis. To make sure that correctly coded forms are completed by librarian and patron for each question, the two forms for each question are attached to each other until they are torn apart at the time the question is asked.

It was anticipated that most libraries using the RTAI would sample their reference questions using cluster samples based on selected periods of time. Within a sample period, every question asked at the service point by walk-in patrons should be included in the sample, thus cutting down on choices and decisions that might affect the representativeness of the sample. This meant that directional questions should be included, as well as reference questions, even though data on answering success and environmental factors are not as important for directional questions. Very brief directional-question forms for patrons and librarians were designed that gather data on question type and patron characteristics (see Appendices D-F).

The patron form for reference questions asks for information about the patron (academic status and area of study or teaching for academic library patrons; occupation, age, gender, and source of the question for public library patrons). A group of questions at the top of the patron form asks about the patron's satisfaction with the information or materials that were provided or suggested in answer to the question. A group of questions on the bottom portion of the form asks about the patron's perception of the librarian and the service received. Other questions ask whether or not the patron feels that he or she learned about reference sources or library use (see Appendices B and C).

The librarian form for reference questions (Appendix A) gathers data about the type of information or materials that the question asks for, including its subject area. The librarian's perception of answering success is recorded, as are several items concerning how the librarian went about answering the question. These include whether the librarian searched with the patron or only directed or suggested sources, the amount of time taken, and the number and type of sources consulted or recommended. The librarian is also asked to indicate factors about the patron, the question, and the situation that apply to the encounter. These include, for example, indications that the patron had special characteristics such as difficulty communicating, that the collection was weak in the area of the question, or that the librarian was busy at the time the question was asked. The staff member is asked to indicate whether he or she is a professional or paraprofessional.

Guided by the objectives mentioned above, several drafts of the RTAI were prepared and were reviewed by practicing reference librarians and managers. A penultimate draft of the academic library version was field tested in the reference departments of fifteen academic libraries of various sizes in the fall of 1983, using a sample of fifty questions in each library.

A primary purpose for consultation with practicing librarians and for field testing was to improve the reliability and validity of the data gathered with the forms. The reference librarians who reviewed the forms attested to their high face validity. Using statistical cluster analysis on the field test data, it was determined that the questions relating to patron satisfaction with the information received and those related to satisfaction with the quality of the service do measure two different factors, further adding to the researchers' confidence in the validity of the form. Data from the field test were also used to assess the reliability of the forms, using Cronbach's alpha and an extension of this estimator, the theta statistic (Murfin & Gugelchuk, 1987, pp. 323-29).

Questions regarding patron and question-source categories for the public library version of the patron form were developed and field tested with the cooperation of reference librarians. Thus, the RTAI set consists of librarian forms for directional and reference questions that are used in both academic and public libraries (Appendices A and D) and patron forms for directional and reference questions that have different patron categories for academic and public libraries (Appendices B, C, E, and F).

Libraries that wish to use the service obtain copies of the RTAI from the project office for samples ranging from 100 reference questions upward (and for an equal member of directional questions), along with instructions regarding the use of the forms. For each question in the sample, the librarian quickly ascertains the patron's willingness to participate (participating libraries have experienced nearly 100 percent willingness), and the question is answered in the normal fashion. At the end of the encounter, the librarian and patron forms for the question are detached from each other, the patron is handed his or her form for completion, and the librarian completes the librarian form (or at least enough of it to allow completion later).

At the end of the survey, completed forms are returned to the project office for reading and analysis of the data. The response rate from patrons (i.e., the percentage of sample reference questions for which both patron and librarian forms are available for analysis) averages 93 percent for public libraries and 85 percent for academic libraries.

The data from each library is analyzed using a complex program on an IBM mainframe computer, and a detailed report is prepared and sent to the library. The report provides information on the library's question-answering success, as perceived by reference librarians and patrons, on the question-answering behavior of answering librarians, and on factors present in the reference situation at the time the questions were asked. The report compares the library's data with data from other participating libraries (either public or academic) of similar size, with all public or academic libraries that have used the service, and with the most successful participating public or academic library so far.

The data are also accumulating in a continually growing database, from which national norms and other useful information can be obtained. Other researchers can have access to this database for their own analysis as well. The participating libraries are a self-selected sample rather than a random sample. However, there is no reason to believe that they are unrepresentative of academic and public libraries in general.

The data on directional questions have not received much analysis. Participating libraries receive frequency counts and percentages for patron categories and types of directional questions. The data on patron categories, taken together with those from reference questions, can give a library a pretty good picture of who is asking questions at the reference desk.

DEMOGRAPHIC INFORMATION

The forty-two public libraries that have participated in the program through September 1990 include libraries in six states. While there is a concentration of suburban libraries, there are also large urban libraries and libraries serving rural populations. Library collections range from 23,000 volumes to over 2,000,000 volumes, and populations served range from 7,500 to over 600,000. For purposes of comparison, libraries have been categorized as small (twelve libraries of under 50,000 volumes), medium (fifteen libraries of 50,000-99,999 volumes), and large (fifteen libraries of 100,000 volumes or more). There are data on some 6,000 reference questions from these libraries.

Table 1 shows the proportion of various patron categories and question sources for reference questions in the public libraries. In interpreting these figures, readers should be aware that some patrons marked responses in both the occupation and student categories and some in only one or the other. Figures for occupation categories are percentages of only those patrons who marked an occupation, while figures for student categories represent percentages for all patrons.

General reference departments in forty-eight public and private academic libraries in twenty-five states and Canada have participated in the Wisconsin-Ohio program through September 1990, and have provided data on over 5,000 reference questions. Participating libraries include twenty-three with collections of fewer than 500,000,

TABLE 1. Percentage of Public Library Patrons and Questions by Category

Category	*Percentage of Questions*
OCCUPATION (% of total responses for occupation)	
Homemaker	22.79
Skilled labor/trades/services	14.97
Secretarial/clerical/office	10.30
Sales/marketing	10.74
Professional/technical/management	27.71
Unemployed	10.77
Retired	7.00
AGE (% of total responses for age)	
Under 18	21.79
18-40	45.76
41-64	26.96
65+	5.69
GENDER (% of total responses for gender)	
Male	39.74
Female	60.35
STUDENTS (% of total patrons)	
High School	19.61
College	20.67
Graduate School	7.74
Continuing Education	7.21
SOURCE OF QUESTION (% of total responses for source)	
Work related	19.66
School/education related	40.82
Recreation related	10.75
Other personal project	33.34

thirteen with between 500,000 and 1,000,000 volumes, and twelve with collections of over 1,000,000 volumes. Table 2 shows the proportion of various patron categories among those who asked reference questions in the academic libraries. In interpreting these figures, readers should be aware that a few patrons marked responses for more than one "status" or "major" category, so that the figures add up to slightly over 100 percent.

REFERENCE QUESTION-ANSWERING SUCCESS

The main figure used to indicate question-answering success, and the figure in which reference librarians and managers seem most interested, is the patrons' perception of whether or not their questions were answered. A stringent criterion for patron-perceived answering success has been established. In order to be counted as successful transactions, the patrons must have reported that they obtained just what was

TABLE 2. Percentage of Academic Library Patrons by Status and Subject Area

Status or Subject	*Percentage of Questions*
STATUS	
Freshman	18.80
Sophomore	17.61
Junior	17.13
Senior	21.16
Graduate student	12.82
Continuing education/nondegree	2.82
Faculty	3.05
Alumna/us	1.35
Unaffiliated with college	5.45
MAJOR OR TEACHING/RESEARCH AREA	
Arts or Humanities	18.29
Business/Management	24.73
Education	7.98
Law	1.76
Other Social Sciences	11.50
Agriculture/Biological Science	5.49
Medicine/Health	7.78
Mathematics/Physical Sciences	2.79
Technology/Engineering	7.12
Interdisciplinary/Other	6.40
Major not declared	6.91

wanted and that they were completely satisfied with the information or materials found or suggested. When the terms *success score* or *success rate* are used for a library or group of libraries, the terms refer to the percentage of questions on which patron responses meet this criterion. By a "significant" relationship is meant that the relationship has been tested statistically (usually with the chi square test for independence) using the .05 probability level to indicate significance.

The success rate across all forty-two public libraries is 60.01 percent. When patrons reporting finding approximately what was wanted are added, the percentage is 71.00. Comparable figures for the forty-eight academic libraries are 56.25 and 67.85. (The success rate in public libraries for higher education students with school-related questions is 61.57 percent.) While the difference between public and academic libraries is small (though statistically significant), one is tempted to look for reasons for it. Two factors on which the two types of libraries differ and that are related to patron-perceived success might be partial explanations. One is the percentage of questions for which the librarians reported simply directing the patron to a potential answering source, rather than searching with the patron. For academic libraries, the percentage of such responses is 22.02, while for public libraries it is 15.24. Also, in academic libraries the percentage of questions on which the librarian reported being busy when the question was asked is 25.72, while in public libraries the percentage is 21.25.

Because data on librarian-perceived answering success is easier to collect than that for patron-perceived success, it is interesting to know how close these perceptions are to each other when both are measured for the same questions (so that one might judge the usefulness of substituting the easier measure for the harder one). In most participating libraries, the librarians reported that the answer was found for a higher percentage of questions than that reported by patrons. The average librarian-perceived success rate across the forty-two public libraries is 72.05 (compared to a patron-perceived success rate of 60.01). For the forty-eight academic libraries, the librarian-perceived success rate is 68.45 (compared to a patron-perceived success rate of 56.25). The overall agreement between librarians and their patrons on "found, "partly found," and "not found" responses is 67.68 percent for public libraries and 64.98 percent for academic libraries.

FACTORS ASSOCIATED WITH SUCCESS OR FAILURE

In order for reference staffs and managers to make wise decisions to improve reference question-answering success, they need information on factors that are related to variations in success. Such relationships have been looked at across the participants in the Wisconsin-Ohio program.

Staffing

One important set of factors in the reference situation is staffing patterns. In this area, one factor that is consistently associated with question-answering success is whether or not the librarian is busy at the time the question is asked. On average, the public libraries lost 6.11 percentage points in their success scores when the librarians reported being busy when questions were asked, as compared to when they were not busy. For academic libraries, there was a loss of 4.82 percentage points on average.

Another staffing issue is the involvement of paraprofessional staff in answering reference questions. Analysis of data from twenty academic libraries that used both paraprofessionals and professionals to answer reference questions (among the first thirty-three academic library participants) showed that, overall, professional staff members were more successful (Murfin & Bunge, 1988). However, the same analysis showed that, with appropriate training and effective policy and procedure backup, paraprofessionals can effectively answer reference questions. While the public library data has not been analyzed with the same detail, the data indicates that, across all public library reference questions, paraprofessionals have been just as successful as professionals. However, some participating libraries have paraprofessionals answer only simple or apparently easy questions, while others have them answer the full range of questions, so that overall findings here must be interpreted with caution.

Time and Effort Spent on Questions

Another group of factors relates to the time and effort spent on questions by reference librarians. The RTAI collects data on whether the librarian searches for information with the patron or merely directs or suggests a strategy. For the public libraries, success scores are on average 9.45 points lower for questions where the librarian directed patrons to a potential source, rather than searching with the patron. For the academic libraries, this difference averages 18.05 percent.

To help reference staffs assess their potential for answering reference questions successfully, the report form that is sent to participating libraries includes the patron-perceived success rate for questions on which the patron was served by a professional staff member who was not busy and who searched with the patron. This allows the staff to see how its success under various conditions compares with its success under these "ideal" conditions (what is called the "potential" success rate). For the forty-two public libraries, this potential success rate averages 66.61 percent (compared with 60.01 overall); for the forty-eight academic libraries, it is 67.79 percent (compared with 56.25 overall).

The number of sources used or suggested in answering a question is of interest, as well. In academic libraries, the data indicates that there is a positive relationship between the number of sources consulted or suggested and patron perceived answering success (at least up to a point of diminishing return). For example, Table 3 shows the average figures for all academic libraries and those for the library with the highest success rate (65.63 percent) among the forty-eight libraries. This relationship does not show up in the same way for public library participants. However, analysis of the data on time spent per reference question in the first thirty-six public library participants showed that, in the nine most successful libraries–the proportion of questions on

TABLE 3. Number of Sources Consulted or Suggested per Question Answered

	Percentage of Questions	
Number of Sources	*All Academic Libraries*	*Most Successful Academic Library*
1 Source	37.90	25.00
2 Sources	30.12	17.86
3 Sources	17.68	32.14
4 Sources	7.40	14.29
5 or More Sources	6.90	10.71

which librarians reported spending less than three minutes (26.38) is significantly lower than for the nine least successful ones (31.47 percent) (Bunge, 1990).

As an aid to reference staffs in interpreting their data from the Wisconsin-Ohio program, Marjorie Murfin has constructed some indexes based on similar factors. Comparative figures for these indexes are reported to participating libraries. For example, she analyzed the data from the thirty-three earliest participating academic libraries to see if patron-perceived success is related to the amount of time and effort that is provided by the answering librarian. An "effort index" for a given library is based on the percentage of questions for which the librarians direct or suggest only (rather than search with the patron), the percentage of questions on which the librarians report working for under three minutes, and the percentage of questions for which only one source was used or suggested. Table 4 shows the percentage of such questions for the eleven libraries with the highest success rates and the eleven with the lowest success rates, along with a column combining what might be called the "negative effort" factors. From this table it is clear that library staffs who spend more effort on questions have higher patron-perceived success rates.

These "effort" factors are related to how busy the reference staff is, of course. It is interesting to note, however, that the percentage of reference questions on which the librarian searched with the patron, even though busy (again, based on data from the thirty-three earliest participating academic libraries), is 73.85 for the most successful eleven libraries, 47.06 for the least successful eleven libraries, and 63.52 for those in the middle range.

Communication

Effective communication between the reference librarian and the patron is crucial to question-answering success. One measure of communication effectiveness is the percentage of questions on which the librarian and the patron agree in their assessment of whether or not the question was answered. For example, across all forty-eight academic libraries, this agreement rate is 64.98 percent, while in the library with the highest patron-perceived success rate it is 77.42 percent. An analysis of the data from the earliest thirty-three participating public libraries shows that in the nine most successful libraries the agreement rate is 78.95 percent, while in the nine least successful libraries it is

TABLE 4. Answering Effort Related to Answering Success

Success Rate (%)	Percentage of Questions			
	1 Directed Only	2 Under 3 Min.	3 Used 1 Source	Average: 1,2,3
MOST SUCCESSFUL				
69.74	18.42	37.33	37.50	31.08
69.59	14.62	15.79	21.74	17.38
68.75	6.25	16.67	23.53	15.48
68.52	11.11	26.32	33.33	23.59
65.63	9.38	38.71	25.00	24.36
63.51	27.03	30.14	33.93	30.37
61.54	15.38	18.42	38.46	24.09
60.78	12.42	20.39	22.38	18.40
60.53	31.58	36.84	47.06	38.49
60.53	28.95	32.43	40.00	33.79
60.26	13.46	34.67	30.28	26.14
Average	17.15	27.97	31.11	25.74
LEAST SUCCESSFUL				
53.08	25.38	46.51	45.00	38.96
52.05	38.36	51.05	50.00	46.47
51.43	22.86	48.57	37.14	36.19
51.35	37.84	37.84	53.84	43.17
50.00	22.22	33.33	50.00	35.18
49.28	26.09	32.84	46.97	35.30
47.17	18.87	48.08	52.00	39.65
45.00	20.00	48.72	32.35	33.69
44.83	27.59	35.71	52.00	38.43
41.67	16.67	44.44	45.71	35.61
34.48	25.86	45.28	24.53	31.89
Average	25.61	42.94	44.32	37.62

63.77 percent. These and other data from the RTAI indicate that there is a greater communication gap between librarians and patrons in less successful libraries.

Type and Source of Questions

One of the most frequently studied sets of factors is the type and source of reference questions. Data on success rates for patrons and questions in various categories are provided in Tables 5 and 6. These figures might be used by individual libraries as norms against which to compare local results. For example, participants in the Wisconsin-

TABLE 5. Public Library Success Rate by Category of Patrons and Questions

Category	Patron-Perceived Success Rate (%)
ALL QUESTIONS*	60.01
OCCUPATION	
Homemaker	59.90
Skilled labor/trades/services	63.72
Secretarial/clerical/office	63.01
Sale/marketing	49.15
Professional/technical/management	60.92
Unemployed	59.54
Retired	63.47
AGE	
Under 18	56.07
18-40	59.74
41-64	61.98
65+	64.42
GENDER	
Male	58.10
Female	60.80
STUDENTS	
High School	54.55
College	58.16
Graduate School	64.88
Continuing Education	59.11
SOURCE OF QUESTION	
Work related	58.75
School/education related	59.68
Recreation related	60.60
Other personal project	61.34

*Excluding questions asking for a specific book, serial, etc.

Ohio program can use such comparison to identify areas for collection and staff development attention.

The librarian portion of the RTAI asks librarians to categorize questions using some fifteen categories. Table 7 shows the percentage of questions recorded in the most frequently used categories (based on all transactions and adjusted by choosing one category per transaction). Some interesting differences between academic and public libraries appear in Table 7. Types of questions that have been hardest for public libraries to answer to their patrons' satisfaction are ones asking for criticism and reviews (51.78 percent success), ones asking for trends, pro and con, how-to-do-it, etc. (51.86 percent), and explanation of the

TABLE 6. Academic Library Success Rate by Status and Question Subject

Status and Subject	*Patron-Perceived Success Rate (%)*
ALL QUESTIONS*	56.25
STATUS	
Freshman/Sophomore	56.55
Junior/Senior	54.76
Graduate Student	51.74
SUBJECT AREA OF QUESTIONS	
Arts or Humanities	58.84
Social Sciences	51.94
Science and Technology	52.25

*Excluding questions asking for a specific book, serial, etc.

TABLE 7. Types of Questions Asked

	Percentage (of all questions)	
Type of Question	*Public Libraries*	*Academic Libraries*
Specific book, serial, etc.	19.09	14.09
Smaller item in larger publication	1.78	2.46
Anything by a particular author	2.36	0.78
Short answer, verification, etc.	4.49	9.71
Facts or statistics	13.42	12.41
Explanation of library, catalog, or particular source	2.28	9.29
Something/anything on a topic	22.43	14.02
Certain type of format of material	7.90	11.35
Criticism, reviews, interpretation, etc.	2.45	6.05
Analysis, trends, how-to, pro/con	3.73	5.37

library, its catalog, or another tool (56.46 percent). For academic libraries, types of questions where patron-perceived success has been lowest are ones asking for trends, pro and con, how-to-do-it, etc. (46.85 percent success), for just something or anything on a topic (48.80 percent), and for facts or statistics (49.08 percent).

The data on the "just something or anything" on a topic type of question are interesting. Such questions have been much more prevalent in public libraries (23.43 percent of all reference questions, versus 14.02 percent in academic libraries). Public librarians seem to have been more successful at ascertaining the real information needs behind these questions and at providing satisfactory answers, achieving a 59.60 percent success rate. In academic libraries, significantly more patron-librarian communication difficulty is associated with these questions than is true for public librarians, and the success rate on them is only 48.80 percent.

Collection Size

Collection size is another factor of interest. Simple correlation indicates no significant difference in patron-perceived success rate by collection-size category in either public or academic libraries. More detailed analysis of the data does indicate that there is a positive relationship between library collection size and success rate. However, this relationship is obscured by the fact that larger libraries tend to be busier and to receive more complex questions, both of which are associated with lower success rates. For example, when one looks at questions for which the librarian does not report being busy, the larger libraries have a much higher success rate than smaller libraries. This and other evidence suggest that larger collections have a greater potential for success, but that this success can be negated by being overly busy.

The size of the reference collection seems to have a curvilinear relationship to answering success. Not all libraries can provide accurate data on reference collection size, and the research team's analysis and interpretation of the data on this relationship have been somewhat impressionistic. However, success rate does seem to go up as reference collection size increases, up to an optimum size (around 4,000 volumes for public libraries and around 15,000-20,000 volumes for academic libraries), after which success rate seems to fall off. Evidence on other factors leads to the speculation that larger collections invite (or require) relatively more directing (rather than going with the patron to the shelves) and that it is harder for reference staff members to gain the mastery over larger collections that is required for quick and effective access to the information in them.

Bibliographic Instruction

One measure of the success of a reference encounter might be whether or not the patron learns anything about information sources as a result of it. The patron RTAI asks patrons whether they became acquainted with any reference sources that had not previously been known as a result of consulting the reference librarian. In academic libraries, 37.41 percent of the patrons who asked reference questions reported learning about two or more sources, 48.54 percent learned about one source, and 14.05 percent reported "No, none." For public library patrons, the figures are 30.04 percent, 44.16 percent, and 25.81 percent, respectively, indicating that more one-to-one bibliographic instruction is occurring in academic libraries than in public libraries. Likewise, when asked if they learned something about the use of the library or reference sources as the result of consulting the reference librarian, academic library patrons responded "Yes" more frequently (76.93 percent) and "No" less frequently (6.76 percent) than did public library patrons (70.01 percent and 12.45 percent).

CONCLUSION

This paper has tried to show that the reference librarian and the patron can both be valuable sources of data on which to base evaluation of question-answering effectiveness if appropriate care is taken in gathering and interpreting this data. Each of these sources is especially valuable for certain perceptions, including perceptions regarding important environmental or situational factors that are related to reference effectiveness. Each also has real or potential weaknesses that need to be minimized in the data collection process and accounted for in interpretation of the data.

The paper discusses the ways in which the Wisconsin-Ohio Reference Evaluation Program has addressed these concerns, including the development and use of the Reference Transaction Assessment Instruments. Data from forty-two public libraries and forty-eight academic libraries that have participated in the program are presented and discussed, including data on relationships between patron-perceived answering success and factors such as staffing patterns, effort spent answering questions, types and sources of questions, and collection size.

The long-range intent of the Wisconsin-Ohio Reference Evaluation Program is to improve the reference services that library patrons receive. This paper is presented in the hope that it will be of value to reference librarians and managers who have the same intent and who wish to evaluate their success at answering reference questions.

ACKNOWLEDGMENTS

Grateful acknowledgment is made to Ohio State University, which provided Marjorie Murfin a seed money grant for this project and whose Instructional and Research Computer Center has provided extensive computer support; to the University of Wisconsin-Madison Graduate School, which provided Charles Bunge research funds to support the project; and to the Council on library Resources for financial support in the form of Faculty/Librarian Cooperative Research Grants.

APPENDIX A

Librarian's RTAI for Reference Questions Public and Academic Libraries

1. TYPE OF QUESTION Select only one category in A-D below that best fits type of answer wanted.

○ Librarian
○ Library Assistant
○ Other Assistant

JOT DOWN QUESTION

A PARTICULAR TEXT(S) OR AUTHOR(S) WANTED
○ 1. Is particular book, serial, etc. in our collection?
○ 2. Smaller item in larger publication (Particular article, speech, quote, poem, law, etc.)
○ 3. Anything (or certain type of thing) by particular author

○ **B** SHORT ANSWER WANTED (AND IS APPROPRIATE) (What, when, where, who, which, yes or no, etc.) (Answer of a few words. Includes verification and meaning of citations, bibliographical form, recommendations, etc., etc., etc.)

○ **C** GENERAL EXPL. OF CATALOG, LIBR., OR PRINTED REF. SOURCE WANTED (Rather than short answer)

D TYPE MATERIALS OR LONGER DESCRIPTIVE ANSWER WANTED (OR APPROPR.) (Answer usually in the form of printed materials)

1. SUBJECT (Mark one)
○ a. Single subject(s)
○ b. Relate 2 subj. or concepts
○ d. Focus on aspect, biog., hist., other
○ e. Requests factual inf. in general (or source containing it) (names, addr., definitions, statistics, ratings, rankings, etc., etc.)

2. ASPECTS (MARK ALL THAT APPLY)
○ a. Something, anything, everything
○ b. Must be cert. time period, currentness, place, country, lang., etc.
○ c. Must be cert. type ref. source, publ., materials, or format (map, pict., etc., etc., etc.)
○ f. Criticism, reviews, interpr., etc.
○ g. Analysis, trends, pro/con, cause/effect, how-to-do-it, how-it-works, & other
○ h. Requests that you compile list of references on a subject

2A RESULTS (MARK ONE)	2B RESPONSE (MARK ONE)	2C TIME (MARK ONE)
○ 1. Found	○ 1. Directed and suggested only	○ 1. 0-3 minutes (i.e. under 3 min.)
○ 2. Partly found	○ 2. Helped with or made search	○ 2. 3-5 minutes
○ 3. Not found	○ 3. Deferred	○ 3. 5-15 minutes
○ 4. Don't know	○ 4. Referred	○ 4. Over 15 minutes

3. SPECIAL FACTORS. DO NOT OMIT MARK ALL THAT APPLY

QUESTION AND PATRON	CONDITIONS
○ 1. Missing information or misinformation	○ 10. Difficult to think of source
○ 2. Concerned with foreign countr./lang.	○ 11. Difficult to find subj. headings
○ 3. Concerned with govt. docs.	○ 12. Books off shelf
○ 4. Inf. needed (or citat.) very recent	○ 13. Source difficult to consult
○ 5. Wants no. of things	○ 14A. Busy ○ 14B. Very busy
○ 6. Difficult citation	○ 15. Cataloging or tech. problem
○ 7. Patron in hurry	○ 16. Collection weak in that area or out-of-date
○ 8. Communic. diff. or confused question	○ 17. Need bks. in another area or location
○ 9A. Needs extra help ○ 9B. Returns freq.	

4. LIB. INSTRUCT. MARK ALL THAT APPLY
○ 1. Expl. sources, citations, search strat.
○ 2. Expl. cat., computer, holdings, locations

5. NUMBER OF SOURCES USED, REC., OR INTERP. — 1 2 3 4 5+ ○○○○○

TYPE: MARK ALL THAT APPLY

○ 1. Indexes to period.	○ 6. Yr. own knowledge
○ 2. Ref. books	○ 7. Inhouse prod. tools
○ 3. Cat. (card, online, etc.)	○ 8. Phone bks., VF, Coll. cat.
○ 4. OCLC, RLIN, etc.	○ 9. Circ bks., period., newsp.
○ 5. Comp. database srch. or CD-ROM	○ 10. Consult someone
	○ 11. Refer

6. QUESTION DIFFICULTY (as perceived)
○ Easy
○ Medium
○ Hard

7. ASPECT (only if applicable)
○ Stat
○ Biog
○ Hist

8. SUBJECT

1st		2nd (if applic)	
	○0		○0
○1	○1	○1	○1
○2	○2	○2	○2
○3	○3	○3	○3
○4	○4	○4	○4
○5	○5	○5	○5
○6	○6	○6	○6
○7	○7	○7	○7
○8	○8	○8	○8
○9	○9	○9	○9

Use separate guidesheet and select subj. Mark boxes with no. of your subject.

EXAMPLE

SUBJ. No. 2		SUBJ. No. 20	
	○0		●0
○1	○1	○1	○1
●2	○2	●2	○2

MAKE NO MARKS IN THIS AREA

14454

FOR OFFICE USE ONLY

APPENDIX B

Patron's RTAI for Reference Questions–Academic Libraries

FILL IN DOT LIKE THIS ——————— ●

The Reference Department is doing a survey of reference use and would appreciate it if you would mark the following brief checksheet.
Thank you!

(Deposit checksheet UNFOLDED in container on leaving this area or on leaving the library.)
THANKS AGAIN FOR YOUR HELP!

USE NO. 2 PENCIL ONLY

STATUS

- ○ Freshman
- ○ Sophomore
- ○ Junior
- ○ Senior
- ○ Graduate student or teaching assistant
- ○ Continuing education or nondegree student
- ○ Alumni
- ○ Faculty
- ○ Staff
- ○ Not affiliated with Univ

MAJOR OR TEACHING-RESEARCH AREA

- ○ Arts or Humanities
- ○ Education
- ○ Law
- ○ Business/Management
- ○ Other Social Sci
- ○ Medicine/Health
- ○ Agric./Biological Sci.
- ○ Math/Physical Sci
- ○ Technology Engineering
- ○ Interdisciplinary/Other
- ○ Major not declared

1. Did you locate what you asked about at the reference desk?
   ○ Yes, just what I wanted ○ Yes, with limitations ○ Yes, not what I asked for, but oth. information or materials that will be helpful ○ Yes, but not really what I wanted ○ Only partly ○ No

2. If yes, how did you find the information or materials?
   ○ Librarian found or helped find ○ Followed suggestions and found on my own ○ Didn't follow suggestions but found on my own

3. Were you satisfied with the information or materials found or suggested?
   ○ Yes ○ Partly ○ No

4. If partly or not satisfied, why? MARK ALL THAT APPLY.
   ○ Found nothing ○ Too much ○ Want different viewpoint
   ○ Not enough ○ Need more in-depth ○ Couldn't find information in source
   ○ Need more simple ○ Not relevant enough ○ Not sure if information given me is correct

5. How important was it to you to find what you asked about?
   ○ Very important ○ Important ○ Moderately important ○ Somewhat important ○ Not important

	Yes	Partly	No
6. Was the librarian busy (e.g., phone ringing, others waiting)?	○	○	○
7. Did the librarian understand what you wanted?	○	○	○
8. Did you get enough help and explanation?	○	○	○
9. Were the explanations clear?	○	○	○
10. Did the librarian appear knowledgeable about your question?	○	○	○
11. Was the service you received courteous and considerate?	○	○	○
12. Did the librarian give you enough time?	○	○	○
13. Did you learn something about reference sources or use of the library as a result of consulting the reference librarian?	○	○	○

14. Did you become acquainted with any reference sources you hadn't previously known about, as a result of consulting the reference librarian?
   ○ Yes, one ○ Yes, more than one ○ No, none

MAKE NO MARKS IN THIS AREA 15914

FOR OFFICE USE ONLY

APPENDIX C

Patron's RTAI for Reference Questions–Public Libraries

FILL IN DOT LIKE THIS ———— ●

The Reference Department is doing a survey of reference use and would appreciate it if you would mark the following brief checksheet. Thank you!

(Deposit checksheet UNFOLDED in container on leaving this area or on leaving the library.)
THANKS AGAIN FOR YOUR HELP!

USE NO. 2 PENCIL ONLY

OCCUPATION (Mark one)
- ○ Homemaker
- ○ Skilled labor/trades/services
- ○ Secretarial/clerical/office
- ○ Sales/marketing
- ○ Professional/technical/management
- ○ Unemployed at present
- ○ Retired

AGE
- ○ Under 18
- ○ 18-40
- ○ 41-64
- ○ 65+

SEX
- ○ Male
- ○ Female

STUDENT
- ○ High School
- ○ College
- ○ Graduate school
- ○ Continuing education

SOURCE OF QUESTION
- ○ Work related
- ○ School/education related
- ○ Recreation related
- ○ Other personal project (hobbies, self-development, curiosity, etc.)

1. Did you locate what you asked about at the reference desk?
○ Yes, just what I wanted ○ Yes, with limitations ○ Yes, not what I asked for, but oth. information or materials that will be helpful ○ Yes, but not really what I wanted ○ Only partly ○ No

2. If yes, how did you find the information or materials?
○ Librarian found or helped find ○ Followed suggestions and found on my own ○ Didn't follow suggestions but found on my own

3. Were you satisfied with the information or materials found or suggested? ○ Yes ○ Partly ○ No

4. If partly or not satisfied, why? MARK ALL THAT APPLY.
- ○ Found nothing ○ Too much ○ Want different viewpoint
- ○ Not enough ○ Need more in-depth ○ Couldn't find information in source
- ○ Need more simple ○ Not relevant enough ○ Not sure if information given me is correct

5. How important was it to you to find what you asked about?
○ Very important ○ Important ○ Moderately important ○ Somewhat important ○ Not important

	Yes	Partly	No
6. Was the librarian busy (e.g., phone ringing, others waiting)?	○	○	○
7. Did the librarian understand what you wanted?	○	○	○
8. Did you get enough help and explanation?	○	○	○
9. Were the explanations clear?	○	○	○
10. Did the librarian appear knowledgeable about your question?	○	○	○
11. Was the service you received courteous and considerate?	○	○	○
12. Did the librarian give you enough time?	○	○	○
13. Did you learn something about reference sources or use of the library as a result of consulting the reference librarian?	○	○	○

14. Did you become acquainted with any reference sources you hadn't previously known about, as a result of consulting the reference librarian?
○ Yes, one ○ Yes, more than one ○ No, none

14454

MAKE NO MARKS IN THIS AREA

FOR OFFICE USE ONLY

APPENDIX D
Librarian's RTAI for Directional Questions Public and Academic Libraries

MAKE NO MARKS IN THIS AREA

FOR OFFICE USE ONLY

- ○ Librarian
- ○ Library Assistant
- ○ Other Assistant

DIRECTIONAL QUESTIONS

- ○ 1. Location of Reader's Guide, Atlases, Dictionaries, Encyclopedias, College Catalogs, Phone Books, Zip Code Directory, City Directory, Periodical Directory
- ○ 2. Asks for book kept on *ready reference* and gives *recognizable title*
- ○ 3. Has call number and wants location
- ○ 4. Location of areas and collections within the building
- ○ 5. Request for use of supplies (stapler, phone, pencil, etc.)
- ○ 6. Location of persons within the building
- ○ 7. Library hours and rules
- ○ 8. Help with machines
- ○ 9. Locate periodical title in library's directory or union list
- ○ 10. Other

1746

APPENDIX E

Patron's RTAI for Directional Questions–Academic Libraries

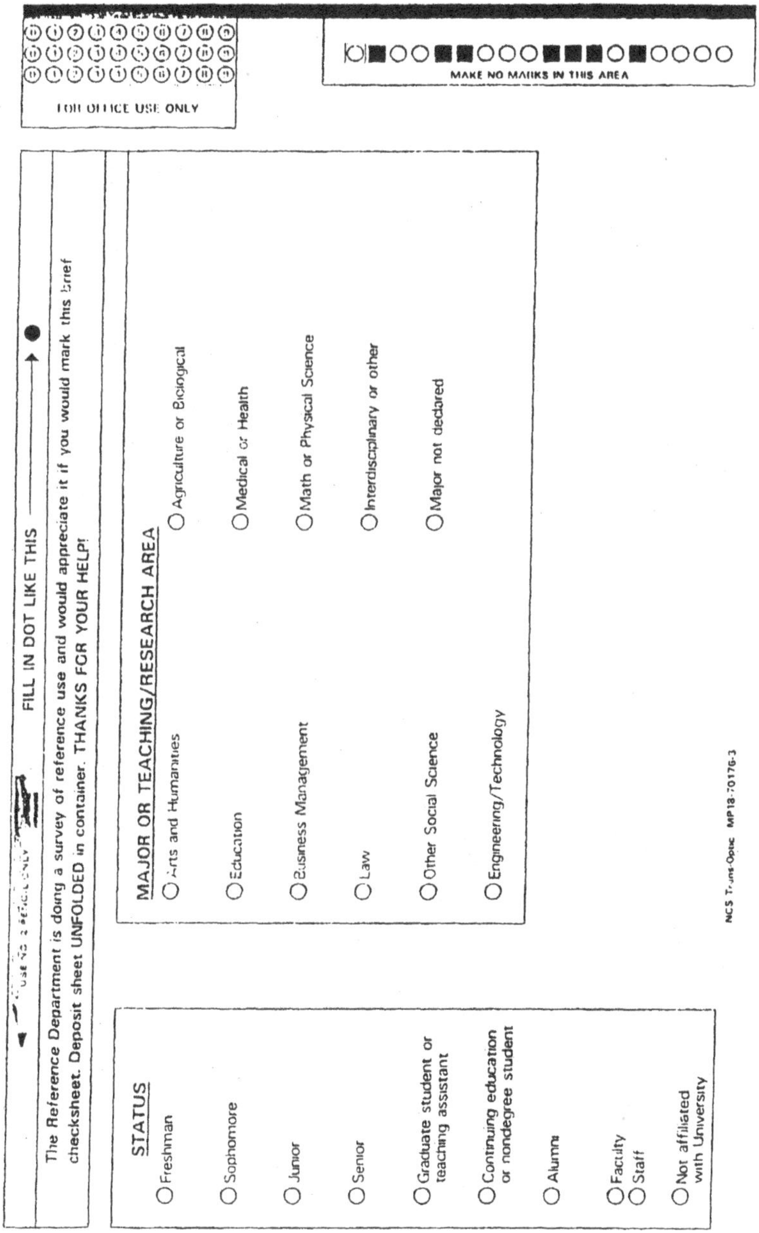

USE NO. 2 PENCIL ONLY

FILL IN DOT LIKE THIS → ●

The *Reference Department* is doing a survey of reference use and would appreciate it if you would mark this brief checksheet. Deposit sheet UNFOLDED in container. THANKS FOR YOUR HELP!

STATUS

- ○ Freshman
- ○ Sophomore
- ○ Junior
- ○ Senior
- ○ Graduate student or teaching assistant
- ○ Continuing education or nondegree student
- ○ Alumni
- ○ Faculty
- ○ Staff
- ○ Not affiliated with University

MAJOR OR TEACHING/RESEARCH AREA

- ○ Arts and Humanities
- ○ Agriculture or Biological
- ○ Education
- ○ Medical or Health
- ○ Business Management
- ○ Math or Physical Science
- ○ Law
- ○ Interdisciplinary or other
- ○ Other Social Science
- ○ Major not declared
- ○ Engineering/Technology

FOR OFFICE USE ONLY

MAKE NO MARKS IN THIS AREA

NCS Trans-Optic MP18-70176-3

APPENDIX F
Patron's RTAI for Dircetional Questions–Public Libraries

FOR OFFICE USE ONLY

MAKE NO MARKS IN THIS AREA

USE NO. 2 PENCIL ONLY — FILL IN DOT LIKE THIS → ●

The Reference Department is doing a survey of reference use and would appreciate it if you would mark this brief checksheet. Deposit sheet UNFOLDED in container. THANKS FOR YOUR HELP!

OCCUPATION
Mark one

- ○ Homemaker
- ○ Skilled labor/trades/services
- ○ Secretarial/clerical/office
- ○ Sales/marketing
- ○ Professional/technical/management
- ○ Unemployed at present
- ○ Retired

AGE

- ○ Under 18
- ○ 18-40
- ○ 41-64
- ○ 65+

SEX

- ○ Male
- ○ Female

STUDENT

- ○ High School
- ○ College
- ○ Graduate school
- ○ Continuing education

SOURCE OF QUESTION

- ○ Work related
- ○ School/education related
- ○ Recreation related
- ○ Other personal project (hobbies, self-development, curiosity, etc.)

Staffing the Reference Desk in the Largely-Digital Library

Steve Coffman
Matthew L. Saxton

SUMMARY. This article examines how a centralized, networked reference service might improve efficiency and reduce costs by addressing two long-standing and seemingly intractable problems associated with the reference process–that librarians spend only a small portion of their time at the reference desk actually answering questions, and that many of the questions they do answer could be handled by paraprofessionals. The authors explore the feasibility of a live, centralized, networked reference service in a library setting by comparing traditional reference services at the County of Los Angeles Public Library with a commercial inbound call center designed to handle the same volume of questions. Applying Erlang C, the standard algorithm used to calculate staffing requirements for commercial call centers, the authors find that a networked reference service based on a call center model could reduce the reference staff requirements at the County of Los Angeles Public Library by 42% or more. These results are very preliminary, and the article cautions against jumping to conclusions until we have much better data on the questions we are answering and the reference process as a whole, but the evidence we do have suggests that networked reference services have the potential to truly revolutionize the way we have been doing reference for the past 100 years. *[Article copies available for a fee from The Haworth Document Delivery Service: 1-800-342-9678. E-mail address: getinfo@haworthpressinc.com <Website: http://www.haworthpressinc.com>]*

Steve Coffman is Director of FYI, the research and information service of the County of Los Angeles Public Library (E-mail: coffman@cerf.net). Matthew L. Saxton is Reference Librarian at the Anaheim Public Library, an Instructor in the Library Technology program at Santa Ana College, and a Doctoral Student in the Graduate School of Education and Information Science at UCLA.

[Haworth co-indexing entry note]: "Staffing the Reference Desk in the Largely-Digital Library." Coffman, Steve, and Matthew L. Saxton. Co-published simultaneously in *The Reference Librarian* (The Haworth Information Press, an imprint of The Haworth Press, Inc.) No. 66, 1999, pp. 141-163; and: *From Past-Present to Future-Perfect: A Tribute to Charles A. Bunge and the Challenges of Contemporary Reference Service* (ed: Chris D. Ferguson) The Haworth Information Press, an imprint of The Haworth Press, Inc., 1999, pp. 141-163. Single or multiple copies of this article are available for a fee from The Haworth Document Delivery Service [1-800-342-9678, 9:00 a.m. - 5:00 p.m. (EST). E-mail address: getinfo@haworthpressinc.com].

In their award-winning article, Chris Ferguson and Charles Bunge predict live, real-time networked reference service as the next logical step in the evolution of the digital library.[1] They point out that as library materials and library users move increasingly onto the Internet, it only make sense that we should move our core reference service there as well to create a seven-day, 24-hour user support system. Operating under the auspices of the library, this service would emanate from a single service point to many libraries, computer rooms, and individual networked users.

Ferguson and Bunge note that such a network-based service would have some obvious advantages over the way we currently do things. It would allow us to provide reference services to users when and wherever they need them. It would increase library collaboration with other departments, agencies, and institutions to offer one-stop shopping for a broad range of information needs and services. It would encourage "holistic computing" by allowing the library to incorporate the tools and software needed for analysis with the information and data needing manipulation, and all from a single interface. It would increase integration of reference with instruction–specific answers with general education–and thereby decrease the boundaries between the library and the classroom. Finally, it would allow us to extend the enduring values that have governed reference services from the beginning–equity of access, intellectual freedom, respect for the user, and the importance of personal service–to the brave new world of the largely-digital library.

The evidence, however, also suggests that networked reference service might have another, less obvious advantage. Judging from the results of similar information services already well-established in the commercial sector, centralized networked reference services have the potential to improve radically the productivity and efficiency of reference service by providing new tools with which to tackle some very long-standing problems with the reference process.

WHAT'S WRONG WITH REFERENCE TODAY?

Reference services traditionally have been plagued by two major areas of inefficiency: librarians spend a lot of time at the desk not answering questions, and librarians spend a lot of time answering questions that don't require their level of training and expertise.

Anybody that has spent much time behind a reference desk knows the workload can be extremely uneven. Sometimes we can be totally swamped with patrons lined up five deep at the desk and two calls holding on the phone. Other times, large portions of an hour can go by without fielding a single question. For example, in a timed study of reference desk work at the UC Davis Library, Jestes and Laird concluded that "despite the fact that there are peak periods during the day which can barely be handled by two librarians, the librarians are, in fact, spending less than one-quarter of their total desk time with patrons or their questions."[2]

Although public library studies in this area are much older, what evidence there is suggests a similar problem. In a study of 33 public libraries in major cities published in 1935, Edith Guerrier found that librarians were spending an average of 20% of their time answering questions.[3] And in a study published in 1941, Emma Baldwin and W. J. Marcus indicate that the amount of time actually spent answering questions at some public library reference desk may be much less, perhaps no more than five-to-eight percent.[4] Admittedly, both of these studies are more dated than one might like, but they are the most recently published data of this type for public libraries. And the fact of the matter is that the way we do reference really has not changed all that much over the past 60 years.

The amount of down-time spent waiting around for somebody to ask a question will vary from library to library, desk to desk, and from day to day. But downtime almost always represents a significant problem in managing reference resources. Despite the fact that librarians try to fill up these slack periods by "reviewing the professional literature" and other odd tasks, down-time still represents a pretty inefficient use of a professional's time.

Busy peak periods don't represent very good service either. Patrons often find themselves waiting in long lines to be served or listening to music while on hold, wondering if they'll ever get through to someone who can help. Bunge, moreover, has found that the performance of reference librarians tend to deteriorate during busy periods, that they often end up giving questions short-shrift as they struggle to handle the increased demand.[5]

Theoretically a networked reference service like that imagined by Ferguson and Bunge could make far more efficient use of professional time by pooling reference staff and offering services to many desks and many users from a single location. Such an arrangement would provide more flexibility in adjusting staffing levels so as to minimize stand-by time while maximizing the time librarians actually spend providing reference service.

If reference services don't make very efficient use of librarians' time, there is also plenty of evidence that they don't make very good use of our training or expertise, either. Numerous reference studies have shown that a large percentage of the questions librarians handle at the reference desk today could better go to paraprofessionals. The Jestes and Laird study of the UC Davis reference desk showed that not only were the librarians spending much of their time not engaged in reference service, but nearly three-quarters of the questions they did get involved non-professional activity.[6] Another study by Jeffrey W. St. Clair and Rao Aluri found that nearly 80% of the reference questions they recorded at the University of Nebraska at Omaha could have been answered by non-professional employees.[7] A number of other studies report that 60-80% of the questions received at academic library reference desks could be handled easily by lower-paid paraprofessionals.

The data on the public library side are not quite as thoroughly researched, but what evidence exists indicates an even greater problem there. For example, an unpublished study of 464 questions collected during 12 hours of one week at the reference and information desks of Anaheim Public Library revealed that only 14.2% could be classified as "real" reference questions that might have required professional assistance. Almost three-quarters of the questions, 74.8%, were either directional questions regarding library rules or facilities, internal referrals from one service point to another within the library, or requests for back issues of magazines or videocassettes which are kept in non-public areas of the building. Approximately 11% were "Do you have . . . " type questions that paraprofessional staff could easily answer using the catalog.[8]

An unpublished analysis of one month of telephone reference logs from the Norwalk branch of the County of Los Angeles Public Library similarly shows that at least 545 or 52% of the 1,041 telephone reference questions received during the month of July, 1992, involved telephone directories, telephone reverse directories, book requests, or holdings questions that would not have required the assistance of professional librarians (see Appendix for a more detailed analysis of this data).[9] Another study reports the results of the Wisconsin-Ohio reference evaluation program, involving 6,000 reference questions from 42 public libraries in six states. In this study, Bunge states that preliminary results indicate that "across all public library reference questions, paraprofessionals have been just as successful as professionals."[10] He notes, however, that these results have to be interpreted with caution since in some cases paraprofessionals are allowed to answer only so-called easy questions.

Some libraries have tried to address this problem by setting up tiered reference services where routine information requests go to paraprofessionals, while librarians handle only those questions that need professional attention. Accomplishing this kind of pre-sorting effectively, however, can sometimes prove difficult in the physical setting of a library. In the first place, there must be a very busy reference desk and a substantial reference staff before one can even think about dividing the work between professionals and non-professionals. And even then, a study by Halldorsson and Murfin[11] suggests that some questions that should be handled by librarians don't always get referred on as they should–often because of problems in the referral process, wherein the librarian is busy, the librarian is not there, the staff doesn't want to bother the librarian with a referral, or other reasons.

The evidence suggests that to make effective use of a tiered reference service, one needs a system that insures adequate numbers of both paraprofessional and professional staff are available to answer questions, and that questions transfer easily and quickly from paraprofessional to professional staff (and *vice versa*) without delaying or otherwise inconveniencing the patron. One would also want a system that permits convenient monitoring of non-professional staff performance to insure the quality and correctness of both answers and referrals.

Networked reference service theoretically should make meeting each of these goals easier to achieve by creating a large staff pool for handling questions from many different users and locations at once, and by turning a referral into a simple matter of pressing a button to transfer a call. This, plus the greater question-monitoring capabilities available in a network environment, could help insure calls go to the right person and that those users who need professional assistance receive it in a timely fashion.

THE INCOMING CALL CENTER AS A MODEL FOR NETWORKED REFERENCE SERVICE

Do all of the possible advantages of a networked reference service outlined so far represent no more than idle speculation? It is not hard to envision such a network, nor to guess about the benefits it might bring. It only makes sense that networked reference services could make better use of staff time and skills. It is more difficult to imagine, however, just how such a reference service might work, or to get a clear picture of the efficiencies it might allow us to achieve, without comparing it to a real-world model.

Unfortunately there has not been much experience with real-time networked reference service in the library field to date. Nobody has yet built a service along the lines of what Ferguson and Bunge describe. True, some libraries offer reference services over the Internet. But with turn-around times ranging anywhere from 24 hours to one week or more, few if any of these could be considered real-time. And the number of questions handled by even the largest of these innovative programs doesn't come close to the daily volume at a busy reference desk.[12] Reference referral networks have long existed among public libraries and second-level reference centers, but these generally do not operate in real-time, do not directly serve the library user, and don't handle anywhere near the volume of questions that one might expect for a large networked reference service. If we want to find a working model of a networked reference service we must look outside the library.

However, we don't have to look very far afield, for there is a comparable model that has been in use in commercial settings for years, a model that most of us already know pretty well. Technically they are called incoming call centers, but we know them better as the customer service desk at a mutual fund, the reservation desk at an airline, the medical advice line at an HMO, or the technical support desk we call when our hard disk crashes. Whatever they may be called, their basic function is to provide business customers with information, assistance, and customer service–very much like our reference services. Unlike our reference services, however, incoming call centers are very carefully designed to perform these functions in the most efficient and most cost-effective manner possible.

The concept of the call center[13]–a centralized facility for handling telephone calls–dates back to the early days of the telephone system, when rooms full of telephone operators physically connected calls. With the introduction of toll-free 800 numbers in the early 1980s, however, incoming call centers really came into their own as information and customer service centers for business. Today incoming call centers are a very large business. Altogether there were some 60,000 to 70,000 such centers in the U.S. at the end of 1995, employing some 3.5 million people or about 3% of the total domestic workforce with an annual payroll of over $60 billion. The growth rate for call centers is estimated at nearly 20% per year.[14]

Although originally designed to handle telephone calls only, many call centers have now expanded to handle other forms of communication as well, such as FAX, email, and now even live assistance on Internet Web sites. Lucent Technologies in fact has even developed a special Internet Call Center that allows the agent and the customer to talk directly with one another using a single telephone line, even while viewing a Web site, much like one might expect to see in a networked reference service. Finally, call centers have even expanded to take over some applications once handled by local, live desk staff. For example, the bank branch inside a supermarket often handles account inquiries and other routine matters over the phone instead of an in-person transaction with a teller. And where once we used to find on-site staff behind the counter at department store credit desks, now we more likely will find a bank of phones connected to the store's call center.

Whatever they may be called, and however disparate their functions, all incoming call centers have some key elements in common. Much like the networked reference service we've discussed, call centers normally feature a large customer service staff centralized in a single location. (Recently, however, we have begun to see the development of *virtual* call centers, which function like a traditional centralized call center even though many of the staff are actually telecommuting and receiving calls at their homes.) Call centers vary in size from very small arrangements of 4-5 employees to true behemoths that may employ thousands of agents in a number of separate facilities located all over the world, with calls automatically switched between the facilities depending on volume, time of day, and other criteria. Many call centers accommodate a mixture of staff with different skill sets, such as sales and technical services personnel, or even nurses and doctors and insurance billing staff. A bank call center, for example, might include a large number of clerical staff trained to handle account inquiries and other routine transactions, plus a smaller number of loan officers and investment counselors to handle calls in those areas.

When you phone a call center, your incoming call routes through the center's automatic call distribution system (ACD), which is programmed to forward the call to the most appropriate agent on the center staff. ACDs can select the most appropriate agent based on such factors as the agent's present availability, the number of calls the agent has handled during the shift, the length of recent downtime, agent skill sets, and a broad variety of other criteria determined by the call center manager. If an agent is not available immediately, the call is placed in a queue until a line is free.

Agents normally take calls at computer workstations where they usually have ready access to databases, lists of frequently-asked questions and answers, pre-written scripts for particular situations, and other tools needed to deliver the information or service. Many centers maintain detailed customer records including a log of questions the customer has asked and other information that pops up on the computer screen when a call comes in. (Just imagine the possibilities for reference service!) In call centers that provide help desk services for computer hardware and software, agents often have access to sophisticated diagnosis software, inference engines, case-based reasoning tools, and other expert systems that make it easier for them to identify and fix problems–software that might have applications in reference services, also.

Unlike the little hash marks most of us make to record reference questions, call centers closely monitor and track all critical elements of the center's operation, much of it in real time. The ACD automatically monitors and reports on the technical aspects of the center's operations, such as number of calls received, number placed on hold, time on hold, number of calls handled by a particular agent, average speaking time on a call, average after-call processing time, and dozens of other details. Agents meanwhile typically log information on the content and disposition of each call and other information into large databases for further analysis and review.

One of the primary objectives in designing and managing an incoming call center is to make sure that the staff, phone lines, and other resources closely match anticipated traffic. Too many staff leaves a lot of employees sitting idly waiting for questions, just as it does at the reference desk. Too few staff, and customers end up spending long periods on hold while agents facing an array of blinking lights can quickly burn out from overwork, also a problem at the reference desk.

Call centers with hundreds of staff handling thousands of calls per hour need precise measures and models for staff demand. Most call centers use a complicated algorithm called Erlang C to determine their staffing requirements. Erlang C was developed in 1917 by A. K. Erlang, an engineer with the Copenhagen Telephone Company, who sought a way to predict the number of telephone operators needed to respond to a given volume of calls. Erlang C, however, will work for any situation in which people wait in a line for service, including the number of staff needed at a call center, the number of tellers required at a bank, the number of toilets required in a stadium restroom, or even the number of librarians required to handle a given volume of reference questions.

The algorithm itself is fairly complex (see Diagram 1 below) and calculating it by hand is a task better left for skilled mathematicians. Fortunately for the rest of us, automated Erlang C calculators are

DIAGRAM 1

Erlang C Formula

$$D(>0) = \frac{\frac{A^n}{n!} \cdot \frac{n}{n-A}}{\sum_{x=0}^{n-1} \frac{A^x}{x!} + \frac{A^n}{n!} \frac{n}{n-A}}$$

Where:

D (>0) = probability of delay;
A = total traffic volume of calls arriving (measured in erlangs);
n = number of customer service officers available; and
B = probability of loss (rejection) (Poisson distribution).

Where the relationship between D and B is described by:

$$D = \frac{nB}{n - A(1 - B)}$$

available in a number of computer programs, and several call center sites even include free Erlang C calculators on the Internet.[15]

In order to use Erlang C, one needs to know several things: (a) the average amount of talking time spent on a call; (b) the average length of after-call processing time (i.e., the time required to log the question, make notes, and anything else necessary to prepare for the next call); (c) the average number of calls received during a particular period (normally a half-hour or hour); and (d) an acceptable service level, normally defined as X number of calls answered in Y seconds, which is really a measure of how long customers will have to wait on average to talk with an agent. Acceptable service levels vary from call center to call center, but an 80/20 service level (80% of the calls picked up within 20 seconds) is considered standard.

TRYING OUT A NETWORKED REFERENCE SERVICE ON THE REAL WORLD

So how might a networked reference service built on the call center model work in a real-world library situation? Suppose, for example, we could design a networked reference service to handle all of the three million-plus reference questions answered each year at the 88 branches of the County of Los Angeles Public Library. What might the network look like? How would it operate? How many staff might we need, according to Erlang C? And how would it compare to the way we handle reference now?

First, let's take a look at the way we do things now. During the fiscal year 1995/1996 (the most current detailed reference figures available), the 88 branches of the County of Los Angeles Public Library answered a total of 3,016,618 reference questions. All of these should be "true" reference questions (i.e., those requiring the use of library materials) because directional/policy questions are counted separately. Staff noted the approximate length of time required to answer each of these questions by classifying reference interactions (the actual time spent with the patron regardless of the number of questions asked) into five time categories: 0 to 3 minutes, 3 to 8 minutes, 8 to 15 minutes, 15 to 30 minutes, and 30 to 60 minutes (see Table A for details).

Now if this were a true call center study, we would want much more detailed information on actual duration of reference interaction–and such other factors as the amount of after-call processing time required

TABLE A. Analysis of Time Spent on Reference Questions, 1995-96 County of Los Angeles Public Library

Questions Length Categories	Average Length of Questions	Number of Questions Asked	Total Minutes	Percentage of Total Time	Percentage of Total Questions
0m-3m	1.5m	2,340,883	3,511,324	40.5	77.6
3m-8m	5.5m	539,362	2,966,491	34.3	17.9
8m-15m	11.5m	101,328	1,165,272	13.5	3.4
15m-30m	22.5m	24,881	559,823	6.5	0.8
30m-60m	45m	10,165	457,425	5.3	0.3
TOTALS		3,016,618	8,660,335		

*8,660,335 minutes = 144,338 reference person hours
Overall average length or reference question = 2.87 minutes
Average questions/hour based on annual operating schedule of 3,276 hours = 920

to get ready for another question. The fact that we don't already have this data is evidence in itself that we have not treated these issues as seriously as they are considered in the business world. For the crude purposes of this analysis, however, we have taken the midpoint for each time period as an average for all the reference questions answered during that time period. Thus, calls classified in the 0 to 3 minutes interval are assumed to have an average length of 1.5 minutes, calls in the 3 to 8 minutes class have an assumed average length of 5.5 minutes, and so on.

Add up all of the reference questions recorded in each time category and multiply them by the average length of time to answer them, and we can derive a very rough estimate that during the 1995/1996 fiscal year County Library staff in all 88 branches spent somewhere around 8,660,335 minutes or 144,338 person hours answering a total of 3,016,618 reference questions, and that the average reference question takes about 2.87 minutes to answer.

As it stands now, the County Library normally has at least one staff member on duty to answer reference questions in each of its 88 branch libraries, and the 28 larger branches in the system normally have two people on the reference desk at all times. So, at any time the libraries are open, then, the County of Los Angeles Public Library has roughly 116 staff detailed to handling reference questions. Most of these are professional reference librarians, although a few smaller libraries are staffed with library assistants, and assistants occasionally share the desk with librarians at some of the larger libraries.

Now let's take a look at what it would take to provide the same level of service using a networked reference service based on a call center model. In the first place, reference service would operate out of one centralized location instead of 88 different desks as at present. Initially that central location might reside within a large print collection to allow the staff ready access to material available only in print. As we move toward the largely-digital library with more and more reference material moving onto the Internet, however, the physical location of the reference center will matter less and less.

Patrons could access the center in a variety of different ways. Some might phone in, just as they do now, others might use FAX and email, but live reference assistance over the Web would probably be the most effective method, since it allows the reference staff and the patron to interact just as they do now in the physical library. And of course one could deliver information to the patron over the Web much easier than by phone, FAX, or email.

We would expect of course that a networked reference service would incorporate an automatic call distribution system and that the reference staff would operate out of workstations that take advantage of all the specialized software and other productivity tools developed for traditional call centers. The real productivity improvements, however, would come from more effective use of staff.

In Table B, we have calculated staff requirements for a centralized reference call center using Erlang C. We have assumed an industry standard service level of 80% of the calls (or perhaps "contacts" would be a better descriptor in referring to communications over the Web) answered on average in 20 seconds. That means that 80% of the callers would wait an average of 20 seconds before speaking to a person on the reference staff. (This is not to say the question would be *answered* in 20 seconds–that's a little fast for even the most efficient librarians!) We are also assuming that the reference network would be open 3,276 hours annually, the same number of hours as the County's larger libraries. All of which means that the center could handle reference questions at the rather significant rate of about 920 per hour.

Based on these assumptions, Erlang C predicts that a centralized

TABLE B. Erlang C Calculations for a Networked Reference Service

Number of Reference Transactions Expected Per Hour	920
Average Amount of Time Per Transaction (In Seconds)	172
Average Post Precessing Time (In Seconds)	60
Service Level Percentage (*X* in: *X* Percent of Calls Answered in *Y* Seconds)	80
Number of Seconds to Answer (*Y* in: Percent of Calls Answered in *Y* Seconds)	20
Number of Minutes in the Interval Being Measured	60
Number of Staff Required	67
Staff Occupancy Rate (%)	89
Average Speed of Answer (In Seconds; Time Average Caller Spends on Hold)	9

reference center could handle all of the 3,106,618 questions received by the County Library with a reference staff of only 67, a 42% reduction of the 116 staff required to handle reference services as we now provide it.

Much of the improved productivity would stem from the fact that the centralized reference service could do a much better job of keeping the staff occupied. It is easy to see this effect in the two tables. Table B, the Erlang C calculations for a networked reference service, shows that the 67 staff would be occupied and answering questions 89% of the time. In Table C, we have given Erlang C the 116 staff we now use to answer reference questions and asked it to calculate the occupancy rate for our current reference librarians. You'll note that our staff are currently only 51% occupied, meaning they are spending half their time doing something other than reference. To be fair here, some of the reference staff in the smaller libraries are doing other things in between reference questions, such as keeping kids quiet, scheduling staff, ordering supplies, presiding over children's story times, check-

TABLE C. Erlang C Calculations for Existing Desk Reference Service

Number of Reference Transactions Expected Per Hour	920
Average Amount of Time Per Transaction (In Seconds)	172
Average Post Precessing Time (In Seconds)	60
Service Level Percentage (*X* in: *X* Percent of Calls Answered in *Y* Seconds)	NA
Number of Seconds to Answer (*Y* in: Percent of Calls Answered in *Y* Seconds)	NA
Number of Minutes in the Interval Being Measured	60
Number of Staff Available	116
Staff Occupancy Rate (%)	51
Average Speed of Answer (In Seconds; Time Average Caller Spends on Hold)	NA

ing books out, and other details of managing the building. Still, this only raises even more fundamental questions about what the true professional functions are in a library, and how and where they should best be performed, questions that go well beyond the scope of this article.

Finally, just in case these productivity improvements are not enough to impress, there is one other area of potential cost savings yet to discuss: savings that might be achieved by reconfiguring the type of staff used to provide reference services. We don't really have all the evidence we need to determine exactly what percentage of those 3,106,618 questions could be handled by paraprofessional staff, but based on figures cited in the literature we could predict that anywhere from 50% to 80% of these questions might not require professional librarians. This doesn't necessarily mean that 50% to 80% of the 67 positions would be held by paraprofessionals, because questions that require professional assistance might take longer to answer and thus might require more staff time and hence more positions than the number of questions alone would indicate. We don't know. But what we do know is that a large percentage of the 67 staff needed to operate the networked reference service would not require professional degrees nor would they require professional salaries. Since most of the 116 staff who are currently providing reference services for the County do have professional degrees, the potential cost savings of a centralized service staffed with a high percentage of paraprofessionals could be substantial.

CONCLUSIONS AND IMPLICATIONS

The evidence indicates, then, that a networked reference service based on the call center model might allow us to provide the same level of service with far fewer staff and at lower salary cost than the way we do it now. Does this mean it's time to begin ripping out reference desks and replacing them with call centers, and that we reference librarians should get busy dusting off our resumes and preparing for new careers?

Well, not quite. Many questions still remain to be answered and many issues still need to be addressed before we can implement something like this. And even though we've been providing reference service for over a century now, we still know so little about the reference process that it may take some time before we can fully gauge the real efficiencies that are possible using the call center model, the true implications it might have for the way we staff our libraries, or for that matter, the future careers of reference librarians.

In the first place, we need to know a lot more about the kinds of questions people are asking us. Much of the efficiency the business world has been able to achieve with the call center model comes from a careful understanding and analysis of the kinds of questions their customers ask. Call centers that handle product information on baby food know that they will get a lot of questions on ingredients, allergic reactions, and nutrition, so they have designed their systems to handle these types of questions quickly and efficiently. They might set up a database of all the ingredients and nutritional information that the customer service staff can access right from their desktops, or they may develop prewritten scripts on how to handle various types of allergic reactions, with referrals to local doctors or allergy associations. Banks know that account balance inquiries are one of the most frequently asked questions at their call centers, so many have taken steps to automate that process so customers can do it for themselves as much as possible. For the questions that do require "human intervention," banks have done research to anticipate the kinds of questions their customers might ask and then have developed databases, scripts, special software, and other tools to help their customer service staff answer those questions as quickly and efficiently as possible. And so it is with call centers for airlines, HMOs, catalog sales, computer help desks, and almost every other industry that is in the business of answering people's questions.

Except, that is, for libraries. Although many of us have a feeling for what our most frequently asked questions might be, and most of us have attempted to create some kind of a ready-reference file to answer some of them, but these have been individual ad hoc efforts at best. The fact of the matter is that for all the years we have been answering questions, we really have done very little serious research on the types of questions people ask us or on the best and most effective ways of answering them. If we hope to achieve the same kinds of efficiencies others have gained with the call center model, our first order of business should be to obtain a much better understanding of the questions we are answering and what people really want to know from us. Otherwise we will simply perpetuate existing problems with reference in a new electronic environment.

Secondly, we must have much better measurements of reference questions and the entire reference process. The figures we used for the Erlang C analysis in this paper are based on the crudest possible data because that's the best data available. And the sad thing is that as crude as our measurements are, they are far better and more detailed than those most libraries collect. Our figure for the average length of time it takes to answer a reference question is a rough calculation at best, and our estimate of 60 seconds for question post-processing time is nothing more than a wild guess. We really have no idea what it is because nobody in the library world has ever thought to measure it. Yet both of these figures are critical to the design and staffing of networked reference services; if we were off by more than a few seconds with either of these measurements, it could have a major impact on our estimates of staffing and costs. Reducing the average question length by just 22 seconds from 172 seconds to 150, for example, would reduce staff requirements by over 10% from 67 to 60 positions. And of course if we underestimated even a little, we would have to add staff. The point here is that we really don't know what the right answers are, and we need to have much more accurate and detailed measurements of the entire reference process if we are ever to figure out how we can improve it.

Next, we need to know much more about the cost of the equipment, network, and other infrastructure that will be required to support the call center model and networked reference in general. We've based our estimated savings for the call center model entirely on an analysis of staffing costs. This ignores the additional and very real costs of the software, equipment, and communications network that would be required to support such a system. One can reasonably argue that libraries will have to install a lot of the communications infrastructure and a good deal of the terminals and other equipment needed to make the system work anyway, just to insure they have adequate access to the Internet and other networked information systems; so many of these costs will be present regardless of the kind of reference service offered. Still, the call center hardware and software itself is not cheap and would have to be weighed along with the potential reductions in staff costs to yield an honest estimate of the potential savings of the call center model. It could be that when everything is added up, the cost savings of the call center approach are less than they appear on the surface and that the real advantages of adopting this model may be in the additional benefits it offers in the way of service to remote users, potential for 24-hour service, potential for consortial sharing of resources and expertise at many institutions, and so on.

Just to complicate matters further, the savings we've calculated in staff costs may also be somewhat illusory. That's because we've limited our analysis to calculating the number of call center staff required to answer *the same* number of reference questions we are handling now. The problem is, the way we are handling reference now actually discourages most people from asking us a question. They either have to come down to the library or try to get us on the phone, and even then our services are available only during regular business hours. A networked reference service has the potential for being far easier and more convenient for our patrons to use. It could be available right on their desktops with a button that could be clicked at any time. And as Ferguson and Bunge point out, a networked reference service could be available 24 hours a day since it is not limited to a particular library or particular staff. Take all of these factors into account, and it is highly unlikely we would be handling anywhere near the same number of questions in a networked reference environment. We would probably be handling a lot more. And it is possible that we might need all our existing staff and then some just to deal with the increased workload. We would of course be serving a much larger number of patrons and answering a lot more questions much more efficiently, but we may not be able to reduce real staff costs that much–and there could still be a bright future for reference librarians!

Finally, we've based all our assumptions and calculations here on the fact that we are dealing with a largely-digital library, where a large percentage of our patrons and the information and content we need to provide reference services is easily accessible over the network. With 88 branches spread over 3,000 square miles, and millions of very real books sitting on thousands of miles of very real shelving, the County of Los Angeles Public Library–and many other libraries just like it–is a very long way from being largely-digital. And if one can judge from the popularity of the new library-style bookstores like Barnes & Noble and Borders, people still love the idea of the library (or a bookstore that looks a lot like it) as a physical place where they can browse the stacks, hang out, drink coffee, enjoy programs, read, and otherwise entertain themselves. So it may be a very long time, if ever, before the County of Los Angeles Public Library becomes largely-digital.

Does this mean that we've just been wasting our time talking about networked reference services? Hardly. There is ample evidence to suggest that networked reference services could help improve the way we handle reference in physical libraries just as well as in largely-digital ones, and that we don't need to wait around until everything becomes electronic to begin increasing the efficiency (if not reducing the costs) of what we do.

One obvious application is in telephone reference services. Here patrons are already on the telephone calling into our libraries, and staff have often complained about the difficulties of handling both walk-in and telephone inquiries at the same desk. A telephone reference call center is a natural response. Preliminary studies at the County of Los Angeles Public Library indicate that telephone reference may account for anywhere from 10% to 20% of total questions asked. Using Erlang C and assuming that telephone questions are like other reference questions, we can predict that we should be able to handle all the telephone reference inquiries received at all County libraries with a staff of nine, assuming 10% of the questions come over the phone; or a staff of 16, assuming 20% of our questions are phone reference. Not only would this reduce the number of staff required to handle telephone questions, but it could make the regular desk staff and their patrons a lot happier, too.

Networked reference services could change the way we handle reference inside our libraries as well. Given the fact that a high percentage of the questions we answer could be handled by paraprofessionals, it might make more sense to staff our reference desks with paraprofessionals and move most of our reference librarians to the network. The paraprofessionals would need to be well-trained to help patrons find the material they want and to answer the most routine questions they receive on the floor. If a question requires professional assistance, however, a live librarian would be only a click away, accessible through a reference terminal that would allow them to interact with the patron directly, using a web browser, voice, and even live video. There is nothing far-fetched about this scenario. Banks, lawyers, insurance companies, stock brokers, doctors and others are already using these technologies to deliver professional services remotely, so why not libraries? And the potential efficiencies–particularly in a system as large as the County of Los Angeles Public Library–could be tremendous.

The advent of the computer and the network has done much in the past 30 years to change the way libraries work. It has truly revolutionized cataloging. Our once-massive card catalogs have been replaced by banks of softly glowing terminals. With shared cataloging records, small technical services staffs can now accomplish the work of huge cataloging departments, and many libraries are now outsourcing this function altogether. Acquisitions, which used to be a very paper- and labor-intensive process, is now largely an automated function. We have made circulation so easy, that we now have self-check machines that allow patrons to do it for themselves. And there have been significant cost savings here as well.

In the midst of all these technological advances, improvements in efficiency, staff reductions, and the wholesale restructuring of entire departments, however, one area of the library has so far remained largely untouched: reference services. Although we have a few new tools like online searching, CD-ROMs, and now the Internet, we still continue to do reference pretty much the same way we were doing it 100 years ago. Reference services were an important but very labor intensive, expensive, and inefficient process when they were first introduced, and they remain so today. Although the jury is still out, many questions remain to be answered, and many issues still need to be addressed, it is readily apparent that networked reference services and call center technologies have the very real potential to change the way we staff the reference desks at largely-digital libraries as well as at the very real ones. And for the first time they might permit us to truly revolutionize reference services even as other core functions of the library have been improved and transformed by new technologies. For our sake and the sake of the millions of people who depend on the information and knowledge we provide, it cannot happen soon enough.

REFERENCES

1. Chris D. Ferguson and Charles A. Bunge, "The Shape of Services to Come: Values-Based Reference Service for the Largely-Digital Library," *College and Research Libraries* 58 (May 1997): 252-65.

2. Edward Jestes and David Laird, "A Timed Study of General Reference Work in a University Library," *Research in Librarianship* 2 (January 1968): 9-16.

3. Edith Guerrier, "The Measurement of Reference Service in a Branch Library," *Bulletin of the American Library Association* 29(1935): 632.

4. Emma Baldwin and William E. Marcus, *Library Costs and Budgets: A Study of Cost Accounting in Public Libraries* (New York: Bowker, 1941).

5. Charles A. Bunge, "Gathering and Using Patron and Librarian Perceptions of Question-Answering Success," in *Evaluation of Public Services and Public Services Personnel: Papers Presented at the Allerton Park Institute, 1990* (Champaign: University of Illinois Graduate School of Library and Information Science, 1991), 65.

6. Jestes and Laird, 15.

7. Jeffrey W. St. Clair and Rao Aluri, "Staffing the Reference Desk: Professionals or Nonprofessionals?" *Journal of Academic Librarianship* 3:3 (July 1977): 153.

8. From a pilot study of reference service at the Anaheim Public Library for a dissertation research study conducted in May 1998. The complete data from the larger study of reference questions in many public libraries will be published with Matthew L. Saxton's dissertation in May 1999.

9. Data from an internal study of telephone reference logs compiled by the reference staff at the Norwalk Public Library of the County of Los Angeles Public Library during July 1992. For a detailed analysis of the data, please see Appendix.

10. Bunge, "Gathering," 69.

11. Egill A. Halldorsson and Marjorie E. Murfin, "The Performance of Professionals and Nonprofessionals in the Reference Interview," *College and Research Libraries* 38:3 (September 1977): 385.

12. The Internet Public Library (www.ipl.org), for example, one of the best known of these services, limits itself to 35 questions per day, according to Joe Janes, founder and director of the IPL, in a presentation at the Southern California Online Users Group annual workshop, "Rethinking Reference and Research," Industry, CA, 29 April 1998.

13. This technical discussion on call centers has been drawn chiefly from three sources: Robert A. Gable, *Inbound Call Centers: Design, Implementation, and Management* (Boston: Artech House, 1993); Brad Cleveland and Julia Mayhen, *Call Center Management on Fast Forward: Succeeding in Today's Dynamic Inbound Environment* (Annapolis, MD: Call Center Press, 1997); and Keith Dawson, *The Call Center Handbook: The Complete Guide to Starting, Running and Improving Your Call Center*, 2nd ed. (New York: Telecom Books, 1998).

14. From an unpublished internal market research study prepared for Lucent Technologies, 1998.

15. A very good example is the Call Center Directory site at www.prefsolutions.com (June 1998).

APPENDIX

Analysis of Reference Questions Received by the County of Los Angeles Telephone Reference Service of Norwalk Public Library, July 1992

	Could Be Handled by Paraprofessionals		May Require Professional Handling			
Subject Areas	Number	Percent of Area	Number	Percent of Area	Total Question in Area	Percentage of Grand Total
Animals			3	100%	3	.03%
Antiques, hobbies			7	100%	7	.07%
Art, architecture			4	100%	4	.04%
Simple Questions: "Do you have. . ." phone directories reverse directories book requests	544	93.6%	37	6.4%	581	55.8%
Biography			11	100%	11	1.1%
Company info.			217	100%	217	20.8%
Consumer, taxes, Blue Book			32	100%	32	3.1%
Education, career			36	100%	36	3.5%
Genealogy, history			12	100%	12	1.2%
Cookery, how to			16	100%	16	1.5%
Law, government			40	100%	40	3.8%
Games, sports			9	100%	9	.09%
Literature, words			16	100%	16	1.5%
Medicine			22	100%	22	2.1%
Music, lyrics			15	100%	15	1.4%
Performing arts			0	100%	0	
Religion, philosophy			11	100%	11	1.1%
Social sciences			5	100%	5	.04%
Physical sciences			4	100%	4	0.4%
Totals	544	52.2%	497	47.7%	1,041	

APPENDIX (continued)

This set of telephone reference questions was collected during July, 1992 by the staff of the dedicated telephone reference service operated by the Norwalk branch of the County of Los Angeles Public Library. The service operated from 10 a.m. to 5 p.m. on weekdays. Over the month, reference staff handled a total of 1,041 telephone reference questions.

During this period reference staff categorized all questions received by subject matter, time of day received, and length of time required to answer (1-5 minutes, 5-10 minutes, and call back). This data is consolidated in the table above. "Simple Questions" includes such routine questions as whether the library had a specific book, telephone numbers, and telephone reverse directory (crisscross) lookups. All told, this category accounts for over 52% of all questions received.

For the purposes of this analysis, we are assuming that the "Simple Questions," virtually all answered in less than 5 minutes, easily could have been answered by paraprofessionals since they entailed simple, straight-forward lookups in the library catalog or in phone directories. It is quite likely, however, that a closer analysis of the other question categories would reveal plenty of other questions that could be handled by paraprofessionals as well. For example, requests for information on business represented the second highest category with over 20% of the total questions. A look at the raw logs shows that many of these were requests for information on specific companies. The County Library today provides that same kind of company information directly to its branch libraries through a centralized business reference service largely staffed by well-trained paraprofessionals. And there are probably similar types of questions in other categories as well. So, while we have derived the 52% figure cited in the paper from the "Simple Question" category alone, the likelihood is that there were actually many more questions than could have been effectively handled by paraprofessionals.

Reference Service: A Field with a View

Linda McCann
Ruth Wallach

SUMMARY. The advent of new technologies raises a question of the value of one-on-one personalized interaction in the reference environment. The first part of this paper briefly surveys leading library literature; the second part reports results of an informal survey of practitioners in the field, designed to elicit their views on the influence of theoretical models and new technologies on reference service. It is suggested that while there is no necessary conflict between integration of technology and existing structures in the reference environment, new technology does raise issues that need to be thoughtfully addressed. *[Article copies available for a fee from The Haworth Document Delivery Service: 1-800-342-9678. E-mail address: getinfo@haworthpressinc.com <Website: http://www.haworthpressinc.com>]*

The basic definition of reference service is the provision of information or assistance in finding information by a librarian/information specialist to a patron/customer upon the latter's request–in a professional manner, in as ample a quantity as possible, and promptly.[1] Alternatively, "the proper role and purpose of the reference librarian is to provide personal assistance to library users in their pursuit of information."[2] These basic statements have been elaborated within

---

Linda McCann and Ruth Wallach are Reference Librarians in the Reference Center, Doheny Memorial Library, University of Southern California, Los Angeles, CA 90089-0182 (E-mail: lmccann@usc.edu or rwallach@usc.edu).

[Haworth co-indexing entry note]: "Reference Service: A Field with a View." McCann, Linda, and Ruth Wallach. Co-published simultaneously in *The Reference Librarian* (The Haworth Information Press, an imprint of The Haworth Press, Inc.) No. 66, 1999, pp. 165-174; and: *From Past-Present to Future-Perfect: A Tribute to Charles A. Bunge and the Challenges of Contemporary Reference Service* (ed: Chris D. Ferguson) The Haworth Information Press, an imprint of The Haworth Press, Inc., 1999, pp. 165-174. Single or multiple copies of this article are available for a fee from The Haworth Document Delivery Service [1-800-342-9678, 9:00 a.m. - 5:00 p.m. (EST). E-mail address: getinfo@haworthpressinc.com].

professional reference literature to deal with evaluation of services, studies of librarian and user perceptions of question answering success, applications of communication and educational theories to reference service, and the development of new service quality concepts. They are based partly on management theory and extend to public services in general and reference service in particular. Many of these developments have been documented, discussed, and studied by Charles Bunge, as can be seen from the bibliographies of and references to his work throughout this volume.

The present paper is concerned with the applicability of reference theory to the actual practice of reference, and is an opinion piece rather than a scientific study. We believe that while the application of social science methods to the study of reference have provided valuable information to generations of reference librarians, what we do not have is a better grasp of reference work as a humanistic endeavor. Since reference service is "characterized by a high degree of personal interaction between library staff members and library users,"[3] and since "the information that the reference librarian produces or suggests will be found useful by the inquirer only in terms of the inquirer's own reality, and the inquirer's specific situation, not merely in terms of how well it matches some typical or normatively defined situation,"[4] we are interested in conceptualizing the ways in which reference librarians define their work and whether the standard reference service definition applies. For that purpose, we questioned a small sample of reference librarians in an attempt to gauge what providing reference service meant to them. Our questionnaire does not represent a statistically meaningful study, but provides a qualitative snapshot of professional philosophy.

LITERATURE OVERVIEW

Beyond the very basic definition of reference presented in the beginning of this chapter, several theories of service have developed. The most common set of theories elaborates on the level and type of service provided. These levels, usually called "conservative," "moderate," and "liberal," define reference service based on the emphasis placed on teaching to find information as opposed to providing the information itself.[5] This theoretical model of service, which is often described in historical overviews of the profession, also serves to separate academic from public and special libraries.

Our profession's interest in defining and measuring the quality of service has given rise to a large body of literature within librarianship, relying chiefly on such social science tools as communication and management. Several studies have brought to the fore considerable differences in perception of the quality of service rendered between librarians and users. It has became clear that while librarians concentrate on the content, correctness, and value of the information retrieved, users cite the quality of the relationship between them and the librarians as an important factor in satisfaction.[6] Other types of studies attempt to evaluate in concrete terms the output produced by reference service. One of the standard figures cited in reference literature is that approximately 65% of reference transactions are satisfactory to the patron.[7] While these and many other studies shed increasing light on a rather murky process of reference service, we would like to consider additional issues.

REFERENCE ISSUES FROM THE FIELD

Collection Development and Reference

The role of reference librarians in defining resource collections and access is often an important factor in reference service, and one that is almost always overlooked in library literature. In many institutions reference librarians function as collection development officers or bibliographers, whereby they define the collection (both reference and circulating) through their understanding of current and potential research needs of their constituencies. More importantly, reference service often depends on the librarian's understanding of the function of the reference collection within specific research needs and vice versa. The questions, in other words, are: Does the reference collection fit the needs of researchers within the institution, and can the needs of researchers fit into the existing reference collection and access framework? This process is one of continuing refinement and redefinition, based on contact with users and on dear articulation of services and needs involved, which is no mean matter.

Whither Interpersonal Relations?

There is a difference between user expectations and user needs, just as there is a difference between the librarian's perception of user needs and the actual needs themselves. It is often the case that the "reference interview" involves either gradual or radical readjustments in expectations on the part of both parties.[8] While the provision of *correct answers* (and the term is in italics, as we feel that the correctness of an answer can be measured in some but not all of the situations) is important to the definition of reference service, the interaction between the librarian and the individual may, in fact, provide the emotional veneer through which *correctness* or *satisfaction* are filtered by both parties. What often creates a positive interaction is the process of research which involves both a librarian and a patron, and which may turn out to be just as important as the final answer. For example: A patron asks a librarian to help her find references to black experiences regarding travel and transportation from the first hail of the century, an issue pertaining to her dissertation that looks at Jack Kerouac's *On the Road* from a cultural, social, and political perspective. After extensive literature search involving both the librarian and the researcher, which reveals very little written on the topic, a special relationship develops between the researcher and the librarian that continues into the future. From our perspective, this story is one of long-term success, or, rather, satisfaction for both parties involved even though it fails to get an answer to a particular research problem.

The Rhetoric of Success

An issue of interest to many reference librarians and library administrators is the question of the effectiveness of reference service. Studies have been conducted in evaluating the success of reference transactions, the perception of success among librarians and among users, and the cost of delivering reference service. A major debate on the latter involves the economic viability of the reference desk versus provision of reference service through other means. This debate often links the cost of provision of reference service with the definition of the role of librarians in the delivery of that service.[9]

With regard to the question of success, many studies show that approximately 65-70 percent of reference transactions may be deemed successful. Most studies, however, do not provide a definition of success. Does the fact that with the help of a librarian an undergraduate found three citations to his or her topic mean the reference transaction was successful? If a researcher and a librarian are unable to trace a citation in various subject-related indexes and catalogs, is the transaction unsuccessful? How does one measure the success of a reference exchange that sends a student in search of elusive statistics to an outside organization known to have studied questions similar to the one the student is exploring? Given the fact that research needs are often varied and multi-layered, and that part of the research process is the generation of new knowledge, how can we evaluate the standard 65% success figure? Should this figure be viewed as a public good, and can librarians continue to justify providing it? We bring up these questions not because we expect there are easy answers that have not yet been properly tracked down, but because we don't think there are answers. These questions are rhetorical; they point to the very complex interaction among researchers, librarians, and information, and they do not lend themselves to structured characterizations.

The Question of Technology

Lastly, we would like to address briefly the role of technology, and particularly of computers, in reference service. The debate about the utility of computers in advancing reference service to improve the process of research and information-seeking cannot adequately be captured here. The optimism expressed by Alvin Toffler's 1980 book, *The Third Wave*, and other such writings is beginning to be modified by economic reality, as it appears now that the broad-based entry of computers into the marketplace has not significantly improved productivity.[10] We are in the very beginning of what might be a transition age, so we have little understanding of the effect new technologies are having on human needs and relations, and whether or not the availability of technology is radically redefining our psychology and our life as Toffler and his followers predicted in the 1980s.[11] To quote from Christine Borgman's Presidential Chair Lecture, "Access to information is not a technology problem. It's a people problem. . . . We've got lots of technology. What we don't have is enough understanding of human behavior and human relationships."[12]

REFERENCE SERVICE SURVEY

As indicated in the first part of this paper, library literature on reference service provides definitions, studies, and analyses of many facets of reference service. We have sometimes felt in reading current literature about reference, particularly literature on academic libraries in a time when much is also written about changes in higher education, that the literature does not always correspond to actual concerns of front-line practitioners. The opportunity to write about the reference environment for this volume on Charles Bunge provided an occasion to contact other reference librarians in the field to see what sorts of patterns emerged from responses to a brief survey posted on several reference listservs.

The immediate goal was to see if any theoretical models from literature or educational training match real-life experiences of reference librarians, and whether this varies among reference environments (academic, public, special, other). This approach does not require the collection of large amounts of statistical data for quantitative analysis, but it does enable a qualitative analysis of reference service across different types of environments in which the respondents work.

We conducted a brief informal survey through postings to two listservs, LIBREF_L and Dig_Ref. We decided to post two general questions to permit respondents to provide their own interpretations. The questions, which informed our own interest in this survey, were: (1) What do practitioners in the field think constitutes excellence in reference service, (2) do librarians base their practice on theoretical foundations or models of reference, and (3) are user expectations of reference an important influence in design and provision of service?

The following survey questions were posted to the listservs in May, 1998:

1. Do you base your reference activities on a specific model of reference? If yes, which model? If no, why not?
2. Do reference services need to be provided in person, or does the availability of technology change the reference model?
3. What type of institution are you from?

Charles Bunge wrote that reference librarians know that "our field is not well supplied with useful standards."[13] This statement was supported in the listserv responses we received to the first question about whether librarians in the field based their practice on a specific model.

Of the total 46 responses received, most indicated either that they did not follow a specific model or were not aware of a specific model. A few named models that they followed: RASD performance guidelines, State of Art Reference (STAR), Maryland Model, Ranganathan's five laws, triage model, or retail/customer service model. Even though most respondents did not refer to a particular model, most answered this question with a description of what they thought guided their provision of reference service.

A few respondents indicated they went to school before models were trendy and one person stated that creative reference was too complex for simplistic models. Other answers describing the reference environment were: (1) providing the best service, (2) focus on the user, (3) personal (synthesized) model or standards customized for a specific environment or clientele, (4) guiding principles (reference interview, active reference, point of use reference, problem analysis), (5) a mentor or a professor's philosophy, (6) experience, and (7) methods (WORF method, Ralph Gers workshops, Kuhlthau method).

The answers to the second question were varied. Most respondents do not think reference needs to be provided in person. A number of responses indicate that while technology provides an additional mode of delivery, it is not a substitute for in-person reference. The most common technologies mentioned are telephone and email, with additional technologies being FAX and the Web. A few respondents feel technology has changed and will continue to change reference service.

A few common themes emerge from this informal survey. Customized or personalized service to individual needs is considered to be a key to effective service. The importance of the process of reference is also emphasized, particularly during either in-person (with advantages of non-verbal cues) or telephone interviews. Asynchronous reference, through e-mail or the Web, provides advantages to personalized service that is not limited to location or time, though many respondents thought it makes the interview process cumbersome and frustrating for both sides because this mode lacks immediate feedback. Some respondents think first-time users may benefit from in-person reference and others think complex questions need human interaction. Several respondents felt that interactivity was important, whether face-to-face or by phone. That suggests that technologies which combine synchronous and remote modes of communication might be preferable to asynchronous modes, where immediate intelligent response is missing.

There were also some interesting observations. One academic librarian states that technology has not changed the model of reference, it has changed delivery and costs. A public librarian thinks it is not crucial that reference be provided *in* person, but important that it be provided by *a* person. A corporate librarian notes that electronic reference is harder to provide in public and academic environments, because for this type of service to be effective the librarian has to know individual customers and their areas of expertise as well as the company.

CONCLUSIONS

The question presented in this paper has to do with what might be described as the essence of reference service–what quality or qualities are essential to the service so that when removed from it, most practioners would agree that reference service no longer exists? It is significant that none of the respondents to our informal survey used the word transaction. Reference transactions are what are measured and described by much of the library literature on the subject. Many of our respondents describe the reference interview as central to the process of reference, and the interview is what most think requires a personal touch if user needs are actually to be met. It is this individualized service that answers specific needs that is seen by some analysts and administrators as expensive because it is not scalable to large groups of users. This may be true, at least for some portion of the service now delivered by reference professionals. The question then becomes whether the values of reference are important enough to the users and the organization so that the service will be afforded.

The most common theme in the answers to our survey is the emphasis on the patron, not on technology. One academic librarian who believes that reference librarians will have new values that result from new technologies states that he learned his reflective practitioner approach of reference service from Charles Bunge. In his writing on the practice of reference, Bunge stresses the importance of building a relationship that "recognizes the professional's superior knowledge and expertise, but also recognizes the importance of the client's competence, authority, and responsibility . . . a 'fiduciary relationship.'"[14] Indeed, many of the respondents to our survey recognize these basic tenets, and they fit new technologies and changing services into variations of the "fiduciary relationship."

With regard to development of public service in libraries into the 21st century, we did not find that reference librarians responding to our survey are committed to a specific theoretical model that might conflict with the use of new technologies and development of new service values. What comes out dearly from responses, and is also reflected in the work of Charles Bunge, is the importance of the personal dimension. While there is not a deep conflict of principle in the intelligent application of new technologies to reference service, preservation of personalized reference as fully as possible should be seen as a value in the integration of technology into reference service of the future. The potential impact of technologies on the reference environment needs further careful study so that core values of reference service can be defined and preserved as both the reference environment and libraries change.

This paper makes no pretense of being unbiased as it is not a quantitative statistical analysis. We do not know the total number of people surveyed or even who the respondents really are, precisely because this is a virtual survey sent to listservs. There is a bias in this paper towards technology and reference service because those who took the trouble to reply to the reference listservs cared enough about reference to do so, and the only means of receiving the survey and responding to it was via Internet listservs and e-mail. While we did not survey user populations directly, most respondents stressed that meeting individual user needs drove their service ethic. What is not addressed in this short survey are underlying goals of reference service and how these change in different environments. It is our belief that there are differences between the types of services provided in corporate, educational, and public environments that need to be studied. For instance, while most respondents in this survey from corporate and public environments feel providing information is a major part of reference, respondents from academic settings stress their roles as partners in research and teaching/learning. This article, however, focuses on our view that reference service in different environments shares some core values. The survey was our reality check.

The roles of reference librarians today as selectors, providers/producers, and teachers will be altered by innovations in technologies, and reference professionals are at the forefront of these trends. The Internet today, which provides relatively free direct access to a wealth of information and non-information, may not be so free in the near future. It will be up to reference librarians to provide a physical or virtual environment for users of tomorrow who find themselves deluged by more and more access to less and less of what they really need at costs they cannot afford.

REFERENCES

1. Martin Sable, "Substantive Factors for a Theory of Reference Service," *International Library Review* 16 (October 1984): 407.

2. Charles A. Bunge, "Information Service in the Real World," *The Journal of Academic Librarianship* 11 (May 1985): 77.

3. Charles A. Bunge, "Reference Services," in *ALA World Encyclopedia of Library and Information Services* (Chicago: American Library Association, 1980), 468-474.

4. Charles A. Bunge, "Interpersonal Dimensions of the Reference Interview: A Historical Review of the Literature," *Drexel Library Quarterly* 20 (Spring 1984): 12.

5. Charles A. Bunge, "The Personal Touch: A Brief Overview of the Development of Reference Services in American Libraries." in *Reference Service: A Perspective*, ed. S. H. Lee (Ann Arbor: Pierian Press, 1983), 1.

6. Marie L. Radford, "Communication Theory Applied to the Reference Encounter:An Analysis of Critical Incidents," *Library Quarterly* 66 (April 1996): 124, 132.

7. Charles A. Bunge and Marjorie E. Murfin, "Reference Questions: Data from the Field," *RQ* 27 (Fall 1987): 16.

8. Brian Quinn, "Adapting Service Quality Concepts to Academic Libraries," *Journal of Academic Librarianship* 23 (September 1997): 363.

9. Karen Storin Summerhill, "The High Cost of Reference: The Need to Reassess Services and Service Delivery," *The Reference Librarian* 43(1994): 71-85.

10. Jeff Madrick, "Computers: Waiting for the Revolution," *New York Review of Books* 45 (26 March 1998): 31.

11. Alvin Toffler, *The Third Wave* (New York: William Morrow, 1980).

12. Christine Borgman, "Presidential Chair Lecture Examines Information Access in a Digital World," *GSE&IS Forum* 2 (Winter 1998): 2.

13. Charles A. Bunge, "Evaluating Reference Services and Reference Personnel: Questions and Answers from the Literature," *The Reference Librarian* 43 (1994): 199.

14. Charles A. Bunge, "Ethics and the Reference Librarian," in *Ethics and the Librarian*, ed. F. W. Lancaster (Urbana Champaign: University of Illinois Graduate School of Library and Information Science, 1991), 45-61.

PART 4: REFLECTIONS ON THE PAST AND FUTURE OF REFERENCE SERVICE

Select Bibliography of Bunge's Publications Related to Reflections on the Past and Future of Reference Service

Sarah B. Watstein

BIBLIOGRAPHY

"Statewide Library Surveys and Plans, Development of the Concept and Some Recent Patterns." *Library Quarterly* 36 (January 1966): 25-37.

Sarah B. Watstein is Assistant Director for Academic Use Services, James Branch Cabell Library, Virginia Commonwealth University, Richmond, VA 23284 (E-mail: swatstei@ucc.edu).

[Haworth co-indexing entry note]: "Select Bibliography of Bunge's Publications Related to Reflections on the Past and Future of Reference Service." Watstein, Sarah B. Co-published simultaneously in *The Reference Librarian* (The Haworth Information Press, an imprint of The Haworth Press, Inc.) No. 66, 1999, pp. 175-177; and: *From Past-Present to Future-Perfect: A Tribute to Charles A. Bunge and the Challenges of Contemporary Reference Service* (ed: Chris D. Ferguson) The Haworth Information Press, an imprint of The Haworth Press, Inc., 1999, pp. 175-177. Single or multiple copies of this article are available for a fee from The Haworth Document Delivery Service [1-800-342-9678, 9:00 a.m. - 5:00 p.m. (EST). E-mail address: getinfo@haworthpressinc.com].

"Library Education at Madison: The University of Wisconsin Library School: Through Its Last 25 Years." *Wisconsin Library Bulletin* 71 (November December 1975): 335-38.

"Reference Services." *ALA World Encyclopedia of Library and Information Services*. Chicago: American Library Association, 1980.

(with J. Krikelas) "Herbert Goldhor: A Tribute and a Bibliography." *Library Trends* 38 (Fall 1989): 295-312.

"Introduction: The man [Rothstein] and His Work." *The Reference Librarian* 25-26 (1990): 1-5.

(with C. Ferguson) "The Shape of Services to Come: Values-Based Reference Service for the Largely-Digital Library." *College and Research Libraries* 58 (May 1997): 252-65.

OVERVIEW

We are fortunate to have Charles Bunge's in-depth and thoughtful reflections on a variety of topics–statewide library planning, library education, the contributions of Herbert Goldhor to librarianship and library education, and, of course, reference services.

In "Statewide Library Surveys and Plans: Development of the Concept and Some Recent Patterns," he discusses national influences on statewide public library planning, state and multi-state influences on state-wide library planning, and recent patterns at the state level. In the article Bunge states that the information presented is based on examination of "well over one hundred such items [published surveys and plans] and several pieces of background information on each of the majority of these." Bunge here succeeds in both documenting the development of the phenomenon of state-wide library surveys and plans, and in paying attention to emerging trends.

"Library Education at Madison" provides an in-depth review of the history of the University of Wisconsin library school from its start in 1906. Bunge's contribution considers the growth of the school's teaching, research and service programs, and the school's quarters and facilities over the last quarter century. He also shows how the school has shared in the growth and development of a "resourceful university."

"Herbert Goldhor–A Tribute and Bibliography" includes both a comprehensive bibliography of the publications of Herbert Goldhor and an essay that provides a brief sketch of Goldhor's life and career plus discussion of two especially important aspects of his contributions: public library service and administration, and scientific research in librarianship. In his conclusion, Bunge comments that Goldhor's "works reflect an inquiring mind, one that constantly seeks explanations." He also states that "much of Herbert Goldhor's work represents an invaluable store of information for scholar-researchers today and in the future." Both statements could be applied to Bunge as well.

Finally, two pieces consist of reflections on reference service: "The Shape of Services to Come: Values-Based Reference Service for the Largely Digital Library" and his encyclopedic essay, "Reference Services." In the first work, Ferguson and co-author Bunge focus their attention on the nature and quality of library service that will be required in a largely-digital age. They hold that "the future is now" and do the reader a service by clearly defining that future and profiling evolving models for reference services. They then focus on the relevancy of those service values for the largely-digital library. The article concludes with thoughtful reflections on the shape of services to come. In "Reference Services," Bunge provides an overview of the historical development of reference services as well as an overview of the role of the librarian in the provision of information services. The essay concludes with discussion of two important concerns that Bunge speculates are likely to receive major attention form reference librarians and administrators: direct user fees for information services and the planning and evaluation of services.

Library Education at Madison: The University of Wisconsin Library School: Through Its Last 25 Years

Charles A. Bunge

The Library School at the University of Wisconsin-Madison is one of over 50 graduate programs in the United States accredited by the American Library Association to award master's degrees in librarianship. The school operates as a department in the College of Letters and Science and has three major objectives: the preparation of students to serve as librarians, contribution to the enlargement of the body of knowledge relevant to the practice of librarianship, and the provision of service to librarians and library agencies in the state, nationally and internationally.

About 25 years ago, the fifth-year master's degree became the standard credential for the practice of professional librarianship. The Library School initiated its master's program in 1951, during the directorship of Rachel K. Schenk. Well over 1,000 students have graduated from the master's program, and persons with degrees from the Library School hold important positions in libraries of all types in every state in the United States and in many foreign countries.

[Haworth co-indexing entry note]: "Library Education at Madison: The University of Wisconsin Library School: Through Its Last 25 Years." Bunge, Charles A. Co-published simultaneously in *The Reference Librarian* (The Haworth Information Press, an imprint of The Haworth Press, Inc.) No. 66, 1999, pp. 179-183; and: *From Past-Present to Future-Perfect: A Tribute to Charles A. Bunge and the Challenges of Contemporary Reference Service* (ed: Chris D. Ferguson) The Haworth Information Press, an imprint of The Haworth Press, Inc., 1999, pp. 179-183.

Throughout its history, the program has expected the entering student to possess a bachelor's degree with a strong component of the liberal arts and sciences.

The curriculum of the master's degree program has been continuously evolving over the years. Periodic major revisions are made, in response to the changing needs of the profession. The curriculum of this one-year program currently emphasizes an introduction to the field of librarianship, preparation in basic skills and knowledge in the field, and opportunity for preliminary specialization in one of its subfields (e.g., practice in a particular type of library or in a particular functional area of librarianship). In the late 1940s and early 1950s the typical enrollment (full-time and part-time) in the school's basic program was approximately 50 students. By the early 1960s this number had grown to 75. During the 1970s, enrollment in the master's program is approaching 200 persons (160 full-time equivalents).

Perhaps the most important development for the Library School in the past 25 years has been the establishment and growth of a program of advanced study in librarianship. This program, which began under the directorship of Margaret E. Monroe, consists of the sixth-year Specialist in Librarianship Certificate and the Ph.D. degree. The aim of the specialist program is to prepare librarians with previous professional experience for positions of advanced responsibility in their chosen areas of librarianship. The doctoral program attempts to prepare scholars, competent in research, who will use their understanding and skills in a diversity of teaching, research and administrative functions in librarianship.

The specialist program was inaugurated in 1966. It combines specialization in librarianship with advanced study in one or more related academic disciplines or professional fields. Throughout the program's history, it has been characterized by flexibility and individually tailored study programs. Students in the program have specialized in such areas as services to children, the administration of special types of libraries, automation of library operations, and library social action programs. Holders of the Specialist in Librarianship Certificate have such positions as heads of libraries, senior specialists in departments of libraries, teachers of librarianship and library consultants.

The doctoral program was also begun in 1966, experimentally under the "committee degree" format, which is used on the Madison campus for disciplines or interdisciplinary areas without fully established Ph.D. programs. After a developmental phase (lengthened by the complexities of the merger of the two state university systems) the program was fully entitled by the Board of Regents in 1974. This program emphasizes the achievement of research competence by its participants, so that they may contribute to the quality of library service in upper-level teaching, research and administrative positions. Graduates of the program are serving as faculty members at leading library schools in the country, as heads of important libraries, and as key administrative staff members in other libraries and library agencies.

Serving as a bridge between the school's teaching mission and its service mission is its continuing education program. The Library School has been fortunate to have a close working relationship with the Library Science Department of University Extension. Working both jointly with and independently of this agency, the School has made available a wide range of institutes, workshops and courses to practicing librarians of the state and the nation. Among such programs have been: The Public Library Management Institutes of the 1950s and 1960s, jointly sponsored with University Extension and the state library agency; a series of adult services institutes during the mid-1960s; an institute entitled 'The Young Adult in Conflict" in 1970; a one-day program on "Assistance to Libraries in Developing Nations" in 1971; and a group of institutes and workshops on library outreach and services to disadvantaged persons, which included a yearlong institute for persons pursuing the sixth-year specialist degree in 1971-72.

In addition to these programs, Library School faculty members frequently conduct workshops for the staffs of individual libraries or groups of libraries, lecture on the Educational Telephone Network programs conducted by University Extension, and participate in other continuing education programs for librarians. The Library School makes some of its formal courses available for credit to librarians who already hold the professional degree but who area not seeking an advanced degree. For those who are not interested in academic credits, two faculty members have made certain components of formal courses available, on a noncredit basis, to librarians of the state, in a venture jointly sponsored with University Extension and the State Division for Library Services. A standing committee of the faculty has continuing responsibility for seeking ways in which the School can better serve the needs of practicing librarians for professional education.

Beyond serving the profession through continuing education programs, the faculty participates in many other service activities. Library School faculty members have served as officers, committee chairmen, committee members, and program participants in professional organizations at the state, national and international levels. Within the past few years, a faculty member has headed the Wisconsin Library Association, another has served as president of the Association of American Library Schools, and others have chaired major divisions of the American Library Association. Members of the faculty have also served as consultants on library problems from the local to the international scenes.

In keeping with the rest of the Madison campus, the Library School considers its research mission very important. Over the past 25 years, research projects carried out by the faculty and advanced students have ranged from a study of the potential for interlibrary cooperation in the Madison area and studies on the feasibility of various patterns of statewide library development to a study of national staffing practices in certain libraries and studies of a historical and bibliographical nature. One major study that has brought several hundred thousand dollars of federal research funds to the University is on the reading needs and patterns of newly literate adults. It has sought to establish criteria that can be used to evaluate reading materials intended for their use. This project has produced a major monographic publication, numerous journal articles, and an institute to disseminate findings to a national audience. Further publications will be forthcoming from the study.

The quarters and facilities of the Library School have grown along with its teaching, research and service programs. Persons familiar with the Madison campus in the 1940s and 1950s will remember the remodeled fraternity house at 811 State Street (Sterling Court). Until the mid-1960s the School was housed in this building. During the rest of the 1960s the former Wisconsin High School building at 425 Henry Mall was the home of the School. In June 1971 the Library School moved into quarters especially planned and built for it on the fourth floor of the new Helen C. White Hall at 600 North Park Street.

These new quarters occupy some 32,000 square feet and contain faculty and administrative offices, a departmental library, student and faculty study and conference space (with a beautiful view of Lake Mendota), laboratory facilities and classrooms of various sizes. The library has ample space to house the School's extensive collection of study and research materials on librarianship and related areas, as well as space for seating of various sorts. The Audiovisual facilities include considerable production, projection and playback equipment, as well as laboratory space to allow students to learn their use. Computer and automation equipment includes a cathode ray tube terminal for on-line access to University and other computing facilities, as well as unit-record equipment.

Of course, the heart of any educational enterprise is its faculty. The faculty of the Library School has grown in strength and diversity along with the programs of the School. In the early 19505 the faculty consisted of seven persons. and by the mid 1960s, this had grown to some ten persons. Currently, the teaching faculty numbers 16 members (excluding teaching assistants), or 13.5 full-time equivalents.

Several faculty members are nationally prominent in their specialties, and a number of specialties are represented by particular strength on the faculty. For example, the area of adult reader and reference services is a strength of the school's curriculum and of its faculty. A specialty of several faculty members is the administration and services of college and university libraries. Another broad field where several faculty members have prominence is that of bibliography and library materials for various client groups. The history of librarianship and its relationship to the society it serves is a further area where faculty members have conducted and published considerable research.

Thus, the Library School has shared in the growth and development of a "resourceful university." Building on the solid base established in its first half-century, the School has used the past 25 years to expand the basic program, to inaugurate and refine new programs, and to maintain its position as one of the leading institutions for library education in the country.

Reference Services

Charles A. Bunge

Reference service, sometimes referred to as "reference and information services" or "reader services," has been defined as personal assistance provided to users in the pursuit of information. As distinguished from other library activities or services, reference service is characterized by a high degree of personal interaction between library staff members and library users, the service is typically provided to individual users or specifically identified small groups of users, and the information needs of the users are known at the time of the interaction.

Reference service has three major aspects or service techniques: (1) information service, which consists of finding needed information for the user or assisting the user in finding such information; (2) instruction in library use, consisting of helping users learn the skills they need to find and use library materials; and (3) guidance, in which users are assisted in choosing library materials appropriate to their educational, informational, or recreational needs. In addition to these "direct" reference services, reference librarians provide "indirect" services. These include building and maintaining a collection of bibliographic tools and other information sources, participating in cooperative programs to provide users access to resources outside the library, and various administrative activities.

Historical Development. Reference service had its beginnings in American librarianship in the last quarter of the 19th century. By the

---

Reprinted by permission of the American Library Association from Charles A. Bunge, "Reference Services," *ALA World Encyclopedia of Library and Information Services* (Chicago: American Library Association, 1980), 468-74.

[Haworth co-indexing entry note]: "Reference Services." Bunge, Charles A. Co-published simultaneously in *The Reference Librarian* (The Haworth Information Press, an imprint of The Haworth Press, Inc.) No. 66, 1999, pp. 185-199; and: *From Past-Present to Future-Perfect: A Tribute to Charles A. Bunge and the Challenges of Contemporary Reference Service* (ed: Chris D. Ferguson) The Haworth Information Press, an imprint of The Haworth Press, Inc., 1999, pp. 185-199.

time of World War II, most of its basic forms and techniques had been developed. Most historians of reference service find it convenient to begin with Samuel Swett Green's 1876 paper, "Personal Relations between Librarians and Readers." Until that time, the predominant view of the function of library service emphasized the acquisition and organization of library materials, and library clientele were expected to use the materials independently. Green, on the other hand, pointed out that library users were unskilled in using the catalogue to find materials and lacked the knowledge necessary to select the materials appropriate to their needs. Personal assistance to such users, said Green, would benefit them and would result in their taking a more positive view of the library.

Green's ideas won widespread acceptance and support. By the 1890's the term *reference work* was replacing the earlier terms *aid to readers* and *assistance to readers*. This was particularly true in public libraries, where by the turn of the century most larger libraries were employing identified reference staffs. The early years of the 20st century saw the establishment of separate reference departments in public libraries, the acceptance of reference questions via telephone and correspondence, the extension of reference service to branches, and the differentiation of reference services by level of complexity and subject field. During the period between the two world wars, public libraries developed methods to deal with the greatly increased number of requests for assistance and began to apply specialized techniques to different types of requests. The "information desk" to deal with the multitude of directional and simple requests, "readers' advisory services" to assist readers in choosing materials for self-education and development, and the growth of subject specialist reference librarians and departments were all features of reference service that developed from 1918 to 1940.

The development of special libraries in the early 20th century, with their concept of amplified service, was fertile ground for the development of reference service concepts and techniques. Especially important in the period before World War I was the application of special librarianship to the field of legislative and municipal reference work. The basis of such work, and the example it held out to reference work elsewhere, was a detailed knowledge by the librarian of the information needs of the clientele, a thorough knowledge of information sources and a willingness to seek out needed information from any source, and an ability to synthesize or otherwise to prepare information for use by the client. During and following World War I, reference work in business, industrial, and research libraries assumed increasing importance. By the 1940's the special librarian frequently offered the following services: answering factual inquiries, preparing bibliographies, scanning and referring incoming literature, preparing abstracts and translations of literature, and doing literature searches.

Rothstein points out that the development of reference services was slower in college and university libraries than in public and special libraries. This was due, at least in part, to the expectation that faculty members and students should be able to find their own materials and information and to the emphasis the scholarly community placed on collection development and subject access to materials through cataloguing. By the turn of the century, in spite of the example of a well-developed reference service established by Melvil Dewey at Columbia University, full-time reference staffs were not yet common in academic libraries. In the early decades of the century the relatively new state university libraries led the way in establishing reference services, and by World War I reference work was accepted as a necessary service in a university library. The years between the world wars saw a great increase in the number and variety of reference questions, the establishment of separate reference departments in many or most university libraries, and their assumption of such duties as special bibliographic and indexing projects and greatly expanded interlibrary loan work.

In the first half of the 20th century proponents of reference services reached wide agreement on the importance of such service and developed the basic concepts and methods of reference work. They also discussed the nature and extent of the assistance to be offered library users–a discussion that continues at the present time. On the one hand, many reference librarians and library administrators, especially in academic libraries, have argued that reference service exists to help inquirers to become independent users of library materials, i.e., to guide and instruct them so they may find their own answers to their questions. Some authors have referred to this as the "conservative" philosophy of reference service.

Special librarians and others have argued that the function of reference service is the provision of information itself to inquirers–information located by the reference librarian and provided in the form needed by the user. This is frequently referred to as the "liberal" reference philosophy. Most public and academic libraries have adopted what can be called a "moderate" philosophy, which balances the desire to provide maximum assistance to each user with the capacity of the staff, in terms of time and training, to do so. In the 1970's there was less debate concerning the "conservative," "liberal," or "moderate" philosophies of service in favor of a recognition that users have different needs at different times and that reference programs should provide services–including instruction, guidance, and information–as appropriate to the needs of a particular user at a particular time.

Instruction in Library Use. From the time of Samuel Swett Green's ground-breaking paper to the present, instruction in the use of the library and library materials has been an important facet of reference service. Contemporaries of Green, both librarians and non-librarians such as university presidents, urged the importance of teaching library users about books and the bibliographic apparatus for their location and selection for use. Throughout the first half of the century, there were frequent references in the literature of librarianship to the need for such instruction and to the nature and content of the programs that were instituted. After a period of debate in the 1960's between those who emphasized "information" and those who emphasized "instruction" as the legitimate role of reference service, there was a resurgence of interest in library instruction in the 1970's, leading to the establishment in 1977 of the Library Instruction Round Table in the American Library Association.

Instruction in library use has had its fullest development in school libraries. For several decades most school librarians and teachers have agreed on the importance of teaching skills in the use of libraries and library materials to elementary and secondary school students. There is fairly broad agreement among school library media specialists on the aspects of library use and information finding skills that should be introduced and taught at various grade levels. Many states and individual school districts have adopted courses of study in library instruction to be integrated with other parts of the curriculum. Recent discussions and developments in the school library field have concentrated on teaching techniques and methods, strategies for obtaining the cooperation of classroom teachers, and the evaluation of instruction programs.

Public and special libraries have emphasized the information and guidance aspects of reference service so that, in the main, their library instruction programs have consisted of basic orientation to the library and to publicity regarding the library and its services. Over the years there has been considerable discussion of the need for more extensive efforts, and there have been specific programs related to individual subject areas, user groups, or projects. However, these have not had much cumulative impact on services in either public or special libraries.

The most important recent developments in library instruction have occurred in college and university libraries. These developments have been concentrated in the 1970's. They include the establishment in 1970 of the Bibliographic Instruction Section of the Association of College and Research Libraries and the issuance in 1977 by ACRL of "Guidelines for Bibliographic Instruction in Academic Libraries."

Several important aspects of instruction in library use have been clarified and developed in the last decade in college and university libraries. First, the philosophy has been enunciated that knowledge and skill in the use of information resources has importance beyond that attached to succeeding in one's college or university career. Indeed, the learning of such skill is important preparation for a lifetime of information use, especially in the post-industrial society, and such learning is an important objective for the curriculum of the college or university as a whole.

Library orientation, a term once used almost synonymously with library instruction, is now generally recognized as only the most basic aspect of library instruction, consisting of familiarizing users with the library's policies, procedures, and layout. Library instruction (frequently referred to as "bibliographic instruction") is of three major types: the separate course, course- or assignment-related instruction, and point-of-use or point-of-need instruction. The separate course or set of learning experiences has been a prominent feature in library instruction. Such a course usually has a combination of content about the use of information materials and biographic tools in general and the specific library resources on the campus where it is offered. In the 1960's and 1970's these courses employed such techniques as computer-assisted instruction, workbooks, media presentations, and other individualized and programmed approaches. The separate course allows a more sustained and in-depth coverage of bibliographic knowledge and skills than do other forms of instruction. Some campuses are reluctant, however, to give academic credit for such courses (almost a necessity if students are to be motivated to take them), and students often have difficulty relating course content to the rest of their academic life and to their general educational needs and goals.

Bibliographic instruction related to specific courses has been found to be an effective form of library instruction. Here the librarian and the classroom teacher cooperate so that the librarian helps students learn about bibliographic methods and library resources as a part of the course and at a time when the students have a need for the learning in order to complete other course requirements. Such instruction can be part of courses that are required of all students, of courses required of subject majors, or of graduate research methods courses. They can involve problem sets, programmed instruction, or other individualized methods. Librarians have found that integration of library instruction with college and university courses enhances student motivation because of its relationship with course requirements and increases retention of learning because of its immediate application to course assignments and projects. However, gaining the full cooperation of classroom faculty is a continuing problem in this instructional method.

Point-of-use library instruction involves the provision of instructional assistance at the time and place where a library user encounters a problem. Examples of this technique include media-based programs on catalogue or reference tool use situated at the catalogue or near the reference tool. Perhaps the most widely known recent development in this area has been the "library pathfinder," which was initiated as part of Project Intrex at the Massachusetts Institute of Technology and which has been widely adapted. The "pathfinder" or "roadmap" is a printed handout that is intended to help an individual develop and follow a search strategy in a specific subject area. Many libraries have developed such handouts to assist students in getting started finding and using library materials on topics that are popular for term papers and course projects. Similar in concept are handouts for library users on such topics as how to find biographical information, how to find book reviews, or how to locate plot summaries. Librarians have found that library users appreciate having assistance at the time they become aware of their need for it and that considerably more assistance and learning can be provided through the provision of point-of-use aids for frequently recurring problems than would be possible with individual user contacts. However, reference staffs have great difficulty finding sufficient time and expertise to prepare effective point-of-use programs and materials.

The concerns of the college and university instruction librarians in the late 1970's were similar to those of the school librarians. These include securing a commitment to the importance of library instruction from those who govern and administer colleges and universities, gaining the cooperation of individual classroom instructors, and developing effective planning strategies, from needs assessment through evaluation.

Guidance. Reading guidance, as a distinct method or function of reference service, includes stimulating reading, identifying and locating appropriate materials, and helping to interpret materials so that readers can choose among them according to their interests and needs. Many public libraries established "reader's advisory" services in the 1920's as a way of dealing with the increasing volume of requests for advice on "best" books and the need to separate such queries from those for specific information. The evolution of an administrative device into a specialized service technique was due to the public library's embracing the adult education movement from the mid-1920's onward.

The hallmarks of reading guidance are the unhurried interview, during which the reader's needs, goals, and reading habits are articulated; reading lists or reading courses, individually designed to meet the reader's need; and friendly follow-up, to see that the reader gets the materials when needed and to see if changes in the list or course are needed. These core aspects of reading guidance are supported and supplemented by annotated booklists and guides that can be used to choose and suggest appropriate materials, book talks and reviews, displays and exhibits to stimulate interest and suggest materials, and a reader-interest file that allows the library to notify readers of newly received books that will interest them.

In the 1940's and 1950's the public library's involvement in adult education activities moved from the era of planned reading programs and reader's advisory service into one of services to groups and finally to one of library-sponsored adult education groups. Separate reading guidance staffs generally began to be replaced by the provision of guidance service by the reference staff. While the literature of the 1950's through the 1970's continued to discuss reader's advisory services and to distinguish between information and guidance techniques (e.g., between the "reference interview" and the "advisory interview"), the separate reader's advisory service was not a prominent feature of reference service.

Recent developments in the guidance aspects of reference services have paralleled the growth of the philosophy "special publics." This philosophy finds inadequate the concept of the "general reader" and the characterization of library users by broad occupational, educational, and socioeconomic traits. Rather, librarians are recognizing that there are a very large number of distinctive user groups among a general library's clientele, each with special needs for specially adapted services. The development of effective reference services to such a special public is based on detailed study of the characteristics of the group that affect reading, learning, and information use; involvement of members of the group in planning the service and setting priorities; the development of collections of materials with particular relevance to the special group, which may involve the use of nontraditional and locally produced materials; and the use of a broad spectrum of information and guidance techniques to assure that materials serve the goals of the program.

Special publics to which particular attention has been given in the 1960's and 1970's include the economically and educationally disadvantaged, the aging, persons with certain behavioral or psychological disfunctions, and those who wish to pursue further education (especially independently and outside the classroom context). Two special guidance strategies, bibliotherapy and learner's advising, illustrate the adaptations that are made to meet the needs of such special publics.

Bibliotherapy involves the use of selected reading materials to help the reader regain health or develop desirable behavior. Much of the literature on bibliotherapy is written within the context of service to persons in such institutions as hospitals or prisons. However, with the recent trend toward "mainstreaming" and returning persons with emotional and behavioral problems to their home communities, bibliotherapy outside the institutional context is gaining in emphasis. In bibliotherapy the guidance process of identifying needs, selecting and interpreting materials, and encouraging their use is often performed by the librarian as a part of an interdisciplinary team of helping professionals. Librarians, psychiatrists, social workers, corrections officials, and others continue to do research and develop principles and techniques to enhance the healthful effect of reading on the reader.

The concept of the reference librarian as "learning adviser" almost brings the guidance function full circle to its early roots in adult education. In the past decade rapidly changing technology and an ever-increasing body of knowledge, coupled with the development of various formats of independent and nontraditional education, have brought to the library needs for assistance in identifying, choosing, and pursuing independent education programs. For example, in 1975 and 1976 nine major public libraries tested a planned learner's advisory program. This experiment and the interest it generated were part of a larger movement among libraries and other agencies to assist the many adults who study and learn at their own pace in their own personal style.

The learner's adviser strategy of guidance consists of the learner and the adviser working together to develop a shared understanding of the learner's goal (e.g., job advancement, academic or high school equivalency credit by examination, self-fulfillment) and the development of a learning plan. The learning plan outlines the approaches that match the goals and learning style of the learner and details the sequence of learning experiences. Implementing the learning plan frequently involves referral to other formal and informal educational agencies and organizations.

Information Services. Most libraries, whether or not they offer instructional or guidance services, provide information to users in response to identified needs. Usually, the provision of such information is made upon a request or query by the user. However, information is sometimes provided to users at the initiation of the library, in anticipation of an expressed need or in response to a need identified or even stimulated by the library.

The amount or type of assistance that a library will provide in response to a reference question varies from library to library and from one question to another, depending on the policy of the library, the staff available, the nature of the question, and other factors. Such assistance can range from merely pointing out materials or bibliographic tools that might be of help to the user to making an extensive search for the needed information and providing it in the form that is most appropriate to the user. The types of questions answered by library information services vary widely. A large proportion of questions asked at most reference desks are "directional" in nature; that is, they ask for information about the library, its facilities and services, and can usually be answered without using reference materials. Many other information needs can be served by the provision of bibliographic information; services provided in this category range from the simple verification or completion of a citation to extensive bibliography compilation and such current awareness services as selective dissemination of information programs. Questions that ask for information itself, rather than citations, can range from simple factual questions that can be answered from a single source to complex questions, whose answers require information from several sources, and requests for library-prepared state-of-the-art reports that require synthesis of information based on critical judgment.

The process through which a reference librarian provides the answer to a reference query has a number of highly interrelated parts. One of the most important of these is the clarification of the question itself, to make sure that it represents accurately the user's information need. This aspect of reference service, often referred to as "the reference interview" or "question negotiation," involves helping the user understand and articulate the information need, and making sure that the librarian understands the terms and meaning of the question.

When the reference librarian and the user have agreed upon the question in the user's terms, the librarian must analyze the question and translate it into the structure and terms of the information system and resources available to answer it. This involves such considerations as the type of information sought, the type of tool or source that is likely to provide the answer, and the index or catalogue headings under which the information might be sought. Using the results of this analysis and translation or question indexing, the librarian formulates a search strategy, considering such matters as the actual sources to be consulted, the order in which they will be used, the combination of terms to be searched, and the relationships among them.

The actual search for information, especially if the user is present during the search, often involves refinement of the search strategy and further analysis of the question as the librarian and the user learn more about the information that is available. Depending on the policies and practices of the library and the wishes of the user, the reference librarian either can perform the search for the user or can provide some suggestions regarding search strategy and potential sources and let the user conduct the search.

There is also wide variation regarding the delivery of the information found by librarians in response to questions. Some libraries or the users they serve prefer to receive only the documents or materials containing the information, with the process of extracting and interpreting it left to the user. Other libraries, particularly special libraries, will extract information and synthesize it into a state-of-the-art report as an answer to a question that requires judgment and interpretation.

While the major features of information services were developed by the mid-20th century, their particular concerns and activities are continually changing, as user needs and information resources change. Three examples will be used to illustrate these changes: cooperative reference services, computer-assisted reference service, and information and referral services.

The borrowing of specific materials by one library from another on behalf of users (interlibrary loan) is a long-standing practice. In recent years, libraries have begun to request assistance from each other in the form of answers to reference questions that have not been translated into specific author-title interlibrary loan requests. Referring reference questions from library to library is a very important aspect of the current trend toward library cooperation and resource sharing, and it introduces some fundamental changes into the question-answering process. For example, in a cooperative reference situation the reference interview is conducted by one librarian while the search is formulated and implemented by another. The search must be conducted in the absence of the user, and the information that is found is delivered to the user without the user-searcher interaction and evaluative feedback that can enhance search effectiveness. Reference librarians and administrators are exploring and developing various means for improving the quality of cooperative reference service, especially the full exploitation of modern communications technology to maintain as much as possible the interaction between users, librarians, and information resources that characterizes effective information service. For example, the format in which the reference question is transferred from library to library (whether it be by mail, teletype, or telephone) should be designed so to capture and transmit as much relevant and accurate information as possible about the user and the information need. At times it is appropriate to have the user in direct contact with the librarian to which the question has been referred. Policies and practices regarding such direct contact, as well as for other aspects of cooperative reference service, will continue to be developed and refined.

One of the most important developments in the information resources available to the reference librarian and the user has been the wide availability of computer searchable data bases, especially of bibliographic data, and the means for searching these data bases at any time and in an interactive mode. An increasing number of user needs can be met, either partially or in full, by conducting searches of data bases via computer. Originally concentrated in the natural sciences, indexing and abstracting coverage of data bases is extending into the social sciences and the humanities.

The role of the reference librarian in assisting users with computer readable data bases is basically the same as with more traditional information sources. The need to clarify the question is still there, as is the need for the identification of and choice between potential answering sources, the translation of the question into the terms of the information source, the formulation of a search strategy, and assistance in conducting the search. On the other hand, there are also some important differences. For various reasons–including the "peep hole" effect, whereby only a small portion of the computerized information source and its structure can be seen at one time, the high cost of "browsing" by computer, and the need to make explicit in a computer search what can be left implicit in a traditional search–the reference process is more formal in a computer search than is typically the case in the ordinary situation.

Often the user for whom a computerized search is to be made will be given an appointment to discuss the information need and the search with a librarian (as contrasted to the "first come, first served" immediate service for other users). The reference interview is usually considerably longer in this situation than for other users. The presearch planning, including choice of potential answering sources (data bases), selection of indexing terms, and formulation of a search strategy (usually a matter of expressing algebraic relationships among the search terms), is done more formally and completely for a computerized search than for a traditional search. It is more common for the librarian actually to conduct the search (i.e., to operate the computer terminal) when working with a computer readable data base than is the case with manual searches in printed sources.

Just as the sheer number of information sources can be a barrier between a person who needs information and the resolution of that need, so can the number and complexity of service agencies be a barrier between a person with a problem and an agency that can help solve that problem. It has long been recognized that persons with needs for assistance (whether persons needing charity aid, persons whose lives are disrupted by war, or persons who could be served by government welfare agencies) fail to receive that assistance because they fail to find or use the agencies that exist. It has also been recognized that information and personal assistance provided by a referral service can effectively link persons who have needs or problems with agencies that can serve the needs or solve the problems. During the last few years an increasing number of libraries, especially urban public libraries, have been including such a service, now commonly called "information and referral service" (I&R) among their reference services.

While the reference function in information and referral services is basically the same as in other information services, there are some differences in particulars. The information provided is not in books or printed sources prepared by others and purchased by the library; rather, it is found in a resource file about community services and agencies that has been created by the library staff. This resource file, commonly in a card or loose-leaf format and with detailed subject indexing, can be supplemented with pamphlets and hand-out information on the agencies.

Another important difference between information and referral service and traditional question-answering service is that I&R service does not stop with the provision of a piece of information. There is usually some sort of additional service to make sure that the link is actually made between the person and the service agency. Depending on the policies of the library and the needs of the user, this might include contacting the agency to make an appointment for the user or even escorting the user to the agency. Most writers on I&R services emphasize the importance of follow-up with the user to see if the service of the agency actually helped solve his or her problem. Such follow-up can help the I&R service evaluate its effectiveness, improve the accuracy of the resource file, help keep service agencies accountable and responsive, and lead to alternative referrals if the user was not helped by the initial one.

Issues. Information, instruction, and guidance services in libraries have had a somewhat short period of development, beginning in the last quarter of the 19th century. Their broad function of providing personal assistance to users in overcoming barriers between them and the information they need has remained the same over the years. Likewise, their essential process of identifying and clarifying the user's need, selecting information or learning resources to meet that need, and assisting the user in finding and using these resources remains unchanged. On the other hand, information, instruction, and guidance services are continually evolving as user needs change and become better known, as information resources change and develop, and as equipment and processes for bringing users and information together are developed and refined.

The key to any personal assistance service is, of course, the staff that provides it. Reference staff members will need to master fundamentals, such as a thorough knowledge of their users and skill in communicating with them and a thorough knowledge of information resources and skill in exploiting them on behalf of users. They will also need continually to be changing, as users change and as the nature and structure of information resources change.

In the immediate future two important concerns are likely to receive major attention from reference librarians and administrators. The first of these is the matter of direct user fees for information services. This has been brought into sharp focus by the financial problems associated with the addition of computer-based searching to reference services. Access to and interactive searching of computerized data bases is quite costly, and many libraries have not been able to increase their budgets to cover the costs of such service. On the other hand, it has seemed unwise to deny the service to those who would pay for it. Since computer-assisted searching is a special service, involving staff time and other service beyond that which is provided to all users and with costs that can easily be associated with specific users, administrators see some justification for direct user fees. Many reference librarians, however, are aware that such service is appropriate to a wide range of users, some of whom cannot pay for it, and find the inequitable access to information caused by fees contrary to their philosophy of reference service. This is a hard dilemma, exacerbated by uncertain economic conditions, which will receive much discussion as reference librarians attempt to minimize barriers between all their users and the information they need.

The other matter of major concern to information, instruction, and guidance librarians is the planning and evaluation of services. Increasingly, reference librarians are recognizing that effective services can be based only on careful identification of user needs. This involves the identification of special target publics and collaboration with members of these user groups to ascertain information needs and to translate these into service objectives and priorities. Likewise, reference librarians are increasingly aware of the need for accurate measurement and evaluation of their services. Most authors of the literature of reference service evaluation admit that the state of the art is fairly rudimentary yet all agree that continued study and development will result in improvement and increased effectiveness in personal assistance to library users in the pursuit of information.

REFERENCES

Samuel Rothstein, *The Development of Reference Services*, ACRL Monograph 14 (ALA, 1955), is the standard history of reference services to the mid-20th century.

William A. Katz, *Introduction to Reference Work*, 3rd ed. (1978). This two-volume work is the standard textbook in the field. Volume 2 is especially relevant to this article because of its good discussions and references to further reading regarding the trends, issues, and current status of the various aspects of reference service.

Marjorie E. Murfin and Lubomyr R. Wynar, *Reference Service: An Annotated Bibliographic Guide* (1977), a comprehensive bibliography of books and articles in English from 1876 to 1975, for further reading on almost any facet of reference service.

Richness vs. Reach: Using Technology to Overcome Economic Impediments to Reference Service

Deborah Holmes-Wong

SUMMARY. The ability of reference librarians to bring library services into new electronic arenas has been constrained by the inherent conflict within traditional approaches between the reach (number of users that can be served) and the richness (complexity) of its services. Increased use of information technology has brought with it increases in traffic at the reference desk without increases in staffing. Through the application of information technology used in electronic commerce and available on the Internet, libraries may be able to offer customizable electronic reference services to their users that increase both the richness of these services and the number of persons who benefit from them. *[Article copies available for a fee from The Haworth Document Delivery Service: 1-800-342-9678. E-mail address: getinfo@haworthpressinc.com <Website: http://www.haworthpressinc.com>]*

Growth in the number of people who acquire or have access to networked information due to decreases in cost of the technology and in the cost of long distance telecommunications will in the next several

---

Deborah Holmes-Wong is Director of Consulting Services, Reference and Instruction, Information Services Division, University of Southern California, Los Angeles, CA 90089-0182 (E-mail: dhwong@usc.edu). She holds an MLIS from the University of Texas at Austin.

[Haworth co-indexing entry note]: "Richness vs. Reach: Using Technology to Overcome Economic Impediments to Reference Service." Holmes-Wong, Deborah. Co-published simultaneously in *The Reference Librarian* (The Haworth Information Press, an imprint of The Haworth Press, Inc.) No. 66, 1999, pp. 201-211; and: *From Past-Present to Future-Perfect: A Tribute to Charles A. Bunge and the Challenges of Contemporary Reference Service* (ed: Chris D. Ferguson) The Haworth Information Press, an imprint of The Haworth Press, Inc., 1999, pp. 201-211. Single or multiple copies of this article are available for a fee from The Haworth Document Delivery Service [1-800-342-9678, 9:00 a.m. - 5:00 p.m. (EST). E-mail address: getinfo@haworthpressinc.com].

years have a profound impact on most businesses and industries.[1] Existing in this global environment with a growing user population and improving information technology leads to two seemingly contradictory trends affecting reference service: Consumers are using computers more and more to access information on their own and are becoming increasingly sophisticated and self-sufficient, and increased use of information technology creates new *markets* for libraries and other information providers.

These trends likely will lead to more people trying to obtain information services on the Internet. When they cannot get these services for free, many will turn to the library. Due to the global nature of the Internet and the perception that libraries are a common good, users may not confine their requests to local libraries, but instead may go to other institutions where they believe they will get expert help. As libraries migrate to the Internet, these two trends may result in a further increase in the number of reference questions that come to the reference desk both in person and through the Internet. This trend toward growth in the number of reference questions asked coupled with about the same size reference staff[2] already is forcing institutions to re-examine reference service and to change the way in which many reference transactions are handled.[3]

REACH AND RICHNESS

Information transactions have two properties, reach and richness. Reach is the number of people involved in the exchange of information. Reach has little to do with distance. An audience of one has the same reach whether the audience is in the same room or across the country. Richness has three components: amount of information being conveyed (bandwidth), degree to which the information can be customized, and interactivity.[4] A television broadcast has a large reach, but the consumer receives information created for the masses, not for the individual. Consumers provide little feedback to the network, so it is not a very rich exchange.

A reference interview on the other hand has low reach, usually one person, but it can be very rich. A dialog occurs between the librarian and the questioner where questions are asked and feedback is provided. The answer is tailored to the user's needs. In his "Potential and Reality at the Reference Desk," Charles Bunge identifies this as the ideal in reference service. When we give someone the exact information they have been searching, we are rewarded by knowing we have helped someone.[5] This individualized service makes reference librarianship a rewarding pursuit, but it also makes reference expensive to provide and difficult to scale up when demand increases. These and other constraints lead such administrators as Jerry Campbell to talk about automating reference service and turning reference librarians into access engineers.[6]

The debate over tradeoffs between richness and reach often takes shape as an argument over quality verses quantity, but it is not. Richness implies quality, and reach implies quantity, but one can have a high-quality product such as a reference guide or a database that is used by a large number of people. Richness should be thought of more in terms of the amount of interactivity and customization involved in providing the service to the user.

A computing services colleague contrasting how computing services and reference services solve problems, notes that when *we* create a product, it serves several thousand people and meets ninety per cent of their needs. We receive dozens of complaints because it never meets all of their needs. When *you* help someone, you help them solve their need one hundred per cent. They are satisfied, while our users are never satisfied." The computing solution focuses on reach, the library solution focuses on richness. When we opt for reach we will not meet all the needs of each of our customers. It is possible that we will not meet anyone's needs exactly. When we offer customized, individual services we help fewer people, but we have a higher likelihood of meeting the needs of those individuals served because we are tailoring our responses to their requests.

Prevailing wisdom holds that one cannot increase both richness and reach using existing resources. Librarians have tried to increase reach and richness through a variety of different strategies: library instruction, handouts and user guides, tiered service, paraprofessionals at the reference desk, and video-conferencing. Library instruction reaches more students than a reference interview and it can be somewhat customized for each class, but it is not customized for each student. Handouts are designed to answer repetitive reference questions and are generic enough to be used to provide help to large numbers of users, but they are not customized to meet a specific user's needs. We extend reach rather than richness when we use the Web to *broadcast* user guides or to create online tutorials. An online catalog with a detailed tutorial is better than one without a tutorial, but not the same as having someone to instruct in its use.

Tiered reference and the use of paraprofessionals, students, and others to free librarians from routine directional questions is an attempt to solve the problem of reach vs. richness. The rationale of tiered service is to allow the librarian to focus on more complex questions while other staff handle the routine questions. This means that overall more questions can be answered, and the more expensive resource is allocated where the exchange needs to be the richest. In this regard, Massey-Burzio concludes that tiered reference works best when reference consultation and other services are clearly delineated for the client,[7] but Whitson points out that when this happens the service may actually be less efficient than traditional reference service because people are reverted from desk to desk instead of being helped at the initial contact point.[8] Using video-conferencing to allow remote users access to reference is extending a current service over the network, yet it has the same problems as face-to-face and phone reference.

LESSONS FROM THE CORPORATE WORLD

The application of information technology to certain business problems, argue Evans and Worster, can make the tradeoffs between richness and reach negligible and create far-reaching changes in the structures of businesses and industries.[9] Two businesses, Encyclopedia Britannica and Amazon.com, illustrate how these changes in an industry can transform previous strengths into liabilities and traditional liabilities into strengths.

In the early 1990s, sales of Britannica's multi-volume encyclopedias dropped dramatically due to competition from Microsoft's *Encarta* and other CD-ROM encyclopedias. In the late 1980s families started buying PCs and stopped buying large encyclopedia sets. Britannica failed to realize that consumers bought encyclopedias out of a desire to educate their children better, not because they wanted to have the world's best content. Britannica produced a CD-ROM and tried several pricing strategies before the company was sold, but no one looked at the fundamental company structure and how information technology could have helped the company. Britannica spent most of its money on a large, entrenched direct sales force while spending about five per cent on editorial content. Evans and Wurster state that had Britannica redirected money from the sales force to establishing an Internet presence, they could have offered a lower-cost product and maybe even become the search engine or content provider of choice on the Internet.[10]

Evans and Wurster contrast Britannica with Amazon.com, a recent start-up currently worth about 2.2 billion dollars.[11] Amazon.com has not yet turned a profit, but market analysts like it because it keeps its costs down by maintaining as small an inventory as possible and by leveraging technology.[12] An automated tracking system lets consumers know the status of their orders, and a recommendation engine registers what repeat customers buy and makes recommendations based on what others with similar buying patterns have bought. Amazon.com uses technology to give the kind of high-quality customer service that would have previously been associated only with a large sales force.

Britannica's decline, Evans and Wurster conclude, shows that such traditional sources of advantage as a strong sales force, a "supreme brand," and the "world's best content" no longer ensure success. Even Amazon.com's continued success is not guaranteed because its formula can be easily duplicated by its competitors as it has been by Barnes & Noble and Borders Books.[13] Due to changes brought about by the rise of networked information systems, even retail booksellers could become obsolete and be replaced by either wholesalers or large media conglomerates.

PARALLELS TO ENCYCLOPEDIA BRITANNICA AND AMAZON.COM

In an article that details how "vectors of change" are exerting forces on the online industry, Stephen and Erik Arnold show how changes in this industry have been taking place since 1977 and project changes out to 2007.[14] Their analysis can be applied to the current reference environment since trends impacting the online industry impact on those of us who use electronic resources. In particular, the business climate is becoming increasingly competitive with new content providers entering the market, the size of that market has grown from hundreds of searchers in the 1970s to millions in the 1990s, and the software required to search these services has become easier to develop and easier to use. Content providers that used to target specialists and librarians are now adapting their products to the consumer market, leading to disintermediation.

Disintermediation, perhaps the trend that most concerns reference librarians, in libraries means that users no longer require someone else to search through the system for them. One could argue that a library with open stacks and catalog that allows users to conduct their own searches of the catalog and stacks is a traditional example of disintermediation. A library with closed stacks where a librarian takes a request from and conducts the research for the patron would be an example of a mediated system. Disintermediation of online searching in libraries began in the late 1980s with the movement in most libraries from mediated searching of online databases to end-user searching of CD-ROMs. It intensified in the 1990s as users discovered the World-Wide Web.[15] Disintermediation is fueled by ever-increasing numbers of people with access to computers and the Internet who believe that the answer to their question is out there if they just look in the right place.[16]

It would be a mistake to dismiss these changes and assume that the impact will be the same on the profession as before because similar changes have happened with minimal impact. The difference now is that a critical mass of online users exists to which marketers and companies want access. This group of consumers does not have to come to the library to retrieve information and, because the market is large enough, online vendors are tailoring information services to these consumers. Arguments can be made that the quality of the information is not the same, the scope and content are different, and that some of the information on the Internet is not credible, but these are the same consumers that were happy with *Encarta* and stopped buying Britannica's encyclopedia.

Academic libraries have witnessed the *Lexis-Nexis phenomenon*. It is the belief by large portions of students and faculty coming to the reference desk that whatever they need can be located on Lexis-Nexis, and these users are reluctant to believe a librarian who tells them it's *not* the best source in the world for their specific needs. In a recent article, Heckart describes what a student's life will be like in 2010, and how this student will use the library.[17] Although Heckart places his student twelve years into the future, his attitude–that anything worthwhile has already been digitized and is available online–is quickly becoming a prevailing notion among school children.[18] Some disciplines, moreover, will probably move to digital collections for most of their reference needs within the next five years, rather than Heckart's twelve-year time frame.

THE PROMISE

Rather than declare defeat and surrender to the barbarians at the gate, reference librarians can take a more opportunistic view of things. The same technology that is causing these changes can be used to help. The most promising developments are in the area of push technology, software agents, and search engines.

Push technology delivers information to a desktop as it becomes available or at intervals the user prearranges. A typical library example of push technology is the sort of table of contents service Dialog has been offering for years, but the difference now is that the user can subscribe to such free services as MyYahoo and MyExcite, which include custom profiles for tracking everything from sports scores and stock prices to current events and horoscopes. These profiles generate lists of current articles from news services and Web-based magazines worldwide. MyExcite encourages the user to mark articles that s/he likes, enabling the system to learn preferences so as better to make recommendations for additional terms for the user to add to the search profile. The user can thereby create a highly personalized current awareness service.

Giving this kind of information to a commercial establishment that may sell it to others presents obvious privacy issues, but libraries could license this technology and create a "MyLibrary" where the patron decides what happens to his/her personal information and librarians provide access to additional resources. For example, in addition to current events and stock information, the patron could have a profile that runs against the library catalog to pull lists of newly-cataloged videos in which s/he might be interested. If the library provides access to full-text or full-image databases, there could be a profile that periodically looks for new items and reports back with lists of links. "MyLibrary" could build a database to organize the information for later use.

Another technology that can aid reference service is that of intelligent software agents. These agents may be present on an individual's computer to assist with a variety of tasks or they can be sent out on the Internet to look continually for information that is of interest to the user. When relevant information is found, it is sent back. When an agent encounters another agent looking for similar information, they share information about where they have looked and what they have found. Crawlers of this kind are used by many of the largest search engines to create searchable databases of Internet links. Another possible use of this technology would be a service in "MyLibrary," where the crawler looks for Web sites and places addresses into a searchable database for either the user to customize or the library to use in the generation of its Web pages. Crawlers may become less useful if large numbers of sites deny them access. Quarterdeck's Web Compass is one example of a crawler that produces a personalized database of Internet links.

Recommendation engines, another tool used to provide personalized service, are fairly simple pieces of software. Used by Web-based businesses like Amazon.com and CD-Now to track what an individual buys and to match them with other individuals who bought the same thing, purchase overlaps form the basis for additional purchase recommendations. In the library setting this would be called a *reader's advisory.* In this case, a recommendation engine might be set up so that if someone looked at a free Internet service on a library computer, a subscription service for which the library paid that contains better information could automatically be recommended. If this product were maintained internally, it could be used to determine if anyone actually used the subscription service after it was recommended or if the free service was considered good enough.

Alexa, a free software agent, tracks and makes recommendations for most sites on the Internet although some of its recommendations can be strange. Since its recommendations are based on usage, it should become better as more people use it.[19] As with other commercial services, though, privacy issues are a concern. But as this technology becomes more robust, it may nevertheless be desirable to license and customize it for local needs.

A final use of this technology might be to have a recommendation agent within a subscription service such as Lexis-Nexis or UMI Proquest Direct. After a user selects an article to save, recommendations saved during previous sessions could be brought back for review, enabling the agent to function as a series of interlocking bibliographies.

Search engines will change over the next several years, allowing users to move beyond text-based searching. Search engines currently look for text using either Boolean logic or relevancy rankings to produce results. Usually the results are text or text with graphics. Widespread use of voice recognition in conjunction search engines is predicted within the next five years, which means telephones as well as computers may become interfaces for our catalogs and databases.[20] Visual search engines that can sift through still and video images are under development, as is the software that can take an entire video and index it section by section. The user thus will be able to access information either through text or by submitting a picture.[21] These new search engines, then, may allow us to access information in ways that are more similar to our own thought processes and present us with a variety of challenges and opportunities as we work with our constituencies.

CONCLUSION

As our collections become increasingly digital, our reference desks and our roles will change. Many of our users will never come to the library to interact with us personally, instead using Web pages, online databases, and tutorials to find what they need. Many will use software like WebCompass and Alexa to assist them with their research before we have the chance to introduce them to these and other tools. When they need help from us, they may already know what they need but be unwilling to pay for it, and so come to us either looking to acquire it for free or to obtain a substitute. Rather than experts, they may view us as peers or partners. Others may view us as surrogate experts, asking for our interpretations of what they have found. There is nothing truly new here, but the number of these types of requests likely will increase dramatically. Users with the relatively easy questions will be visiting our Web site and obtaining what they need without our knowledge.

Others we will see in the library are those for whom the library is an information provider, clients without the technology at home or office who either cannot afford it or choose not to use it. This could be a housewife who wants to start a small business or a retired faculty member pursuing-her own interests. As our populations become increasingly computer literate and our resources become computer-focused, these individuals will require proportionately more of our time to help. We will have to decide how best to serve these patrons and our communities. Given the existing system, we will have to decide whether to teach them how to use the technology, do the research for them and print it off, keep print reference collections for them, or refer them to other libraries with the resources to maintain both print and online reference collections. Providing service to these populations may depend on our ability to make our systems easier to use for the people who want to use the technology from home.

These challenges brought on by emerging technologies will be both the impetus to change and the means that allow reference librarians to increase the richness and the reach of their interactions with the public. Even with the support of student employees, volunteers, and paraprofessionals, we cannot avoid the fact that anyone working on the desk needs weeks of training and practice before they achieve even the minimal competency in our current environment. We must find ways to leverage technology so as to make our systems easier to use for everyone, including ourselves.

We must realize the promise of a networked information environment and begin to think and act globally. Reference librarians are very good at taking someone else's solution (such as a bibliography) and customizing it for a local constituency. Before the Internet, that made sense. For certain communities and certain types of information this may still make sense; for others it does not. We do not have the resources for every library in the world to generate its own version of Yahoo!, and with the Internet this is not necessary. The same solutions that will allow us to make a database of Internet links, and quickly to customize it for local use, can be used by some of our patrons to create their own databases in association with similar constituencies in other libraries.

These technologies cannot completely replicate the richness of the reference interview. Their chief benefit is that they can be scaled to offer to large numbers of users services that can be customized to their needs. As these technologies emerge, we need to adopt the ones that give our users the flexibility to gather the information they need, when they need it, in the format they need it, and with as little fuss as possible. The ones we choose should be the ones that help us serve our communities better and lead us to a future library that is more than a static data repository accessed through services severely limited in richness or constrained in their reach.

REFERENCES

1. Frances Cairncross, *The Death of Distance: How the Communications Revolution Will Change Our Lives* (Boston: Harvard Business School Press, 1997), 23-24.

2. Association of Research Libraries, "Service Trends in ARL Libraries, 1991-1997," http://www.arl.org/stats/arlstat/Pubsre97.gif (June 1998).

3. This is the thesis of a number of articles including Virginia Massey-Burzio, "Reference Encounters of a Different Kind: A Symposium," *Journal of Academic Librarianship* 18:5 (November 1992): 276-86; Beth J. Shapiro and Kevin Brook Long, "Just Say Yes: Reengineering Library User Services for the 21st Century," *Journal of Academic Librarianship* 20:5/6 (November 1994): 285-90; and William L. Whitson, "Differentiated Service: A New Reference Model," *Journal of Academic Librarianship* 21:2 (March 1995): 103-10.

4. Philip B. Evans and Thomas S. Wurster, "Strategy and the New Economics of Information," *Harvard Business Review* 75:5 (September/October 1997): 73-74.

5. Charles A. Bunge, "Potential and Reality at the Reference Desk: Reflections on a Return to the Field,'" *Journal of Academic Librarianship* 10:3 (July 1984): 128-29.

6. Jerry D. Campbell, "Shaking the Conceptual Foundations of Reference: A Perspective," *RSR: Reference Services Review* 20:4 (Winter 1992): 33-34.

7. Massey-Burzio, 279.

8. Whitson, 108-09.

9. Evans and Wurster, 74.

10. Ibid., 81.

11. Ouicksource, "Amazon.com, Inc. Stock Price Data as of Close 05/29/98" in *Quicksource Report*, accessed through Wall Street Research Network, http://www.wsrn.com/home/dataset/quicksource.html?symbol=AMZN&page=1 (May 1998).

12. Evans and Wurster, 80-81.

13. Jacqueline Doherty, "Trading Points: Amazon.com, No Earnings in Sight and Competition Looming Prepares Junk Offering," *Barron's* 4 May 1998, MW20-21.

14. Stephen E. Arnold and Erik S. Arnold, "Vectors of Change: Electronic Information from 1977 to 2007," *Online* 21:4 (July 1997): 18-31. UMI item number 03324310 retrieved from UMI Periodical Database via USC's USCInfo, May 1998.

15. Arnold and Arnold, p. 1 of printout.

16. Cairncross, 105-06.

17. Ronald J. Heckart, "Machine Help and Human Help in the Emerging Digital Library," *College and Research Libraries* 59:3 (May 1998): 254.

18. Elliot Soloway and Raven Wallace, "Does the Internet Support Student Inquiry? Don't Ask," *Communications of the ACM* 40:5 (May 1997): 11-16. UMI item number 03252741 retrieved from UMI Periodical Database via USC's USCInfo, May 1998.

19. Thomas E. Weber, "A Closer Look," *Wall Street Journal*, 28 May 1998, B7, Western edition.

20. Ian H. Witten, "A Public Library Based on Full-Text Retrieval," *Communications of the ACM* 41:4(1998): 71-75. UMI item number 03669192 retrieved from UMI Periodical Database via USC's USCInfo, May 1998.

21. Boon-Lock Yeo and Minerva M. Yeung, "Retrieving and Visualizing Video," *Communications of the ACM*, 40:12 (December 1997): 43-52. UMI item number 03531157 retrieved from UMI Periodical Database via USC's USCInfo, May 1998.

Information Literacy in the Reference Environment: Preparing for the Future

Hannelore B. Rader

SUMMARY. The academic information environment is changing greatly as we enter the millennium. These changes are affecting libraries and, specifically, reference services. In the past and even in recent times librarians have been concerned with library orientation, library instruction, and bibliographic instruction. Now they have to worry about teaching students and others viable information and computer skills to cope effectively in the information society. Reference work as practiced this century will undergo major changes in the electronic information environment, and the teaching of effective information skills will become a very important component of reference services. The challenges thus presented to academic librarians will be great but success in this area will mean effective professional survival.
[Article copies available for a fee from The Haworth Document Delivery Service: 1-800-342-9678. E-mail address: getinfo@haworthpressinc.com <Website: http://www.haworthpressinc.com>]

Making information available is not enough. Making information useful is the key. Personalized attention, training, and after ser-

---

Hannelore B. Rader is University Librarian, University of Louisville, Louisville, KY 40292 (E-mail: h.rader@louisville.edu).

This article is based on the author's earlier publication, "Reference Services as a Teaching Function" (*Library Trends*, 1980) and on many years of experience both in reference and information literary.

[Haworth co-indexing entry note]: "Information Literacy in the Reference Environment: Preparing for the Future." Rader, Hannelore B. Co-published simultaneously in *The Reference Librarian* (The Haworth Information Press, an imprint of The Haworth Press, Inc.) No. 66, 1999, pp. 213-221; and: *From Past-Present to Future-Perfect: A Tribute to Charles A. Bunge and the Challenges of Contemporary Reference Service* (ed: Chris D. Ferguson) The Haworth Information Press, an imprint of The Haworth Press, Inc., 1999, pp. 213-221. Single or multiple copies of this article are available for a fee from The Haworth Document Delivery Service [1-800-342-9678, 9:00 a.m. - 5:00 p.m. (EST). E-mail address: getinfo@haworthpressinc.com].

vice responsiveness are now competitive requirements. Using communication and information technologies to make people more information literate is a viable approach.[1]

INTRODUCTION

Technology and the electronic information explosion are having a major impact on society as a whole–business, education, and libraries in particular. People need new skills to learn and to cope with the expanding information in their lives. They need to acquire these new skills and learn how to obtain, evaluate, and apply information to solve problems and address important issues in the workplace and in their daily lives. There are no definitive methods to address these information dilemmas although businesses, schools, post-secondary institutions, and libraries are attempting to offer solutions and training.

Helping people to be successful in finding and using information in the electronic environment is an extremely complex process. Public and academic library users now want efficient and effective one-stop shopping in a seamless access environment. They do not want to read complicated manuals, study the complexities of databases, or know about complicated search mechanisms. To deal with this situation, librarians have to provide library systems designed to facilitate access and information skills instruction at the time of need. Reference services are especially affected by these new needs and demands in the electronic information environment, and reference librarians will have to rethink their service goals and outcomes fairly quickly to stay viable in this highly-competitive information environment.

HISTORY

Discussions about reference service and what exactly it should entail have been documented in the library literature and conferences since the late 19th century. These discussions often address reference service as a teaching function and provide rationale for it.[2] This trend has been especially strong in the 1980s and the 1990s. Charles Bunge provides a thorough definition and theory for reference services and its relationship to library instruction from the 19th century to the

1980s and explains the role of the reference librarian as learning advisor and information facilitator. He also discusses the impact of computer applications and the need for good planning and evaluation of reference services.[3] Kathleen Gunning provides a thought-provoking discussion regarding the impact of user instruction and computer searching programs on reference. Results found more complex organizational structures, additional training needs for reference librarians, and more fully integrated public service programs.[4] Advocates of an integrated public service model, including computer searching and user instruction programs, made their ideas clear to their fellow professionals at the ACRL Third National Conference in Seattle in 1984. Several papers addressed extended reference services models in order to provide reference services in a complex environment and changing user needs.[5] Throughout the historical development of reference services, discussions have occurred on a regular basis whether or not library instruction should be a part of reference services. Many librarians have felt that guidance and instruction of library users occur regularly in reference work on an individual basis and group instruction is a natural progression. Although throughout the last three decades several academic libraries incorporated bibliographic instruction into reference services, this did not become a major trend and organizational issues often clouded the service mandates.

PRESENT SITUATION

Libraries have been part of a major information revolution for more than a decade and must now rethink all their functions, services, and organizational structure. The impact of the electronic information environment and constantly changing technology are increasingly forcing librarians to deal with major changes. While librarians have to remain in a continuous learning mode to keep up with new trends and sources, they must rethink how they do their work and how they provide their services. Librarians traditionally have provided information and reference services on their terms and expected users to abide by those terms. Now, however, librarians must begin to understand the changing desires and needs of their users as related to acquiring knowledge and using information. More and more people now have access to computers at work, at home, or in school. They are experiencing immediate information access and delivery through the Internet and expect the same quick results from libraries. They may, however, need guidance, advice, and instruction in getting the specific information they need and want, especially in handling the information effectively and critically.

A study at Duke University to ascertain the library model of the future found among a variety of other things that people characterize a good information source as:

- accessible.
- fast.
- labor saving.
- free.
- computerized.
- networked with other libraries.
- comprehensive.
- available expertise.[6]

These findings are important for viable and successful reference services, and librarians are beginning to experiment with new and different types of reference services. Most of these services are integrating various new or non-traditional activities in creative ways to address user needs.

- Users need help with technology so "help desk" pieces are becoming parts of reference services.
- Users need instruction in accessing, organizing, and using information, so information literacy is being incorporated into reference services.
- Users need help remotely, so electronic communication, including video conferencing, is being integrated into reference work.
- Users want assistance at their location, so reference librarians often roam around the library to accommodate these needs or they go to faculty offices to provide needed services.

Changes and innovations are needed fast because of competition from information technology, vendors, the World Wide Web, and other types of information providers. The changes are also needed because of pressures from funding sources, accrediting groups, and administrative mandates. Yet these changes are difficult and slow to implement because they will have to overcome traditional services and mind sets. Librarians have performed reference services in a certain manner for many years, they have not been trained to perform some of the new services, and, frankly, some are not eager to change.

The impact of technology on reference services and bibliographic instruction continues to be discussed in various publications but usually separately, not in an integrated mode. Although strong relationships and connections are described between bibliographic instruction and reference services, the impact of technology on the two is usually treated separately.[7]

The evolving electronic environment has certainly influenced both reference services and bibliographic instruction. The need for librarians in academic as well as public libraries is documented by the fact that library users now often need professional help and guidance in the chaos and overabundance of electronic publications. In recent years it has become more obvious that public librarians similar to academic librarians need to offer instruction in information skills to their clientele. Users of academic as well as public libraries need expert help and instruction in order to navigate through the World Wide Web and the multitude of other electronic information formats. Librarians are the expert professionals in the current complex information environment to assist people with their information needs within a carefully selected collection of resources, in an open, equitable access environment, and at no cost. Library professionals are closely tied to the principles of democracy, allowing freedom of choice, access to all types of views and thoughts, and offering life-long learning opportunities.[8]

In January 1998 the Library of Congress sponsored an Institute on Reference Service in a Digital Age (http://lcweb.loc.gov/rr/digiref/neworlns.html) in New Orleans during the meeting of the American Library Association. Presentations and discussions centered on the role of reference in the electronic environment and how to prepare for the future. A variety of scenarios were described from traditional reference desk models to reference service in a totally remote video conferencing environment. Most of the scenarios included some type of user instruction on a one-on-one basis. Reference librarians now are called upon not only to supply expert advice, training, and assistance with information questions, but also with technological and networking problems.

During the Institute it became clear that reference services in whatever format will continue to be needed in the electronic environment and that librarians, because of their training and experience with information, are uniquely qualified to provide these services. Human interaction in the reference environment will continue to be important and necessary for successful information assistance. Training and development for librarians will be mandatory for them to stay current in their reference work.

The Internet Public Library, begun in 1995 at the University of Michigan, demonstrates that librarians need to:

- set clear guidelines for electronic reference services.
- build close cooperation among reference librarians.
- identify remote clientele and their needs.
- obtain extensive training and development.

The Interactive Reference Service at the University of California, Irvine describes how reference service was expanded beyond the reference desk using video teleconferencing technology (http://www.ala.org/acrl/paperhtm/a10.html). This type of service will be an effective substitute for distance problems in communication and personal user-librarian interaction. The experiment is important so that it can be ascertained:

- how desktop video teleconferencing can provide remote reference services.
- how reliable is such technology.
- how effective communication is between librarians and clients.
- how such technology can be integrated into regular reference service.
- how this service will affect staffing.
- how to instruct the users of this service.

Challenges librarians will have to address in providing the desktop video teleconferencing reference service include communication etiquette, training, technical problem solving, and others. The experiment at UC Irvine will be well worth watching.

The present reference and instruction environment is definitely in a state of flux. Basically stated, reference services provide the human touch in guiding information users in the digital environment while information literary (an expansion of bibliographic instruction) is the most critical enabler for lifelong learning and effective information use. In the digital information environment, reference services and information skills instruction need to become integrated to offer library users and information seekers the most convenient and supportive learning environment. In fact, integrating these two important public service components in libraries will ensure that librarians remain a viable and important sector of the information and education environment.

THE FUTURE

As librarians prepare for the millennium, reference and instruction services will increasingly gain importance if the following factors are considered:

- realistic assessment of users' needs and requirements.
- user convenience.
- availability of integrated and well-functioning information technology.
- efficient assistance with technology.
- available network of subject expertise.
- expert information guidance in libraries and remotely.
- quick and convenient instruction in information skills.

Limited availability of user survey data indicates that people generally are used to one-stop shopping and expect similar convenience from libraries. Information is wanted quickly, seamlessly, and with expert human guidance. These expectations constitute a major challenge for librarians who have usually provided services at their convenience, not always quickly, nor seamlessly. Rethinking and realigning will probably have to occur from the way libraries are organized, to how quickly they place information into their customers' hands, and to what extent they use customer service attitudes. Each one of the service parts needs to be scrutinized and conceivably changed. That is hard and very challenging work in the complex library and technology environment.

INTEGRATION OF USER INSTRUCTION AND REFERENCE

To integrate user instruction and reference services, organizational structures will have to be changed so librarians have responsibilities in various professional areas such as reference, instruction, collections, and technology. This necessitates major training and development initiatives for the staff; perhaps as much as 5-10% of staff time might have to be allocated to training for a period of time. In addition to professional training, librarians need people and teaching skills, knowledge of print and electronic databases, basic technology and networking skills, and knowledge of information sources in the surrounding areas. Librarians have to build partnerships with teaching faculty, computer experts, and other information specialists to provide the best information access for their clientele.

Information skills instruction should be provided as needed on an individual basis or in groups. Such instruction needs to be convenient and to the point. Depending on user needs, it can be:

- in person,
- interactively online,
- in print, or
- in an electronic classroom situation.

It is during the reference process that librarians frequently determine the user's needs for information skills. During the reference interview, librarians assess whether or not a customer has the skills to access information, evaluate it, collect it, and use it. It is at that point that the reference librarian can best offer and supply necessary instruction in these areas. Some users need simple computer skills, some need Internet instruction, and many of them need to learn about different types of information sources.

As librarians work in partnerships with others, and perhaps in team environments, they will be able to provide the reference and instruction services needed by their clients. Changes in organizations and services, however, take time and are difficult to institute. For example, the selection and implementation of an up-to-date library automation system is a costly and time-consuming process, as is organizational change to partnerships and teamwork, a process that could take several years. Librarians, unfortunately, do not have a great deal of time to accomplish some of the changes. Technology is forcing institutions and organizations, including libraries, to move more quickly to respond to change. Competition in the information environment is adding to the pressure. Funding issues and new information supply models are also having a major impact.

Yet librarians are uniquely qualified and trained to address these challenges and to provide the type of information and instruction services needed and desired by their clientele. Librarians have many talents and they have a reputation for providing good, reliable service to all people. Librarians are uniquely positioned to provide these important information and instruction services in the next century and to become a significant component of the information age.

REFERENCES

1. Karen T. Quinn, "Information Literary in the Workplace: Education/Training Considerations," in *Information Literacy: Learning How to Learn*, ed. J. Varlejs (Jefferson, NC: McFarland, 1991), 19.

2. Hannelore B. Rader, "Reference Services as a Teaching Function," *Library Trends* 28 (Summer 1980): 95-103.

3. Charles A. Bunge, "The Personal Touch: A Brief Overview of the Development of Reference Services in American Libraries," in *Reference Service: A Perspective*, ed. S. Lee (Ann Arbor: Pierian Press, 1983), 1-16.

4. Kathleen Gunning, "The Impact of User Education and Computer Service Programs on Reference Services," in *Reference Service: A Perspective*, ed. S. Lee (Ann Arbor: Pierian Press, 1983), 79-88.

5. Charles R. Martell et al., "A House Divided: Public Services Realities in the 1980's," in *Proceedings of the ACRL Third National Conference* (Chicago: American Library Association, 1984), 85-101.

6. Jerry D. Campbell, "In Search of New Foundations for Reference," in *Rethinking Reference in Academic Libraries*, ed. A. G., Lipow (Berkeley: Library Solutions Press, 1993), 3-14.

7. Harvey Sager, "Implications for Bibliographic Instruction," in *The Impact of Emerging Technologies on Reference Service and Bibliographic Instruction*, ed. G. M. Pitkin (Westport, CT: Greenwood Press, 1995), 49-62.

8. Anne G. Lipow, "Thinking Out Loud: Who Will Give Reference Service in the Digital Environment?" *Reference and User Services Quarterly* 37 (Winter 1997): 125-29.

Index

